FIVE-POINT STAR

My Life as a Secret Service Agent

RON WILLIAMS

Five Point Star
My Life as a Secret Service Agent
All Rights Reserved.
Copyright © 2022 Ron Williams
v1.0

The opinions expressed in this manuscript are solely the opinions of the author and do not represent the opinions or thoughts of the publisher. The author has represented and warranted full ownership and/or legal right to publish all the materials in this book.

This book may not be reproduced, transmitted, or stored in whole or in part by any means, including graphic, electronic, or mechanical without the express written consent of the publisher except in the case of brief quotations embodied in critical articles and reviews.

Secure Strategies International, LLC

ISBN: 978-0-578-26827-9

Cover and Interior Images © 2022 Ron T. Williams. All rights reserved - used with permission.

PRINTED IN THE UNITED STATES OF AMERICA

"This book is for everyone. I truly couldn't put it down.

With Ron Williams words, history comes alive and speaks to us. **Five Point Star: My Life as a Secret Service Agent** *takes the reader on a journey behind the scenes of the Secret Service with an understanding of the humor, fellowship, sacrifice, training, courage and yes, the danger.* **Willing at any** *moment to take a bullet to save another's life whether it was the Pope a President, a former President, a visiting Head of State or a candidate for national office…the ultimate sacrifice. Ron's storytelling ability takes you to an eye-opening look inside a day in the life of a Secret Service Agent that few have ever experienced. He allows us to understand that we are capable of having more faith in ourselves while being brave when required, never quitting, and finally, allowing us to understand that God never gives us a heavier load than we are able to bear. It is a powerful, inspiring book about a man who served his country with unwavering courage, honor and integrity.*

William J. Canary
Former Special Assistant to President George H.W. Bush
Former president and CEO
American Trucking Associations
And, author of **LEAD-ER-SHIP**: *No Reserves. No Retreats. No Regrets.*

"Ron William's insider story, "5 Point Star", offers a very insightful and revealing personal account of his 22 years with the U.S. Secret Service. Beginning with his early years as a young U.S. Secret Service Agent, to the sunset of his distinguished career, his memoir narrative captures his committed and patriotic service protecting four U.S. Presidents, world dignitaries, and investigating criminal cases against the financial infrastructure of the United States,"

Shawn Cassidy – Leadership, Strategist and Author
From Fears to Freedom – The H2G Revolution

Table of Contents

Introduction: My Beginning	i
Chapter 1: Goin' to Kansas City, Kansas City Here I Come	1
Chapter 2: My First Case – The Civella Brothers	4
Chapter 3: Meet Harry Truman	7
Chapter 4: My First Arrest-Cojetta Jackson	10
Chapter 5: Spiro Agnew	13
Chapter 6: Part of the Job-Medical Center for Federal Prisoners	15
Chapter 7: All In A Day's Work	18
Chapter 8: George McGovern Detail	20
Chapter 9: Wichita	27
Chapter 10: Mamie Eisenhower	33
Chapter 11: Major Baldo	40
Chapter 12: The $1,000 Queen	44
Chapter 13: The Christmas Monster	48
Chapter 14: Lon Nol	54
Chapter 15: Steve Ford	57
Chapter 16: Friendly TWA	60
Chapter 17: Welcome to LA	63
Chapter 18: The Murder of Julie Cross	65
Chapter 19: Chase To Down Under	72
Chapter 20: Bad Pennies Always Turn Up	89

Chapter 21: Juan and John—The Robertson Coincidence	99
Chapter 22: Lady Luck	106
Chapter 23: The Sparrow Has Landed	118
Chapter 24: Marcos	132
Chapter 25: The Hapless Hacker	139
Chapter 26: Rudy Montoya	145
Chapter 27: ATM Assault	156
Chapter 28: "Don't Open the Trunk!"	161
Chapter 29: This One Takes the Prize	167
Chapter 30: BCCI Bank-London	172
Chapter 31: Fidel Castro	176
Chapter 32: Smokey the Bear	180
Chapter 33: Shorty	185
Chapter 34: Mariposa—A "Royal" Tragedy	189
Chapter 35: The Counterfeit Counterfeiter	217
Chapter 36: Robert Mugabe	229
Chapter 37: The Highlight of My Career: Protecting the Pope	233
Chapter 38: President Richard Nixon	240
Chapter 39: President Ronald Reagan	244
Chapter 40: The Last Campaign	251
Case Closed	263

Introduction

My Beginning

My father was born in Tallapoosa, Georgia, a hotbed for the Ku Klux Klan. An alcoholic and a wife abuser, he died a tragic death at the age of forty-two. I was twelve when I learned that he mysteriously died and was found in a hotel room in Chicago.

The only memory I have of my father was when he and his brothers came one night to my grandparents' house in Tallapoosa, a log cabin with no running water and no electricity. There was a potbelly stove in the kitchen that heated the cabin, and a weatherworn outhouse that sat next to the well in the yard.

Around midnight, I was fast asleep on a quilt made by my grandmother Hanna, a full-blood Creek Indian from Alabama, when I was awakened by the sounds of cars and raucous men outside the cabin. I heard doors slam and several men cussing and in general raising hell. I walked out onto the porch to see my father, his two brothers, and four other men all dressed in white sheets. Several of the men still had the white hoods on. My grandmother suddenly appeared beside me on the porch with a double barrel shotgun cradled in her arms.

"Get those goddamn sheets off and get your asses in the house."

My father and his buddies laughed at my diminutive grandmother dwarfed by the shotgun. Not to be intimidated, Hanna raised the gun in the air and fired a shot that sounded like a grenade exploding. The kick from the shotgun blew Hanna back through the door where she landed on her butt. The sound was so deafening that I soiled my pajama bottoms. The men might have too. They tore off their sheets and made a run for their cars.

I didn't see my father again.

My mother was a beautiful five-foot-tall woman born in Murrieta, Georgia. She left school after the sixth grade to work in the cotton mills, where she'd met my father. My mother divorced my father when I was five and moved me and my grandmother to Florida.

When I was seven, my mother met and married Jim Baker, an enlisted airman in the Air Force. Jim's dedication to me and my mother over the years saved me from a life of tragedy and defeat. He spent time with me and made sure I attended to homework. He taught me discipline and order. Since I was a good athlete, he made sure I participated in football, baseball, and basketball.

But I was an unruly kid, full of anger. In the fifth grade I got kicked out of school twice for fighting and once for cutting a girl's ponytail off at the rubber band. However, my stepfather never lost faith in me and hung in there with me while I terrorized my teachers and classmates.

I graduated from high school in Wiesbaden, Germany, in 1964. While I excelled in sports, I was a mediocre student because school was not particularly interesting to me. I felt like the only thing I could do was to join the military like my stepfather.

Jim said to me the day I graduated, "Go to college for one year. If you don't do well or don't like it, then you can quit and decide what you will do for the rest of your life. No one in my family has ever graduated from college, and I want you to be the first."

So, I enrolled in the University of Maryland night school at Wiesbaden Air Force Base. I worked for the Air Force base athletic department during the day with my buddies and took classes at night. Unlike high school, I found college challenging and rewarding. I read everything I could get my hands on, and I studied incessantly. At the end of the first semester, I had one A and three B's, and astounded my parents.

But I still had a wild streak. I hung out with other college guys on the base, and to say we were military brats would be giving a compliment to military brats. We were beyond out of control.

Our antics were legendary. One event included one of my buddies dropping his trousers and mooning us, which we found hilarious, so we had him do it again. We took a picture of his big butt with him looking through his legs and had the picture blown up. We then, wearing rubber gloves to thwart fingerprints, climbed a tall ladder to affix the large photograph to the theatre screen on the base.

That night, we assembled with a packed house for a particularly good show. When the National Anthem began playing and the curtain pulled back, soon the patrons realized the picture of someone's big ass taped to the screen and pandemonium ensued.

An investigation occurred by the Air Force base police, and we claimed our innocence. With no fingerprints on the photograph, the police could not make a case. However, my Wiesbaden experience ended in August 1965 when my pals and I got arrested by the German police for disruptive behavior at a strip club in downtown Wiesbaden. The general informed our parents we were to leave Germany within thirty days.

Two of my friends were headed to the University of Oklahoma, so I applied too, but my application was received too late. So, I immediately sent applications to every college within fifty miles of the University of Oklahoma. In a week I received a letter accepting my application to Bethany Nazarene College in Bethany, Oklahoma.

My mates assured me I would be expelled from this Christian college within a week. The plan was for me to go to Bethany one semester and then transfer to the University of Oklahoma and join my buddies from Germany.

The day I arrived at the Oklahoma City airport, I took a cab to Bethany. I lit a cigarette in the back seat. The driver asked if I was attending the Nazarene College and advised that the school did not allow smoking, drinking, or other acts of sin on campus. I replied, "I'm gonna quit when I get there."

As we pulled up to the campus, I tossed what was left of my cigarette out the window and handed the driver my unfinished pack of Camels.

His parting words were, "Good luck, young man. You're gonna need it."

Chapter 1

Goin' to Kansas City, Kansas City Here I Come

It was August 10, 1970 and the Vietnam War was still raging when I was sworn into the Secret Service at the Federal Building in Kansas City, Missouri. Special Agent in Charge Bob Lilley, tall, handsome, with a square jaw and jet-black hair, reminded me of Clark Gable, or Sean Connery of 007 fame. Nicknamed "Silky," he wore expensive suits and Italian-made shoes and ties. When he entered a room, Silky glided in with an announced debonair sophistication. I thought then and now Bob Lilley was the consummate ideal of what a Secret Service agent should look and act like.

I was twenty-three years old and had spent two years in seminary after college, convinced I wanted to be a Navy chaplain and save souls, until one day sitting in theology class, I realized I did not have the empathy to be a man of the cloth.

Withdrawing from seminary, I went to work for Mobil Oil Corporation in their credit department as a credit analyst and while there applied to the FBI and the Secret Service. Eight months later, after several interviews, tests, and an extensive background check, I received a call from the Secret Service with my reporting date.

After an initial week at the Kansas City Field Office, I reported for Treasury School in Washington, DC. My class of fifty new hires began our training in investigations, surveillance, arrests, searches and seizures, shooting weapons, and physical fitness. After eight weeks, we graduated and returned to our home field offices.

Two months later I was back at Secret Service school in DC for more intense—and more interesting—training. We received instructions on how to conduct a presidential advance, how to work a principal through a crowd, conduct a counterfeit money investigation, and how to investigate a threat against the President of the United States (POTUS).

It was during this training that many of our class discovered the Navy Officers Club at Twenty-first and R Street. One Thursday night eight of our agents were at the club when a young Navy officer took exception to their presence even though we were allowed to be in the club. A fight broke out and our guys, overmatched by two to one, returned to the hotel with black eyes and battered faces.

The next night, thirty of our class, including yours truly, decided to seek revenge. Off we went to the "O" Club to engage the enemy. On arrival, we purposely bellied up to the bar and began challenging any Naval officers we thought had put a whoopin' on our boys the night before. I don't recall what started the fireworks, but suddenly we were throwing fists, elbows, and headbutts all up and down the bar. The Navy officers were no match for us, and they soon retreated down the stairs and out into the street. All I recall about that night was seeing one of our guys walk back to the hotel wearing an admiral's hat that he had confiscated during the melee.

On Monday morning our class coordinator ordered all agents who had been at the Club on Friday to remain in their seats while the other agents were dismissed. At this point, the agents who remained in the room assumed we were going to be fired and sent home.

John Simpson, assistant director of investigations, who was later appointed director of the Secret Service, marched into the room straight from Headquarters. He had received a call from a Navy admiral complaining of the conduct by a cadre of Secret Service agents who apparently beat up a number of Navy officers on Friday night.

Mr. Simpson, a former college football star, was no stranger to physical contact. He eloquently berated us for our lack of professionalism and our poor representation of the Secret Service. As I looked around while he was blasting us, I saw both fear and embarrassment in my colleagues' eyes. He finished by advising us that each of us would be responsible for paying for the damage we did at the club, and that the club was now off-limits to our class.

A small price to pay, we all agreed.

The next week, walking to class with a fellow agent trainee, a hulking six-foot-three, 240-pound former college linebacker with massive shoulders, crew cut, and a chiseled jaw—John looked like a baby bull—we came upon a small group of protestors.

This was the era of Vietnam war protests and unrest in the Capitol. A block ahead, three hippies were carrying a door down the sidewalk. John, seeing them hit folks with the door and forcing people off the sidewalk, dropped his gym bag and took off at a sprint. His tie was flying and his suit coat flapping as he picked up speed. The three demonstrators failed to see the baby bull bearing down on them until John lunged, knocking them upside down under the door. Not satisfied, John jumped up and down on the door, squashing the startled hippies. They crawled out from under and fled down the street. John had a huge grin on his sweat-laden face and a look of triumph like he had saved America.

Chapter 2

My First Case – The Civella Brothers

I RETURNED TO my home field office in Kansas City a full-fledged agent ready to go to work.

The first major case I was involved with was a counterfeit money case involving organized crime figures Corky and Nicholas Civella. It was well-known in law enforcement circles that the Civella brothers ran the mob in Kansas City as well as a number of criminal activities in Las Vegas.

An informant had provided sample counterfeit $100 bills to one of our agents. He stated he got them from a man named George Kalas who ran a bar in downtown Kansas City for the Civella brothers. The informant agreed to introduce Kalas to one of our undercover guys.

Agent Bill Williamson from DC was brought to Kansas City. Williamson went to the bar night after night. Finally, after ten meetings, Kalas trusted Williamson enough to give him several sample counterfeit $100 bills. Williamson struck a deal to buy $1,000,000 in counterfeit $100 notes.

The deal went down at a hotel in downtown Kansas City. Williamson was wired and the surveillance units waited for the signal that the deal had been consummated. While my partner and I were secreted in the parking lot, I spotted two wise guys in a car that looked like a countersurveillance. With the signal from Williamson, experienced agents moved in and arrested Williamson and Kalas. The countersurveillance suspects suddenly sped out of the parking lot. So, we gave chase. However, the street leading out of the parking lot was covered with snow, and a right turn took us downhill. I slid down the hill sideways, spinning to a stop. The bad guys in the countersurveillance car got away. Real life doesn't always look like the movies.

After a long night of interrogation, Kalas finally broke and discussed the manufacture of the counterfeit money, naming the printer and that the Civella brothers paid for the operation.

The next day we arrested the printer, who said he'd been forced to print the counterfeit money or was told he would be put in cement shoes. Yes, he really said that. He also fingered the Civella brothers as the kingpins of the operation. Unfortunately, the printer's girlfriend found him hanging in the closet. Was it suicide, or a planned murder? We will never know.

Based on his and Kalas's sworn statements, we arrested the Civella brothers at one of their many places of business in the Kansas City area. Of course, they called their lawyer immediately and refused to cooperate.

Besides the statements of the two participants, the lab in DC found fingerprints of both Civella brothers on a number of the counterfeit bills. The government sent an organized crime strike force attorney out to Kansas City to try the case. As a rookie agent, I got to sit in the courtroom and watch the trial.

The government attorney diligently laid out the facts against the Civella brothers' day after day. After two weeks, he rested his case.

It was clear he had proved a prima fascia case and there could be no doubts as to their guilt.

However, the day of closing arguments, renowned attorney F. Lee Bailey flew into Kansas City from Boston and delivered a passionate defense of the Civella brothers. As he waxed eloquent, with a polish and a passion (and a fat paycheck, I assume), I looked over at the jury and realized he was creating doubt.

The jury was out for several days before they came back with a hung jury in favor of guilty by 10-2. It was speculated that the Civella brothers had identified the jury members and been able to bribe two of them.

It was decided to try the Civella brothers again in another city, and Kalas and his wife were put in the U.S. Marshal's protection program. Their names were changed, and they were moved to Anchorage, Alaska, where George worked as a bartender under an assumed name.

Unfortunately, while waiting to retry the case, George Kalas and his wife were found dead in Anchorage, shot in the back of the head. Since the star witness was now dead, the Civella brothers escaped being tried again on the counterfeit case.

It was frustrating to see how the government's strong case had been waylaid. Honestly, I was really angry that the government's case in the first trial had not gone like I thought it should have.

The wheels of justice turn slow, but they keep rolling. In 1977, Nicholas Civella was convicted of illegal gambling charges and sent to prison. He died of lung cancer six years later. Corky Civella was finally convicted in 1984 of skimming operations in Las Vegas casinos throughout the 1970s and sent to prison where he died in 1994.

And I was getting more and more seasoned as an agent.

Chapter 3

MEET HARRY TRUMAN

IN 1971, I was sent to Independence, Missouri, to stand in for a vacationing agent who was on the detail for former President Harry Truman.

On the first day, Paul Burns, the Secret Service Detail leader, asked me if I would like to meet President Truman. Since I had been a history and political science major in college, I immediately said yes, I would love to meet Harry Truman.

Mr. Burns told me to be at the command post at 7:15 the next morning even though I was not scheduled to be on duty until eight. Burns said that Truman went for a walk every morning at 7:30. He cautioned me not to open the gate when Truman approached. Burns said the president always insisted on opening the gate himself.

The next morning, I was at the command post, a small three-bedroom house across the street from the Truman residence. The Truman house was not a mansion or an estate. The two-story home sat in a residential neighborhood with an iron rod fence surrounding the property with a gate that led to the sidewalk.

On this very cold morning, I stood with Paul Burns outside the fence near the gate. At precisely 7:30 a.m., the door opened, and Harry Truman emerged in an overcoat, top hat, and carrying a cane in his right hand.

When the president opened the gate and stepped on the public sidewalk, Burns addressed him. "Mr. President, I want to introduce Ron Williams, a new agent, to you."

Harry Truman put his cane in his left hand and extended his right hand to shake. I stepped forward and grasped his hand. Truman said, "Secret Service, huh? I've always liked the Secret Service, and that's no shit, boy." The president then turned and walked down the sidewalk.

Burns looked at me and smiled. "Well, you just met the president."

As Harry Truman's health began to deteriorate, the Secret Service sent Agent Lew to be by the president's side at all times. Lew had been a Navy corpsman in the military, and this assignment with President Truman was to watch over him and provide emergency care in the event he collapsed or had a heart attack. Lew would sit for hours and talk to Harry Truman. Occasionally, Lew would tell us about his conversations. I asked Lew if Truman ever discussed the decision to drop bombs on Hiroshima and Nagasaki. Lew said Truman told him he never regretted ordering the nuclear A-bombs dropped. Lew said Truman's exact words were "Hell no, and I'd do it again."

One day we took Truman to the hospital to have a physical examination. I stood post outside his hospital room, and Paul Burns relaxed in a chair in the nurses' station. Several hours had gone by when the door opened and Harry Truman stepped out in the hallway wearing a blue hospital gown and said, "I wanna go for a walk."

Burns and I followed the president down the hall. At the end of the hall was a closed door with a blue light and a DO NOT DISTURB sign. Truman headed for the door and had his hand on the handle when Burns said, "Mr. President, I don't think you are supposed to go in there."

The president responded, "I'll go where I want to go."

Truman opened the door and was confronted by a man lying in bed in traction. It was apparent he had been in a serious accident. As the man stared back at Truman, it was clear he recognized Harry Truman. Truman still standing at the door looked at the man and said, "Hell boy, you're in worse shape than I'm in." As the door closed, we heard the man painfully laughing.

My temporary assignment with Harry Truman ended when the other assigned agent returned to his post. Back in my field office in Kansas City in December 1972, I got the call from my boss to drive to the airport to pick up Margaret Truman, the president's daughter, and take her to Research Hospital in Kansas City, where Harry Truman had been hospitalized. It looked like he was entering his last days. I was to remain at the hospital and protect Margaret Truman while she was there.

Margaret and her mother, Bess Truman, sat in a room that had been reserved for them, and played gin rummy while the agents stood post and guarded their door. Late that evening, about 10:30, a doctor came to the room and advised Bess and Margaret to come to Harry's bedside.

Bess and Margaret Truman returned forty-five minutes later and told the agents that "the president is dead." Bess Truman then passed a flask around and asked the agents to have a drink to honor the president.

I raised the flask to my lips and realized it was straight Jack Daniel's. My thought at the time was Bess and Margaret Truman were strong, independent women with true grit. I passed the flask and silently toasted, "Give 'em hell, Harry."

Chapter 4

My First Arrest- Cojetta Jackson

New, inexperienced agents cut their teeth on investigating forged government checks as part of the Secret Service investigative obligations. One of my first cases involved a $5,000 IRS refund check that had been stolen, forged, and cashed. The perpetrator had used false identification in the payee's name and cashed the check at one of the many check cashing businesses in Kansas City. The check cashing company had taken a picture of the person and a picture of the false ID.

I went to a variety of businesses in the depressed areas of Kansas City, Kansas, known as the ghetto, showing the picture of the perpetrator and looking for leads. After I had spent several days showing the photograph, an informant called me and said the person I was looking for was Cozetta Jackson, a twenty-five-year-old woman who lived in the projects.

After running Cozetta for a criminal record, I discovered she had been arrested multiple times for theft, forgery, and prostitution. Her rap sheet had several addresses. Dick, a new agent like me, accompanied me to look for Cozetta in the projects. On our fourth stop at one of her known addresses, we approached what appeared to be an abandoned, rundown, one-story house next to a dilapidated, five-story apartment building. As I approached the door, I heard voices inside the house. I noticed the door was slightly ajar, so I slowly opened it. Inside were eight men sitting on the floor. Sitting on a windowsill across the other side of the room was Cozetta Jackson.

The men in the room appeared to be drunk, and Cozetta was holding a bottle of Canadian Mist. I shouted to Cozetta to get out of the windowsill and come across the room and that she was under arrest. Cozetta complied and staggered across the room. I turned her around and handcuffed her. The drunks in the room suddenly realized that their Cozetta was being arrested.

They staggered to their feet and shouted that I couldn't arrest their woman. Dick stood at the door as I grabbed Cozetta from behind and backed out of the house with eight drunk men advancing on me. Apparently, the drunks had made enough racket that some folks in the apartment building heard. They came to their windows and started yelling at us too. They threw eggs, tomatoes, and rocks at us.

I pulled my badge and gun and demanded the advancing men to halt their pursuit and that they were interfering with a federal agent. I was naïve enough to believe they would actually stop if I showed them my badge. This was my first lesson in law enforcement. The badge means very little to the criminal element.

Dick got to the car and started the engine. I backed up to the rear passenger door and was able to get Cozetta in the back seat with me. Dick floored the pedal, and we roared off with eggs, tomatoes, and other food missiles pelting the car.

As we drove, Cozetta simultaneously threw up and shit her pants. Even though it was thirty degrees outside, Dick and I rolled down the windows, gagging. Traffic was heavy and we moved at a snail's pace. We finally got to the Federal Building and turned Cozetta over to the U.S. Marshals.

This was our first arrest, a cause to celebrate, but both Dick and I were tired and sick, and definitely not hungry.

Chapter 5

SPIRO AGNEW

SECRET SERVICE AGENTS investigate counterfeit money, government check forgery, credit card fraud, identity theft, cyber violations, and threats against the president. In my first such assignment, it was a threat against the vice president.

Late in 1971, I was sent to Washington to work as a shift agent on the Spiro Agnew vice presidential detail. Agnew had sustained a number of threats from the anti-war crowd, and he was a controversial figure. On my first week, I stood post at the vice president's residence.

To understand what it is like to stand post, put on your best suit and tie, strap on a gun, put a radio on with an earpiece, and go stand in your garage for hours. Very boring. But take into consideration that you are there in the event someone wants to kill the second most important person in the United States. That provides incentive and a feeling that you are accomplishing an objective.

Another agent and I were posted outside Spiro Agnew's door at his office in the Old Executive office building next to the White

House. About 10 p.m., the door opened, and the vice president stuck his head out. "I'm hungry for pizza. I'm ordering now. What do you want on yours?" I was impressed that the vice president would take the time to talk with us and order pizza for us.

After the first week, I was then placed on the day shift. The vice president decided to travel to Palm Springs, California, and stay at Bob Hope's residence. On the flight on Air Force Two, Spiro came back to the rear of the plane and sat with the agents and told jokes and enjoyed being a regular guy. He was personable, and the agents on his detail were loyal.

When Spiro Agnew died in Palm Desert, California, his widow, Judy Agnew, requested six retired Secret Service agents who served on the Agnew Detail be his pallbearers. She said the Secret Service agents were the only folks who remained loyal to her husband after he left office in disgrace.

Although there were no incidents while I was assigned to Spiro Agnew, it was exciting to be with the vice president and to be exposed to real protection.

Chapter 6

Part of the Job-Medical Center for Federal Prisoners

Perpetrators who threaten the president or vice president can be charged under Title 18 USC 871 and sentenced to five years in federal prison. Those prisoners are housed at the Medical Center for Federal Prisoners (MCFP) in Springfield, Missouri, which was in our jurisdiction in Kansas City. While I was assigned to Kansas City, thirty-five prisoners were incarcerated at MCFP for threatening the president.

The Secret Service had a policy that every person convicted of threatening the president should be interviewed on a quarterly basis. Being the new kid on the block, I was assigned to go to MCFP for a week and interview the incarcerated prisoners.

When I arrived on a Monday morning after a long drive from Kansas City, I was stunned with the beauty of the facility. The outer perimeter was lush with green grass and flowers. Once through the gate, the facility was clean, the halls were waxed, and the walls were freshly painted with a stark white hue.

I was ushered into a sterile room, and the files on the prisoners were provided for my review. As I recall, out of thirty-five prisoners, twenty-two of them had actually killed someone. One particular person had dragged his mother out of the house into the backyard and chopped her head off with a shovel. Another prisoner had walked up behind a couple on a street corner in Houston and shot them in the back of the head.

From Monday through Friday, I interviewed each prisoner with a set of questions that in reality were quite ridiculous. An example: "What are your current thoughts about the President of the United States?" Some prisoners laughed, but many of them would yell and scream and call the president vile names. At first, I didn't understand their reaction until one of the guards explained that by making new threats, they hoped to prolong their stay at MCFP rather than being returned to state prison, where the living conditions and food were inferior.

One particular prisoner really bothered me. His first name was George. When George was brought in for me to interview him, he had belly chains and his legs were chained. A guard entered and stayed close by because George had just stabbed another inmate in the mail room that morning.

George was six-foot-seven and 340 pounds with a shaved head. When he walked in, he had a Bible under his arm. Before I could identify myself, he began to cite scripture and ended by identifying himself as a reverend, and that if I did not declare Jesus as my savior, I would go to hell.

George was the prisoner who had shot the Texas couple in the back of the head. After he settled down, I read the threats he had made to sexually violate Pat and Julie Nixon. The threats were graphic and heinous. When I concluded, George lowered his head and said, "It was a moment of weakness, my son."

I had no doubt that if released, George would kill again.

At the end of each day while I was at MCFP, I found myself in a state of depression from being with human beings who were sociopathic psychopaths. I saw firsthand man's inhumanity to man, and it disturbed me.

And yet I knew, it was part of the job.

Chapter 7

All In A Day's Work

"I have information on a counterfeit operation." The caller told me the operation was directed by organized crime.

"Why don't you come to the Federal Building so we can discuss these allegations?" I asked.

"I can't come near the Federal Building. If anyone associated to this group sees me enter the Federal Building, I'll be dead. Meet me at Union Station in the morning."

He advised he would be wearing a red flannel shirt and that he had brown hair and a mustache. I in turn gave him my description and verified I would meet him inside the station near the front entrance.

The next day Agent Dave Harris and I went to the station early to make sure there was no countersurveillance and that we were not being set up for an ambush. In the 1920s, a mob hit had occurred at Union Station when several mobsters machine-gunned down gang rivals. Bullet holes are still in the wall as a monument to the assassination.

At 9:30 a.m. I told Harris to stay near the front because I had to go to the bathroom. Union Station was a huge, old, beautiful, cavernous facility. When I entered the men's room, I noticed the old white tile on the floor. There were approximately fifty stalls with no doors. The bathroom appeared to be empty, so I walked down to about the fifteenth stall.

I took off my suit jacket and hung it on a hook, dropped my pants, and sat down on the toilet to do my morning constitution.

Shortly after I sat down, I heard what sounded like tennis shoes padding on the tile floor coming toward my stall. Sure enough, a short, bald man wearing a brown suit with a carnation in his lapel, wearing Hush Puppies shoes, walked slowly past me and grinned at me. As he walked past, I had a hunch he would be back.

After padding all the way to the end, I heard him coming back. He stopped in front of my stall and stood in the doorway leering at me. I inadvertently grinned because I had this mental image that I would have to fight him off with my pants around my ankles. My grin was interpreted as an invitation, and the intruder took one step into my stall. I reached down and pulled out my .357 Secret Service-issued revolver and thrust it in his mouth, saying in a loud voice, "Bite down on this one."

The little fat man screamed and vaulted backward, landing on his butt. He jumped up and ran out of the bathroom.

My partner, hearing the scream, drew his weapon and ran in the bathroom, bumping into the little fat man and knocking him down. The guy started screaming again and jumped up and ran. Harris came around my stall with his gun drawn, pointing it right at me. I was still sitting on the toilet with my gun drawn.

We almost pulled the trigger and shot each other.

The informant never showed, and I'm not sure to this day how it could have been explained that two Secret Service agents shot each other at Union Station while one was sitting on the toilet. What can we say? It's all in a day's work.

Chapter 8

GEORGE MCGOVERN DETAIL

EVERY FOUR YEARS becomes a campaign year for politicians seeking the office of President of the United States. In 1972, I was assigned to George McGovern, senator from South Dakota. On our first trip from Washington, Jim, my partner and roommate throughout the campaign, and I sat in the back of an old C47 Gooney Bird. As we rumbled down the runway in the World War II airplane, Jim looked at me and said, "We won't be on McGovern long; he'll be gone from the race in a month."

McGovern was the most unlikely candidate in the Democratic field, and his campaign started on a financial shoestring. Miraculously, as the campaign wore on, McGovern picked up steam. We went from state to state, city to city, like a traveling circus with George as the barker. For nine months, our shift worked four weeks on the campaign, and one week at home.

On one trip, I traveled with Mrs. McGovern on a Gulfstream. As we approached Chicago's Midway Airport for a landing, I looked out the window, and the fog was so thick I couldn't see anything.

All of a sudden, I saw the rooftop of a house. The plane jerked up violently, and I felt a force press me back down in my seat. Mrs. McGovern screamed. Bottles and other items sailed through the air. When we finally landed, the pilot and co-pilot emerged with faces white as sheets. I later asked them how close we came, and the pilot meekly replied, "Inches."

My partner Jim, a big, rough Irishman from Gary, Indiana, kept me laughing and entertained throughout the campaign. Jim had worked his way through college in the steel mills carrying hot pods. He was six-foot-three, 220 pounds, big, strong, and ugly. But Jimmy had the gift of gab. He was brilliant, with a wicked sense of humor. He could talk on any subject and be credible as an expert. He read incessantly. One night in a bar in Boston, he convinced a group of six nurses that he was a brain surgeon.

Later in his career, Jim was assigned to the presidential detail for Ronald Reagan. One day while standing post at the White House, the shift leader told him to go to the Old Executive Office Building to be interviewed by the psychologist the Secret Service hired to conduct a study on agent morale.

When Jim entered, the good doctor asked him to be seated. The doctor's first question was "Jim, what do you think about when you are standing post guarding the President of the United States?"

Without missing a beat, Jim said, "I dream about having sex with a seagull."

The doctor pushed his Coke-bottle glasses down his nose and asked Jim to expound on his dream. Jim said he "sees himself running down a deserted beach in the Caribbean, naked, chasing a seagull. He catches the seagull, spreads its wings, and mounts it. The seagull goes eh, eh, eh."

The doctor told Jim he had no other questions and that he could leave. When Jim arrived back at the White House, the shift leader told him to report to the special agent in charge (SAIC).

"What did you say to that psychologist?" the SAIC asked as soon as Jim entered his office. "I just got a call, and he says to take away your gun and badge—this guy is nuts."

After Jim explained that he was screwing with the doctor, the SAIC ripped him a new one and then told him to get his "ass back out on post."

That is my pal Jim.

George McGovern was not big, strong, or funny. He always started his speech with the same phrase, "I was a bomber pilot in World War II." I came to understand that he used the phrase because he had to appear macho since he was such a wimp and milquetoast.

During the campaign, there was a flood in Sioux Falls, South Dakota, that destroyed parts of the city and killed a number of people. We took an emergency trip to South Dakota for McGovern to survey the damage. Once we arrived at the airport, we boarded a helicopter and flew around reviewing the damage. It was horrible. Many had lost loved ones, and the city was in grief. After the helicopter trip, we went by motorcade to get a firsthand, up-close examination of the carnage.

We pulled up in front of a fire station where firemen and emergency responders were getting some reprieve from working around the clock recovering bodies. McGovern jumped from the limo wearing his nice crisp suit and strolled into the fire station to glad hand the firemen and get a photo op. Most of the firemen turned their backs on McGovern and refused to shake his hand, showing their resentment that he would take this opportunity to grandstand. You could see the trauma and dirt and grime on their faces. These heroes had been dealing with death and destruction, and deserved respect and compassion. I felt embarrassed for McGovern and ashamed of him.

As we headed back to DC, this time on a sleek, modern jet, my shift leader advised that he and I would drive McGovern to his tax accountant, and the rest of the contingent and agents would return to the McGovern residence. McGovern got in the back seat of the limo, and I drove to the Capitol Hill address he gave us, which turned out to be a large, stylish, and expensive apartment building.

The senator got out of the car and told us he would be back in an hour. My shift leader told the senator we would have to go with him to know exactly where he was in the building. I could tell the senator was nervous, but he did not object. McGovern pushed a button to one of the apartments. A sultry, sexy voice answered and said she would have to come down and let the senator in the building because the electronic locking device was broken. My shift leader looked at me with raised eyebrows as we both waited intently to see what was behind that voice.

When the elevator door opened, a gorgeous blonde stepped out wearing a slightly revealing, thin nightgown. It was clear that with her newly applied red lipstick and musk perfume that floated through the air and caressed our nostrils, she was not ready to prepare taxes. As we stepped into the foyer, McGovern again tried to shake us by stating that he would be down in an hour. Again, my shift leader told him that we needed to know exactly where he was in the building, so we rode up the elevator several floors. No one spoke during the brief trip, but the perfume caused me to begin sneezing. The senator and his "tax accountant" exited the elevator, and my shift leader and I followed them down the hall. When she opened the door to her apartment, we could hear Frank Sinatra serenading with one of his love songs. The senator did not look at us as he slid through the door.

Senator McGovern appeared about an hour later looking refreshed, with a new spring in his step. I speculated that his accountant had been able to deliver a tax credit or refund. On the ride to his house, I was tempted but did not ask the senator if I could get my taxes done with his accountant.

Maybe he was not as milquetoast as I thought.

In the last stages of the campaign, we arrived in New York City. One of the first stops on a Saturday was at a synagogue. McGovern gave his standard canned speech and then opened it up for questions. A small, elderly Jewish woman rose, and a microphone was thrust in her hands. She asked Senator McGovern, "If Israel is attacked by Arab countries, would you, as President, come to the military aid of Israel?"

McGovern dodged giving a straightforward answer. On Sunday morning, the headlines in the *New York Times* read, "McGovern Waffles on Defense of Israel." We were scheduled to go to Brooklyn at 2 p.m. for a street rally in a Hasidic Jewish neighborhood. I was in the command post in the hotel when the advance agent radioed and stated, "The senator should not come to this event. The Jewish Defense League is here in the street, and they want to tip over McGovern's limo on arrival with him in the car."

The Secret Service Detail leader briefed the senator and told him that he thought it was too dangerous for him to go to Brooklyn. McGovern turned to his chief of staff, who was Jewish, and asked him his opinion. He replied, "My people will not stop us from winning this election."

McGovern said, "We're going."

Our detail was advised by the advance agent there were at least 2,000 people in the street and about fifty were Jewish Defense League (JDL) who were intent on harming the senator. On arrival we were to form a circle around McGovern and move him quickly to the front of a drugstore where he was scheduled to shake hands and make a brief speech.

On the trip over to Brooklyn, we agents in the trail car were tense and quiet. When we made the turn onto the street where the senator was scheduled to speak, there were hundreds of people waiting for our arrival. When the limo with McGovern in it came to a stop, we jumped from the follow-up car and ran to the limo.

The JDL screamed at McGovern, and the noise became deafening. After the senator exited the limo and walked about forty feet, the JDL attacked us. A woman came at me, flaying her fists and arms at me. I pushed her back. She came at me again only this time she raked my face with her long nails, sending blood and skin into the air. I pushed her back again. Two of the JDL men picked her up and threw her at me. This time I caught her in midair with a fist to her nose. I splattered her face, and blood rushed out of her nose as she fell to the pavement unconscious.

Meanwhile, other agents were fighting for their lives. The circle was starting to collapse because we were severely outnumbered. One of the JDL grabbed the sleeve of my suit and ripped it off at the shoulder. I glanced at McGovern, and he was white as a sheet and scared. My buddy, Jim, was single-handedly kicking everybody's ass who got in his way.

A news reporter, David Shumacher, who was hated by the agents, was purposely jostling the crowd and getting his camera crew to record the confrontation. As the fight continued, I got close enough to Shumacher to deliver a punch to his solar plexus. He dropped to his knees and came close to getting trampled. Later, at the hotel, he complained to our detail leader that an agent deliberately punched him during the melee. He got no sympathy and instead was told that he should have stayed out of the way and that he was lucky he didn't get seriously hurt.

Just as the pocket started to collapse, I looked up the street and saw four New York City police officers on horseback coming down the street in full gallop mode. It was like being at the Alamo and seeing the cavalry coming to the rescue. When the horses hit the crowd, people went literally flying through the air. The JDL scattered from the scene, and we ran back to the motorcade with McGovern in tow. When we got safely away, I realized my white shirt was covered with blood, and I had a swollen jaw. Several of the other agents were licking their wounds, but no one was seriously injured.

We were shaken and stirred but not hurt. The McGovern staff then laid out a schedule for the next three days in New York City that had at least six campaign stops a day. On one of the days,

Coretta Scott King arrived to make several stops through the African American community. One stop was Harlem General Hospital for a tour.

Tenement buildings lined the street of the neighborhood. After McGovern finished shaking hands along the rope line, he stepped into the street and walked to the sidewalk opposite the hospital to shake a few more hands. I was positioned to McGovern's immediate left flank. I looked up and saw a Black man wearing a white tank top T-shirt hanging out a window about ten floors up, waving a bottle of whiskey.

I was concerned that he would either drop or throw the bottle down on McGovern. But instead of the bottle, the man suddenly lurched and barfed. His ingredients were headed directly at me. I stepped to the left to avoid the vomit, and yelled, but McGovern stepped right in the spot I vacated. The loaded barf hit McGovern right on the top of his head and cascaded down his face onto his expensive suit and tie. Some of the splattered barf splashed onto Mrs. King.

McGovern appeared shell shocked and traumatized. We rushed McGovern and Mrs. King into the hospital and found a room and towels to clean up the mess. To his and Mrs. King's credit, they both continued the tour of the hospital. The agents kept their distance, but we could smell the foul odor emanating from them both. After the hospital stop, we returned to the hotel, where they both cleaned up and continued with their campaign stops.

The campaign lasted nine long, grueling months. When I rotated home to Kansas City, I still had to report to the office and resume my investigative duties until I rotated back on the McGovern detail. While the pace was tiring, I was young, and the campaign was an exciting experience. Nixon won the election in a landslide, and McGovern returned to the Senate, and I will always be grateful that I got to be where the action was.

Chapter 9

WICHITA

AFTER THE ELECTION, I returned to my normal duties in Kansas City, but not for long. In 1973, the boss told me I was to be assigned to a long-term protection detail. At that time, I had a two-year-old little girl, and my wife, Diana, was four months' pregnant. Knowing that I faced at least three years of nonstop traveling on a protective detail, I asked if there were any other options.

That is how I ended up in the two-man office in Wichita, Kansas.

We bought a home in the farming community of Clearwater, seventeen miles outside of Wichita. The Secret Service office was located in the Federal Post Office in downtown Wichita and consisted of three rooms. One room was dedicated to a prisoner processing room, and the other two were offices for the two agents. The resident agent in charge was Bob Horan, a fine gentleman who immediately took me under his wing.

In the fall of 1974, we were notified President Nixon would be visiting Wichita to make an appearance at a convention and would be staying overnight. For a small Midwestern city like Wichita, this was huge news.

Having POTUS in Wichita meant dropping everything else. The Secret Service presidential advance team includes a lead advance agent who is in charge of all the security planning, a transportation agent in charge of motorcades, an intelligence agent to work with the local police department and sheriff's department to track known threats and to respond to any other threats that would affect the visit, and site agents at the airport, hotel, and the venue where the president will speak. The White House Communications Agency arrives with tons of communication gear to set up a virtual secure communication system. A presidential visit is bigger and more complex than a Ringling Brothers Barnum & Bailey circus.

Our job as local field office agents was to coordinate liaisons with the local police and sheriff's departments and to provide support wherever it was needed. We were the go-to guys.

Three days before the visit, the Wichita local newspaper asked if they could do an article on the local agents and their duties. The Kansas City Field Office was called, and they in turn called Headquarters in Washington and passed the request to Liaison Division. The special agent in charge from Kansas City was given permission to come to Wichita to give a brief statement on the duties of the Secret Service and to acknowledge there were two agents assigned to the Wichita office, which covered the entire state of Kansas. Somewhere in the briefing it was disclosed that an agent lived in Clearwater, although I was not identified by name.

The next day the paper ran an article on the two Secret Service agents assigned to the Wichita office with a lengthy explanation on our duties in Kansas. Bob Horan and I were not mentioned by name in the article.

That afternoon I was busy coordinating the visit with the advance team when I got a page to call home. I could tell by the tone of her voice that my wife was scared and that something had happened. Diana explained that she had been out with our daughter for most of the day, and when she returned home, the next-door neighbor alerted her that a large white man had pulled up in front of our house. The man had taken a shotgun out of the bed of his pickup truck and proceeded to knock on the door. When no one answered he paced our front yard with the shotgun on his shoulder. Fortunately, after an hour, the unknown man got into the truck and drove away. The neighbor was smart enough to get the license plate number. But not smart enough to call the police.

I instructed my wife to lock all the doors and go down in the basement with our daughter and to lock herself in the washroom, which had no windows. I told her I would be right home.

Running the license plate number, I was stunned to see the owner had an extensive criminal and mental history. His twelve-page rap sheet disclosed multiple arrests for kidnap, extortion, taking over a radio station in Wichita, and threatening to kill several people at the station. He was identified as a suspect in a homicide a year ago when a victim was shot with a shotgun. Each time he was taken into custody, he was sent to the state mental hospital for the criminally insane and incarcerated for a period of time until a psychiatrist determined he was cured and could return to society.

I immediately called the police chief in Clearwater and notified him of my situation and my findings. Clearwater was a small farming town of 2,500 people, so the police chief and his deputy were not very sophisticated. The chief said he knew the suspect in question and confirmed that he lived in Clearwater. He said they had had numerous run-ins with the subject but had nothing to hold him on.

I got in my Secret Service government car and raced to Clearwater. When I arrived at home, I got my wife and daughter and took them to a rest home for the elderly two blocks away, where my wife worked as a volunteer. I then went to the police station and asked the police chief and his deputy to accompany me to the suspect's house to interview him. When we arrived, no one answered the door and there was no vehicle in the driveway. The chief of police left and told his deputy, who reminded me of Barney Fife, to stay with me while we waited for the subject to come home.

About an hour later, the subject rolled up in the pickup truck. He got out and reached in the bed of the truck and retrieved a shotgun. The man was indeed large. Six-foot-seven and 350 pounds. Although he had not detected the deputy and me across the street, I drew my Secret Service .357 revolver and took a position behind the engine block and yelled at him to drop his weapon.

The local deputy froze behind my car, petrified, and did not take his gun out of the holster. The suspect stared at us with the shotgun on his shoulder, and it appeared he was deciding whether to shoot or to drop the weapon. Several seconds passed with me yelling for him to drop the shotgun. I had already decided that if he lowered the gun, I was going to shoot. It was an intense standoff, as I knew that a shotgun blast from a distance of fifty feet could cut me in half.

I yelled at him one last time, "This is your final warning. Drop the weapon to your side or I will shoot you."

He must have realized I meant business, and he threw the shotgun to the ground. I slowly approached him, shouting for him to turn around and get on the ground. When I got close, I kicked the shotgun away. By that time, the chief of police had arrived, and together we handcuffed the subject. His deputy was still quivering behind my car, frozen in fear.

We put the suspect in the chief's squad car and drove to the tiny Clearwater police station. We took him into an office, and I questioned him about why he had parked in front of a home in Clearwater and waited on the front lawn with a shotgun. I did not reveal to him that I was a Secret Service agent and lived at the home he stalked. He replied that God had directed him to the home to kill the Secret Service agent who lived there. He said he read in the paper that an agent lived in Clearwater, and after asking around town, he discovered where the agent lived.

It was obvious that he was mentally ill and suffering from delusions and psychosis. I requested a sheriff's squad car to transport the subject to a mental hospital in Wichita. I signed a form admitting the subject as a 5150—a person deemed dangerous to himself and others. He was placed on a seventy-two-hour observation hold. I then went to the head of psychiatry and advised the doctor of my investigation and concerns. He said they would keep him until a court hearing determined his mental state of mind evaluation.

Thirty days later I was notified a hearing would take place in a judge's chambers regarding what should be done with the subject. Present at the hearing was a young psychologist representing the State of Kansas, the judge, the subject of concern and his court-appointed attorney, and of course, me.

The judge began the proceedings by questioning me as to the facts and why I took the subject into custody. I provided a detailed account of my actions on my findings and how I felt the subject was a danger to himself and others.

The psychologist was then asked to present his findings on the mental state of the subject. The doctor, wearing wire-rimmed glasses and a long beard, tried to look and act as though this were a classroom where he could wax eloquent and inform us neophytes of his superior insight into the human psyche. The good doctor proceeded to tell the judge he found no basis for the subject to be considered dangerous and opposed holding him any longer in a mental hospital. His testimony directly conflicted with my actions and observations.

A long pause ensued, and I could tell the judge was pondering the conflicting testimony. The subject's court-appointed attorney looked at me and nodded. He then turned to the judge and asked if he was interested in what the subject might have to say about his confinement. The judge gave the subject permission to speak. For the next thirty minutes, the subject told the judge, his attorney, the doctor, and me how God had directed him to kill the Secret

Service agent as well as other people in Clearwater. His testimony was chilling.

The judge silenced him and turned to the psychologist. He told the psychologist he did not know where he got his education, but he clearly was wrong about the diagnosis of this individual. He berated the doctor for his lack of common sense and for potentially putting people (me and my family included!) at the risk of a person who is clearly insane.

The judge ordered the subject to be taken to the State Mental Hospital for the Criminally Insane with a directive that he never again be allowed to leave. The judge also recommended that the young psychologist be terminated from the hospital. A move that I heartily embraced.

Chapter 10

MAMIE EISENHOWER

IN THE SUMMER of 1974, the Wichita Resident Agency was notified that Mamie Eisenhower, wife of the thirty-fourth President of the United States, Dwight Eisenhower, was coming to Abilene, Kansas, to visit the Eisenhower Library and Museum. The teletype advised that Mrs. Eisenhower would be traveling by vehicle and would stay at nearby Fort Riley in the VIP Officers billets. I was assigned to conduct the advance arrangements for her visit.

I made an appointment with the general in charge of Fort Riley, as well as the manager of the Eisenhower museum, and drove up for the meetings the following day. When I arrived at the general's headquarters at 12:30 p.m. for a 1 p.m. meeting, I was instructed to wait in the lobby. At 2 p.m., I was ushered into his office. After I showed my credentials and introduced myself, he ordered me to have a seat. I could tell by his demeanor that he was not overly enthused about having Mamie Eisenhower on his post. The general, a large man in an impeccably starched uniform with shiny medals adorning his chest, was a warrior made for leading fighters, not hosting wives of former presidents, even though Dwight Eisenhower had been a five-star general in his army.

After some forced pleasantries, I was informed that a second lieutenant, recently graduated from West Point, would be the coordinator for the visit. The general picked up the phone on his desk, and immediately there was a knock on the door. A young officer with spit-shined hair and spit-shined shoes, looking like a poster boy for the Army, marched in and saluted. Introductions were made, and the lieutenant set a record for "yes sirs" and "no sirs" in a ten-minute conversation. It appeared this might be the lieutenant's first assignment, and he was poised to impress. In other words, his panties were too tight.

The lieutenant and I adjourned to a conference room to discuss the arrangements for Mrs. Eisenhower's visit. The lieutenant continued to be wired tight and replied to me in yes sir and no sir terms. Based on the fact he was my age, his manners made me uncomfortable. I attempted some small talk, but his cryptic replies with no emotion caused me to return to an official mode of communication. Okay, no more small talk to break the ice.

We went over to the Officers billets and viewed the living quarters for Mrs. Eisenhower. The quarters were like most government apartments, utilitarian without any austere pictures or other amenities.

The next day I went to the Eisenhower Presidential Library in Abilene and conducted a walk-through. The library was not a large facility but had many of President Eisenhower's memorabilia and the history of his presidency plus his past as a five-star general who commanded the Normandy invasion in World War ll.

The third day, the lieutenant and I positioned ourselves in front of the billet on the Fort Riley post at 1 p.m., awaiting the arrival of Mamie Eisenhower at two. At approximately 1:30, Tom and Gary, two agents who I had gone to Secret Service school with, rolled up in a station wagon full of suitcases and other items. When I introduced them to the lieutenant, he gave a sharp salute before shaking their hands. Both Tom and Gary looked at me as if to say, "Is he for real?"

Gary took me aside and said this Secret Service detail was like no other he had ever been on. The Mamie Eisenhower detail had four supervisors who had been with Mamie for twenty years, and she treated them as her family. In return, the four agents, Jim, Bob, Dick, and the detail leader, Herb, viewed her with affection and as a mother figure. Gary also said they always traveled by car because Mrs. Eisenhower was deathly afraid of flying.

At 2 p.m., two black limousines pulled up in front of the billet. The lieutenant and I positioned ourselves on the sidewalk to greet the party as they walked in. The first three were agents, followed by Mrs. Eisenhower, with the detail leader, Herb, close behind her. After Mrs. Eisenhower was introduced to the lieutenant, Herb loitered back and allowed Mrs. Eisenhower to enter the residence before he stepped forward to shake the lieutenant's hand. As Herb grabbed the lieutenant's hand, he lifted his right leg and unloaded a loud, staccato-sounding fanny burp. I gave him a solid nine for tone quality. The lieutenant's face melted down into his spit-shined shoes, and I could tell he knew then this assignment was not going to get him promoted to be a general.

The incident had a good effect though on the uptight lieutenant. After things settled down, he started laughing and realized Herb had probably been holding the fart for a lot of miles.

That night, just as Gary had predicted, all four supervisory agents took turns going up to Mrs. Eisenhower's room to say good night.

The next day we traveled to the Eisenhower museum, and I invited the lieutenant to accompany me in my Secret Service vehicle. By this time, he had let his hair down, and he became quite personable.

As we strode around the museum, I watched as Dick took pictures of their group much like a family outing. To them, it seemed it was. I could tell there was a great deal of affection created by all those years together between the four agents and Mrs. Eisenhower. In many respects, while not completely professional, their personal relationship and devotion were refreshing. I'm glad I was able to be witness to it.

TODAY Chance of showers, 70s
TONIGHT Chance of showers, 60
TOMORROW Chance of showers, 70s
Details, Page 2

TV listings: P. 34

NEW YORK POST

FINAL LATEST PRICES

TUESDAY, OCTOBER 2, 1979   25 CENTS   © 1979 News Group Publications, Inc.   R R   Vol. 178, No. 271

DAILY SALES NOW EXCEED 630,000

HUNT GUNMAN STALKING POPE

By CARL J. PELLECK

POLICE today launched a massive manhunt for an armed and "extremely dangerous" man who was called a security risk to the Pope.

An all-points bulletin was issued this afternoon for a man identified as Alphonso Gustav, who was travelling with a small child and a woman in a Volkswagen or a Mazda.

The police bulletin warned officers to use "extreme caution."

The dramatic message was transmitted every 30 minutes on all security frequencies to officers throughout the metropolitan area.

The bulletin told police: "You are to stop and detain the occupants and take them to the nearest stationhouse for questioning."

Gustav, 36, is described in the message as a Hispanic, 5-foot-2, 140 pounds.

The message, which sent shock waves through police stations around the city, said Gustav "may be in company with a female Hispanic and male child" aged 7.

The alarm alerted officers to look for two cars. A two-door red 1976 Mazda bearing New Jersey license plates 555KSI and an orange 1977 Volkswagen bearing New Jersey plates 381FSV.

The alert was triggered by the FBI and Secret Service. The Secret Service, which went to Gustav's home in Elizabeth, N.J., found a Thompson semi-automatic machine gun, empty boxes which had contained 9 mm and .357 magnum shells, plus four other boxes of live ammunition.

Post photo by Robert Kalfus

Delirious crowds chant "Viva il Papa!" and hero Pope John Paul II salutes them as his motorcade makes its way to the UN.

Chapter 11

Major Baldo

"**I am Major** Baldo Christovis," the beribboned Army officer trumpeted as he extended his hand to grasp mine.

"Ron Williams, Secret Service…"

Thus began one of my most bizarre Secret Service experiences.

I had been summoned to the first floor of the Wichita Federal Building by some postal workers who, in a panicked tone, reported that a "nutty" soldier was screaming derogatory remarks about the president.

"Please hurry!" they implored.

I rushed down five flights of stairs, bypassing the slow elevators. At first, I couldn't see the suspect because he had been surrounded by a small crowd of curious onlookers. But I could hear him blathering away incoherently about the president.

Major Christovis wore a badly wrinkled Air Force uniform, and he clutched a tattered briefcase "full of top-secret orders." His too-short pants revealed white socks whose elastic had lost any semblance of elasticity, baring his bony ankles, and his brown shoes were untied and badly scuffed. The gray Rapid Transit District hat he wore looked as though it might have been forcefully removed from the head of a bus driver, then run over several times in a muddy gutter.

If this sartorial ensemble weren't enough to convince me he wasn't an authentic military officer, the one-foot-tall missile glued to the bill of his cap and poised for launch gave it away. "Major Baldo Christovis" was a certifiable nut case, but probably not dangerous, according to all the behavioral profiles which the Secret Service has compiled over the years.

Major Baldo was accompanied by his *aide de camp,* an equally disheveled man, slightly smaller, who nodded his head in silent agreement at each of Baldo's ravings.

"Mr. Williams," Baldo whispered conspiratorially. His breath did more than whisper; it screamed cheap wine. "I am a government employee. I work for a top-secret group. I came to this building to warn about a possible threat to the president."

"This is very important to the security of our nation, Major," I placated him. "Please come with me to my office so that you can tell me more. You just may be a hero, sir." After listening to the major for an hour, I thanked him for his extraordinary patriotism and ushered him out the door. I did not see Major Baldo Christovis again, or hear of him…until four years later, after my reassignment to Los Angeles in 1979.

Baldo showed up unexpectedly at the Federal Building in downtown LA one day, and it was like instant replay. The same uniform. The same briefcase. The same missile ready to blast off from the brim of his hat. The same rancid breath. Only his partner had changed. This time, he was a she—a toothless, bedraggled street woman whom I suspect had been released from a state hospital and left to wander the sleazy alleys of downtown LA. It was obvious she and the "major" shared the same bottle of vino. Again, I let Baldo go.

I didn't see or hear of Major Baldo Christovis again…until May 1992.

"Ron Williams, Secret Service," I answered the phone perfunctorily.

"Mr. Williams, my name is Bill Brough. I need your help."

"How?"

"My brother, John Brough, is in the hospital."

I strained to remember who John Brough was. "I don't know anybody by that name, Mr. Brough," I said finally.

"How about Major Baldo Christovis?" he asked.

I admitted that I knew Baldo.

"He's in for triple bypass surgery," Mr. Brough explained. "The reason I'm calling you is that he won't give permission for the doctors to operate until 'Ron Williams of the Secret Service gives permission.' My brother insists that he works for you, Mr. Williams, and that you're his super-secret contact. He talks about you all the time."

"You're kidding!" I exclaimed in disbelief.

"No, he says that he's got lots of top-secret work to do, and he'll consent to the operation only if you give the word. Will you give your consent, Mr. Williams?" the major's brother implored.

I called Room 107 at the hospital.

"Is this Major Baldo Christovis?"

"Yes, sir! I'm at your command. Who is this?" Baldo asked.

"Ron Williams, Secret Service."

"I've been awaiting your call, sir," the major snapped officiously.

"Major, you have my permission for open-heart surgery."

"Thank you, sir," the major replied crisply, adding, "but how do I know it's really you?"

"Call me back at this super-secret number," I answered.

Sixty seconds later, my secretary said, "Mr. Williams, there's a Major Baldo Christovis for you."

"Major, I've talked to the president. Let me assure you that he awaits your full recovery. You may go ahead with the operation."

"Thank you, sir," the major barked. I could almost see him snap to attention in his bed.

I imagine I should have checked to see if he had survived his open-heart surgery. No matter what happened or where he is now, I give him a salute.

Chapter 12

THE $1,000 QUEEN

AS ONE OF two agents assigned to the minuscule bureau in Wichita, I frequently traveled throughout the state investigating a surprisingly large number of counterfeit cases, threat incidents, and government check forgeries. After one particularly tedious five-day circuit, I returned to my office to find a note on my desk to call Postal Inspector Mark. In many instances, the Secret Service and the Post Office Department have overlapping jurisdictions, especially when they investigate mail theft and the theft includes U.S. government checks that may be forged and cashed.

As it turned out, this was the reason for Mark's call. We had received a copy of a forged check that had been negotiated at a local convenience store in a seedy part of Topeka. Mark and I drove to the establishment to begin our investigation. It was simpler than I thought it might be— the cashier had a Regiscope photograph of the payee. The endorsement on the back of the check was magnificently feminine. Even the fixed lens and harsh, straight-on strobe lighting provided by the security camera couldn't erase the uncommon beauty of our suspect: white, faultless complexion, impeccable makeup, blonde, in her late twenties, early thirties. We had a face—what a face!—but no name. Her ID obviously had been falsified.

With a copy of her photo, Mark and I began to sleuth the neighborhood. We covered restaurants, coffee shops, beauty shops, clothing stores, grocery stores, and bars. After a couple of days, we struck gold. A bar manager ID'd her as a cocktail waitress whose name fit her image: Kimberly Crisp. A great name for an aspiring actress, we agreed, or a hooker. We obtained her address and a warrant for her arrest an hour later.

Walking up to her apartment house, we read the mailbox: "Ken and Kimberly Crisp." I wondered if Kimberly's husband was mixed up in this crime too.

Wrapped in a terry cloth bathrobe, Ken answered our knock. We observed that he was very small in stature, hardly the stud we imagined that the incredible Kimberly would choose to bed with.

"Is Kimberly Crisp in?" Mark asked. We showed him our identification.

Ken became visibly agitated, unsure of what to say. At that point, we felt that Kimberly might be hiding upstairs, so Mark and I just walked on into the living room.

"Is anyone else here?" I asked Ken.

"No."

"Mind if I go upstairs?" I asked, even though it was unnecessary for me to do so. I didn't wait for his answer. Mark stayed with the obviously nervous Ken.

I checked the bathroom. A fine selection of creams, powders, perfumes, and other cosmetics rested in perfect order on the counter. The combined fragrances of these products were gentle and seductive. No Woolworth water in this bathroom.

Next, I walked into the bedroom, expecting (and hoping) to see her there. This woman had great fashion sense. One of the most beautiful outfits I had ever seen lay on the bed, ready to sheathe her incredible body. But it would have to wait until she came home. A check of the rest of the house proved that Ken was telling the truth. She was not there.

I went downstairs to ask a few questions.

"Is your wife coming home soon?"

"I'm afraid I'm not married."

"Is your sister coming home soon?"

He shook his head "no."

"Well, is your sister named Kimberly?" I showed him her picture, at which point he began to sob almost uncontrollably.

"Please, Mr. Crisp, try to get some control," I said as soothingly as possible. We waited for a couple of minutes.

"I…I…" he stuttered, "I am Kimberly Crisp."

Our mouths dropped.

"I did it. I needed the money," Ken said. "I'm a part-time student and I work as a cocktail waitress at night. I earn just enough money for tuition." He began to cry again.

"We've got to take you downtown. Please go upstairs and get dressed," Mark said.

For obvious reasons, the Service has a policy that after an arrest is made, suspects are never left alone. So, I went upstairs with Ken.

Ken chose to dress as a woman. I stood transfixed as the transformation took place. I was either in the dressing room of a sideshow, or in a chrysalis as caterpillar metamorphosed into butterfly. To this date, I've not spoken with another Secret Service agent who has had the opportunity of witnessing a suspect turn into a "suspect-ette."

When I escorted Ken—Kimberly—downstairs, Mark's eyes almost fell out. "She" was arguably one of the most beautiful women we had ever seen. Certainly, the most gorgeous thing I had ever placed in cuffs.

As Mark and I marched Kimberly into the federal building, she obviously set off the hormone alarm in one of the federal protective guards. He grabbed me by the arm and ooh la laa'd, "Who is *that*? How could you arrest anybody that beautiful!"

"We're going to process her. Want to meet her after we're finished?" I teased.

"You bet!" he drooled.

The guard moved his post so he could watch Kimberly's every move in the processing room. The poor guy was transfixed. He angled himself so he could watch her sign papers; then he realigned himself so he could watch us fingerprint her. His eyes never left her as we took her to be photographed.

When Kimberly stood in front of the camera, big tears welled up in her eyes. An expression of sadness and concern crossed the guard's face.

"Face the camera, Kimberly," I commanded. *Snap, flash.* "Now a profile." *Snap, flash.*

The guard hadn't moved.

"One more thing, Kimberly," I said.

"Yes, Mr. Williams," she replied meekly.

"Without the wig. Perhaps you would like to step away from the door for a moment to take it off," I suggested.

Kimberly-Ken complied, removed the wig, and placed it on a nearby desk. She turned back to the photo station, and I moved toward the door to watch the guard, who could hardly contain himself until she returned. When Kimberly stepped up gracefully to the backdrop for the next set of mug shots, I saw the guard's expectant smile dissolve into a snarl of fury as he realized he had been duped.

"You son of a bitch! You asshole!" he roared, stomping out of the foyer.

Was he angry at the hapless wretch we locked up for mail theft and forgery…or at me? I didn't care. It was worth the chuckle, and the story I continue to love to tell.

Chapter 13

THE CHRISTMAS MONSTER

CHRISTMAS MORNING, 1974. The phone rang. "Got a Christmas present for you," the duty officer said.

"What is it?" I asked, annoyed that my holiday was interrupted.

"Got a guy you've got to visit in Hays, Kansas. He's threatening to kill the president."

Kansas State Highway Patrol had pulled over a male suspect for a routine speeding ticket, when the offender announced stridently that he was en route to Vail, Colorado, to kill President Gerald Ford, who was spending a skiing vacation there with his family.

Eight hours later, after an exhausting drive through a punishing blizzard, I arrived in Hays, where a disgruntled, disinterested gas station attendant lethargically pointed me toward the sheriff's office. I think the jail was the newest building in town, and it had to have been constructed in the mid-1800s.

I was greeted by a deputy wearing farmer's overalls who seemed as disgruntled as the pump jockey was for having the misfortune of having to work on this holiday. The deputy told me that the suspect was in the jail.

"What do you know about the suspect?" I asked.

"Nothin', only that he's in the jailhouse."

"Let's go see him."

Conditioned by countless cowboy movies, I had expected to see the jail cells through the next door. But the door we went through led outside to a fairly large blockhouse with thick bars laid across glassless square openings that served for windows. A light snowfall powered by mild winds blew snowflakes into the cells.

I handed my gun to the undersheriff and told him to let me in to interrogate the suspect.

"Are you nuts?" he barked.

"No problem, Sheriff," I assured him, not knowing that he had been sworn in as a lawman less than three weeks ago.

I walked into a darkened cell, which was illuminated only by a weak lamp outside the back door of the sheriff's office. It took me maybe twenty seconds to adjust to the shadowy world in this frozen cell.

When my eyes finally focused, I saw a man against the wall who appeared to be about my height. Politely, though looking at him eye to eye, I introduced myself. "I'm Ron Williams of the Secret Service." I took out my Secret Service credentials and showed them to him.

Then the prisoner stood up. And up. And up. I felt as David must have felt when he confronted Goliath. My Goliath was an absolute giant whose stoic facial features were like something from a comic book or movie.

He advanced slowly toward me, approaching to within six inches. I could smell his hot, foul breath blowing down at me with force. Then, with incredible speed, he grabbed my credentials from my hands and rasped, "Mr. Williams, I'm going to keep these and kill you…"

Trying to keep my wits, along with a steadiness in my voice, I told this monster coolly, "If you don't give me back my credentials, I'm not going to talk to you." When I said that, I flashed briefly on the childish warning, "If you don't give me back my ball, I'm not going to play with you…"

He looked down at me without emotion. I could see the dim light reflecting in his staring eyes. Without a word, he handed them back.

"Who are you?" I asked.

"Why, I'm Mickey Mantle. No, I'm Joe Louis…" he answered.

Then he shoved me gently toward the steel door of the cell, which I learned later he had dented with many a powerful kick. (I doubt if Kung Fu movie legend Bruce Lee could've dented this door, but he had.) My entire body tightened up at the thought of the power of this man.

Nevertheless, I got him to talk. He told me how inner voices had directed him to eliminate the president, that as a former Army Green Beret he must follow orders from his superiors.

"You must be an excellent soldier," I complimented him. He thanked me.

I don't have the faintest idea what electro-chemical processes took place within his brain or what chemistry might have occurred between him and me, but all of a sudden, he became my docile buddy, and he slumped down on his cold cot.

"Would you mind if I go outside for a moment?" I asked.

"Not at all, Mr. Williams," this obedient Green Beret answered.

Liberated, I stumbled into newfound freedom. I don't know whether it was the cold Kansas Christmas air or my fear taking over, but I stood in the sheriff's office, clutching a steaming cup of coffee, and shivered for ten minutes.

"Told ya he was big, didn't I?" the undersheriff drawled, as if he had just remembered he left out an important piece of information.

I don't know why there would be, but the FBI had an agent stationed in Hays. I called him and he offered me some Christmas dinner and his typewriter to type up the affidavit and arrest warrant. The bureau agent accompanied me to the home of the acting U.S. Magistrate, a successful attorney representing wheat farmers. It was obvious that whoever owned this rambling home was extraordinarily well off—especially for this part of the globe.

The magistrate invited us into his home "office." We found ourselves in a spacious room brimming with antiques set atop fine furniture, all highlighted by the whitest, plushest wool carpeting my feet have ever had the pleasure of trampling. An indoor/outdoor pool about fifteen feet away compounded the ambiance of wealth. With a solid gold pen, the magistrate swirled his signature across the affidavit and complaint.

After I filed the complaint, I drove eight hours back to Wichita and a belated Christmas dinner. Soon after, the federal court assigned two federal marshals from Wichita to pick up the defendant for violation of Title 18 U.S. Code 871: threatening the President of the United States.

One of the marshals stood almost as tall as the Goliath. But where the suspect was as chiseled and sculpted and solid as Michelangelo's David, this marshal suffered the malady commonly called Dunlop's disease. That is, his stomach "done lopped over his belt." A sense of humor definitely was missing from this marshal's genes.

Both marshals went into the dreadfully cold jail house and brought out the suspect, who they discovered was barefoot. Handcuffing him with his hands in front, they ushered him into their car and took him to the home of the magistrate for arraignment.

Standing at attention as only a proud Green Beret could do, our prisoner listened passively as the charges against him were read by the magistrate. Then, as if a Viet Cong sapper had booby-trapped his mind, the Beret went berserk. He screamed, "Fuck you! I'm not guilty." At the same time, he unleashed a vicious, arcing heel kick down on the magistrate's desk. That's how we discovered the prisoner was also a karate expert.

The Beret's foot came down onto a glass Kansas Jayhawks ashtray, shattering it to shards. He cut his foot badly. Blood spattered everywhere, painting the shocked magistrate and violating the virgin white carpet.

"Get that son of a bitch out of here! Get that son of a bitch out of here! Get that son of a bitch out of here!" the magistrate yelled repeatedly.

Perhaps weakened by his loss of blood, the Beret quieted down and walked almost sheepishly to the marshals' car, where they stanched the bleeding and bandaged his cuts before beginning the long, snowy drive to Wichita.

Moments after they began to roll, the Beret suddenly launched a fresh storm of his own. "Kill! Kill! Kill!" he shrieked nonstop for more than an hour. "Kill, kill, kill, kill, kill, kill…" Neither of the officers could get the deranged prisoner to quiet down.

Finally, the marshal slammed on the brakes, walked around to the suspect's side of the car, pulled him out, and tried to punch his lights out. Fortunately for the marshal, the suspect was still manacled. Hitting him was like hitting a punching bag. An insane, rock-hard punching bag.

But the Beret wouldn't shut up. So, the agents drove to the nearest hardware store, where they bought a roll of duct tape and sealed his mouth shut. It worked well enough until they delivered him to the Salina, Kansas, jail, where they removed the gag from his face. Instantly, the insane screeching began again.

There was no sleep for anyone in the jail that night, and in the morning the Salina police chief told the marshals in very clear terms to "get this nut out of my jail."

With their prisoner muffled once again by duct tape, the marshals drove on to Wichita. A young aggressive assistant U.S. attorney, Ben Burgess, wanting to impress a local federal judge, invited the jurist to the holding cell to see this monster-sized would-be assassin.

The marshals warned both to look but not get too close to the cell. However, with a bravado forged from the safety of being on the correct side of the bars, the young attorney approached the cell door, grabbed the bars, and looked in at the poor Beret sitting slumped on his jail cot. Then, with the speed of a viper striking an unsuspecting varmint, the suspect leaped from his cot and, with unerring accuracy, punched him in the face, knocking him unconscious.

"Get that son of a bitch out of here," the judge squealed. I don't know if he was referring to the Beret or the attorney. But in any case, the same pissed-off marshal had to go in the cell and wrestle the Beret into a straitjacket and apply more duct tape before taking him to the Medical Center for Federal Prisoners (MCFP) in Springfield, Missouri.

On checking out this prisoner further, I learned that he had been an outstanding scholar athlete at Denver University before joining the Army Special Forces. Though an incredible physical specimen, he was too weak to fight off the effects of drugs to which he (and many other Vietnam-era soldiers) had become addicted while in Nam. Because of his drug-induced insanity, he did not stand trial for threatening the president. Ultimately, his family removed him from MCFP and had him committed to the Veterans Administration hospital in Denver, where his father was a surgeon.

Wherever he is now, I truly hope he's okay. For all I know, this "monster" might have been a hero in Vietnam.

Chapter 14

Lon Nol

A TELETYPE MESSAGE to the Wichita office notified me that I was being sent to Hawaii to protect Lon Nol, who was escaping Cambodia to get away from the Communist Khmer Rouge.

Lon Nol ruled during the Vietnam war years and hosted both South Vietnamese and U.S. troops in an aerial and ground offensive to wipe out the North Vietnamese Communists, who had virtually appropriated the northern reaches of Cambodia for their supply routes and for safe haven. Simultaneously, the Cambodian Communists—the feared Khmer Rouge—engaged in full-scale war against Lon Nol's regime, gaining the advantage in the early 1970s. By 1975, this murderous faction took total control of Cambodia, the same year that South Vietnam and Laos fell to the North Vietnamese.

The U.S. slipped Lon Nol and his immediate family out of beleaguered Cambodia via U.S. Air Force transport, and landed them safely at Hickam Air Force Base, Hawaii. The Khmer Rouge meanwhile stormed Phnom Penh (Cambodia's capital) like vermin raiding a grain depot and began a pogrom unlike anything seen since Hitler's planned extermination of Jews during World War II.

I was assigned to the Nol protection team—a fairly easy job since he and his party were secure in VIP quarters at the heavily guarded Air Force base in Honolulu.

The Nols appeared to be a quiet group of people—my opinion perhaps being somewhat slanted by the fact that I had pulled the late afternoon-to-midnight watch. I spent two weeks with them in an assignment that would have been ordinary, except for two events that will forever remain with me.

Over the days, I had noticed a wooden footlocker situated in one corner of the screened-in porch of the Nol quarters. *A pretty piece of inlaid woodwork*, I remember thinking to myself one evening between yawns. The still, humid Hawaii evenings didn't help to keep one's eyes open, so I had to walk around the compound constantly just to stay awake.

One evening, I watched one of Lon Nol's assistants stroll out to the porch and cock his head to listen, much as a deer does when about to take a sip at a stream. He looked around; then he unlocked the trunk. I had been walking the perimeter of the compound stealthily, so he had not been aware of exactly where I was. I stopped and watched curiously as he took out a key, twisted it into the padlock, and lifted the lid.

Half expecting a deadly cobra to emerge and sway to some exotic rhythm, I gazed transfixed at what had to be millions of U.S. dollars piled to the brim of the trunk. Hundred-dollar bills literally cascaded down its front and sides as the man tilted the lid back swiftly. He gathered a fistful without so much as counting, jammed the cash into a cloth bag, and looked around again before scooping up the fallen bills and dropping them back atop the stash. He closed the lid, locked it, then retreated into the home.

I just stood there staring, thinking that retirement and I were separated only by a rusty screen.

A few days later, we escorted a State Department employee to Lon Nol's quarters. Minutes later we heard screams and wailing. My partner and I rushed to the front door. People cried hysterically, hugging each other, falling limply to the floor. Now sad-faced, the State Department man left. He told us that he had to break the news to the exiles that the Khmer Rouge had marched their families, friends, and close associates into the central square in Phnom Penh, and beheaded them en masse.

How do you react to that? I couldn't even imagine such news. I stood there numbly, listening to the moans and wails that seemed to go on forever. And I could do nothing except stand my watch.

The families cried almost nonstop for several days.

In all my years in the Secret Service, this was one of the saddest moments I have ever encountered, and one of the strangest. Here we had a man with so much money stashed on the back porch that he probably could have been counted among the world's richest people. In the end, how much money we have stashed does not truly matter. With countless swings of sharpened machetes 5,000 miles away in Cambodia, the exiled president lost that which really counts.

Chapter 15

STEVE FORD

AFTER TWO YEARS in Wichita, I got the call in October 1975 stating I would be given a presidential protection detail. I resigned myself to the fact that I would be moving my family to Washington, DC. I received orders to report on January 2, 1976.

A week later, I got another call asking me if I would rather be assigned to protect one of the president's children, specifically, Steve Ford, who was attending Utah State University in Logan, Utah. I was told the children's details were more informal and I would enjoy being with a nineteen-year-old guy who was also training for the rodeo. I immediately said yes. We sold our home in Kansas and moved to Logan, Utah.

The Steve Ford detail was made up of ten Secret Service agents. I immediately bonded with my partner, Russ, an agent from San Francisco. Since there were always two agents with Steve at all times plus an agent manning the command post, Russ and I planned the schedule so we could work together. Russ and his wife, Kathy, also had two little girls the same ages as our daughters. Diana and Kathy became instant friends, and we as couples frequently spent time together off duty.

Life in Logan was different. The small city was built around the university, and the population was 95 percent Mormon. Our neighbors were friendly and did everything they could to include us. Several of the ladies brought food and desserts to our home, and the men asked me on more than one occasion to go snowmobiling in the mountains, but since no one in our neighborhood drank alcohol, or cussed, I was like a fish out of water. When we went to a restaurant, Russ and I had to bring our own bottle and hide it when we poured ourselves a drink to avoid dirty looks from the teetotalers.

Steve Ford was a nice young man, shy and introverted, and totally unprepared for college. He lived in a dormitory on the Utah State campus, so we worked out of a dorm room as our command post. Because we were not that much older than Steve (I was twenty-eight), we all became his buddies and played basketball with him. He had to be under guard at all times, so we went on dates with him too. Steve drove his Jeep and we followed close behind in a Secret Service vehicle.

He did not like school and Steve was not a good student. We had to pry him out of bed to get up and go to class. Midway through the first semester, it was obvious that Steve was not happy at Utah State and this was not his future. We traveled back to the White House with him so he could talk with the president and his mother. After several days in Washington, we went to Camp David, where Steve spent his time skeet shooting and hanging out. It was at Camp David that Steve told us he was dropping out of school.

Steve informed us he was moving to Newport Beach, California, where he had been invited to live with a millionaire and his wife on Linda Isle. Steve wanted to pursue his rodeo career with a trainer who was located in Mission Viejo. Russ and I tried to talk him out of moving and to stay in school to get an education. But Steve's heart was not into school, and he thought he wanted to be a cowboy. It was then that I realized I made a mistake and should have taken the detail in DC. I think we all felt that way on the Steve Ford Detail. However, the Secret Service was good about helping us to prepare for the next transition to Southern California.

In December, Steve went to Vail, Colorado, for Christmas to be with his family where they loved to vacation and spend holidays, so the agents on his detail had to work into the presidential detail rotation. Standing post in the snow at Christmas in Vail made me realize how fortunate I was to be assigned to Steve.

When we got back from Vail, Steve packed up his belongings at Utah State and drove out to Newport Beach, California. Our protection detail went with him and left our families back in Logan to sell our homes.

Steve moved in with the wealthy couple, and the Secret Service detail rented five two-bedroom apartments across the way. Six days a week we followed Steve to a ranch in Mission Viejo where he would ride, rope, and train to be a cowboy. At night we accompanied him to a local nightclub. Even though he was only nineteen, the club let him in. Steve was tall, fit, blond, and handsome, so he frequently left with an attractive woman to keep him company through the night. Since our command post was in a bedroom located downstairs, we often met a young lady on her way out the door in the morning.

Steve Ford then decided he needed more exposure to rodeo, so he went to San Diego Country Estates to train with Casey Tibbs, once the world's best all-around cowboy. I sat on the fence day after day watching as a bull or bronco threw the president's son through the air and heard the air go out of his lungs as he hit the ground with a hard thud. I kept thinking we would lose our protectee on one of his lethal rides.

I have to give it to Steve though; he had no quit in him no matter how hard he hit the ground. But it sure was painful to watch.

Chapter 16

Friendly TWA

Steve Ford then had to hit the campaign trail for the reelection of his father, Gerald Ford. The Republican Party rented Steve a motorhome, and the Secret Service rented a small motorhome to follow Steve around. A member of the Secret Service Detail drove Steve's motorhome while the other agents followed behind. Steve was assigned to hit all the western states such as Wyoming, Montana, Idaho, North Dakota, South Dakota, Utah, Nevada, and Colorado. Steve, although an introvert, did quite well with young people and focused his appeal to gatherings of folks who would have normally been missed in a campaign. We went from town to town, with Steve preaching the gospel according to the Republican Party to get his father elected.

After months of campaigning, Kansas City was chosen for the Republican Convention. Since I started my career in Kansas City, I was directed to go there as a member of the Presidential Advance Team. I had the dubious honor of finding accommodations for the 200 agents who would be brought in from field offices all across the country for the convention.

Everywhere I looked the hotel rooms were sold out. I went over to my old office and asked if anyone had ideas where to put the agents up for the convention. It was suggested to contact the nearby TWA academy, where they trained flight attendants (then known as stewardesses) in nearby Overland Park to see if they had any dormitory space. They did.

The academy had five dormitories, and only three were currently being used. By doubling up in each room, the 200 agents we had slated to arrive for post standing duties could be accommodated in the two vacant dormitories. I was given a tour by the lead administrator and noticed all the pretty young ladies on the campus. I should have detected trouble ahead.

Two days after the arrival of the field agents, I got a call from the head administrator to come to the TWA Academy immediately. Although she would not tell me what was wrong, I could sense that not all was pleasant at the academy.

When I arrived at her office, her first words were "You have to do something with those animals you brought on my campus." She escorted me to the pool in the center of the academy where two empty beer kegs were floating.

The administrator said that the agents had a pool party on the first night of their arrival, and the party soon got out of control. She advised that the "animals" had violated her young ladies. She admonished me to do something to keep the agents away from her stewardesses.

I went to see the agent in charge at his dorm room. He explained to me that when the agents arrived, they went out to the pool, and twenty minutes later the ladies came flooding from their dorm rooms, wearing skimpy bikinis and toting a boombox playing loud music. He said it became an instant party that went well into the night. He said he would talk to his men, but someone should tell the ladies to stay in their dormitories.

In the meantime, I got the opportunity to see Ronald Reagan

challenge Gerald Ford at the convention. Although I did not know much about Reagan at the time, I was impressed by his demeanor and ability to communicate.

The election of 1976 saw the peanut farmer from Georgia, Jimmy Carter, win the election for the Democratic Party. The protection detail for Steve Ford ended. The agents assigned to Steve were given a choice to stay on the presidential detail and transfer to Washington or apply to go to the field office of our choice. Four of the agents chose to go to DC. Six chose to return to the field, including me. But I was the only agent who chose the Los Angeles Field Office. I did not want to move my family again, and we liked living in Southern California. Besides, if you enjoyed working criminal investigations, which I most certainly did, LA was the place to be.

Chapter 17

WELCOME TO LA

SPORTING A PINSTRIPE suit, I reported to the Los Angeles Field Office and sat outside the office of the special agent in charge for four hours waiting to meet with Bob Powis, known as a tough but respected taskmaster. Finally, I was instructed to go in.

Mr. Powis was one tough cookie. A former tank commander in the military, he had a commanding presence. Without any pleasantries, he proceeded to inform me of what he expected of me: work hard, be truthful, and compete with other agents to make cases and arrests. After admonishing me for an hour, Powis grabbed a street atlas and threw it at me.

"There's a counterfeit surveillance case going on in Anaheim. Check out a car and get out on the street."

I checked out an old Rambler that had no air-conditioning and proceeded to roam the streets wearing my pinstripe suit in 105-degree heat. It took me about two hours to finally join the surveillance team. While I knew the exercise was to test my ability to endure, I was ecstatic to be back in the field looking for bad guys. The other agents on the surveillance were in baggy street clothes with long hair and beards. They looked at me in disdain with my suit and short-cropped hair. They knew I just came off the presidential detail, and I knew I had to prove I belonged on the street with these LA veterans.

I couldn't wait to dive in.

My time in LA was interesting, to say the least. I worked a lot of cases, some frustrating, most fruitful, and I learned plenty. There are too many cases to recount, but some have made it into this book. And there are some that left me forever changed.

Chapter 18

THE MURDER OF JULIE CROSS

SINCE THE INAUGURATION of the Secret Service in 1865, only three agents had been killed in the line of duty as of June 3, 1980. But on June 4, that number would be increased by one, and the total number of female agents at that time would diminish to twenty.

Julie Cross, born in Bradford, Yorkshire, England, in 1954, to an Irish father and an American mother, grew up in South Dakota and then moved to California, where she graduated high school and went on to earn a bachelor's degree in Criminal Justice. A prime candidate for any law enforcement agency, Julie began her life's work in 1977 with the San Diego Police Department. Two and a half years later, Julie entered the United States Secret Service, assigned to the San Diego field office.

It was there where I first met Julie, during a presidential visit by Jimmy Carter. I was immediately struck by her professionalism and her maturity. She didn't display any of the tendencies often associated with fledgling agents, like being enamored by their own image of self-importance or getting goo-goo eyes around political bigwigs.

Though she dressed conservatively, unrevealingly, there was no doubt in any man's mind that Julie was 100 percent woman, and, also, simultaneously, there was no question that she could take care of business. I found her to be somewhat introverted, yet she was a good conversationalist. Most of our chitchat centered on the job of being a Secret Service agent. Her questions were penetrating, and I had little doubt that Julie Cross was going to be a first-rate agent.

I had confidence that I could depend on her to back me up in a tight situation. She had real instincts—street smarts. I wasn't the only one to think so. Julie was quickly transferred to the Los Angeles Field Office, which was quite unusual for a rookie agent to be assigned to a major city, let alone the elite counterfeit squad.

The agent who would become her partner had also entered the Secret Service after serving as a patrolman in the police department. Lloyd, from Laramie, Wyoming, spent several years at the Denver, Colorado Field Office, then transferred to Los Angeles, where he worked the check forgery squad. In 1979, Lloyd made it to the counterfeit investigation team and became Julie's partner.

On June 4, 1980, Cross and Lloyd were assigned as a "perimeter chase team" and were parked in an unmarked car, a nondescript Buick Electra 255. Several other agents were stationed on the other side of the apartment complex in the surveillance van.

I was not part of this operation. That night I was home, and I did what I always did at 10 p.m., turned on the news. The first story was a breaking story. The lady street reporter, broadcasting live from the scene, related that a Drug Enforcement agent had been killed in Inglewood. Of course, this wouldn't have surprised me, since DEA agents are forever busting violent criminals in what has to be one of the deadliest jobs in law enforcement. But something just wasn't right in the telling of the story. The "facts" didn't match the image. And then it hit me: I recognized the white van in the background of the picture. That was our surveillance van. I knew that truck inside and out from numerous stakeouts. Before the reporter even signed off, I was on the phone to the duty agent, and he confirmed that Julie Cross had been killed. I had never felt so weak, so shocked, so wordless, so angry.

What we know of that night is mainly from Lloyd's recollection. At approximately 8:45 p.m., Lloyd observed a rusted '72 Pontiac or Buick cruise around the corner, occupied by two Black men sitting low in their seats, one wearing a dark-colored stocking cap. They circled the block once more before parking about forty yards ahead of the agents.

The two men exited their car and entered the apartment complex, disappearing down a driveway shielded from view by a plant-entwined cyclone fence. It is assumed that the two suspects worked their way to where Agents Cross and Lloyd were positioned and watched them from the security of the thick foliage.

A few moments later, the suspects returned to their car and drove off. It is now presumed that they circled three-quarters of the way around the block, where they left their car to stalk the two agents silently from the rear. A further assumption is that the murderers made the agents as two ready-to-rob lovers.

Julie first spotted the two men in her rearview mirror, skulking up behind the stakeout car. "Somebody's coming up behind us," she said as she grabbed her .357 Smith and Wesson and bailed out of the car and ordered the man in front of her to stop and put up his hands. Taking advantage of Lloyd's attention to Julie, the second suspect yanked open the driver's-side door and jammed his pistol against Lloyd's head.

"Hey, hold it," Lloyd said. "I'm a police officer." Lloyd raised his hands.

The suspect responded, "I'm a police officer too."

"Why don't you show me your badge, and we'll straighten this thing out," Lloyd offered.

"Shut the fuck up," the assailant answered.

It was the proverbial Mexican standoff: Julie had one robber covered; robber number two had the drop on Lloyd.

"Show me your badge first. She's not going to drop her pistol until you show me your badge," Lloyd said.

The suspect shoved the gun into Lloyd's left temple and said, "Tell her to drop her gun or I'll blow your fuckin' head off right here!"

Lloyd said he shouted, "Don't drop your gun, Julie! He's going to have to show me his badge."

At this time, Lloyd said he heard Julie order her suspect to "get your goddamn hands on top of the car!"

But what happened next remains unclear, not uncommon in what is termed "the fog of battle." The assailant came around to Lloyd's side of the car and reached across Lloyd's lap to grab the Secret Service shotgun that had been resting between the two agents on the front seat. Lloyd recalls the suspect retreating with the weapon, and he says he remembers the pale light cast by a streetlamp revealing a deathly expression on Julie's face as she leaped into the passenger side of the front seat—as if she knew her life was to be violently obliterated at that moment.

And it was. Two deafening shotgun blasts shattered the tense quiet of the drama. The first blast hit Julie and knocked her into the back seat. The second slug was aimed at Lloyd, but the rifle slug went through the left front door, barely missing him.

Lloyd managed to grab the pistol barrel and leap out of the car and wrestle the other suspect in the street. In the cloud of confusion, of survival, Lloyd heard a couple of blasts. Then he heard his guy scream, "Shoot the motherfucker," followed by the reply of "I can't—you're in the way!"

Lloyd struggled to keep the second suspect between him and the shotgun. The perpetrator threw Lloyd to the pavement, and this presented the opportunity the shotgunner needed. He rushed up, pointed the muzzle to Lloyd's face. Lloyd pleaded, "Don't shoot," as he turned his head to the side. That's when the Remington went off, blowing a hole in the asphalt and nicking Lloyd in the ear. Thinking they had killed Lloyd, the two murderers ran full sprint into the darkness, sure that Lloyd's head had been pulped by the double OO gauge pellets.

Though bloodied by the asphalt that flew up from the blast, he had not been shot. Lloyd was more dazed at the realization that he was alive than from the trauma he had lived through. He picked himself off the street, retrieved his pistol, and began to chase the two killers.

Lloyd did not catch the suspects and returned to the car and discovered Julie in the back seat dead. The agents on the other side of the building had not heard the shots due to the noise of low-flying planes so near to the airport. Tips started pouring in almost immediately. Two names that catapulted to the top of our list were brothers Charles (Chino) and Terry Brock. Both were convicted felons with rap sheets as thick as dime novels. Several days after the killing, they were arrested for parole violation, and subsequently placed in a police line-up. Agent Lloyd's eyes kept returning to the face of Terry Brock. He studied it for a long time and said that Brock looked like the man with whom he had wrestled. But he just couldn't be sure. The brothers were held on the separate charges. Interestingly, though frustratingly, a police artist's composite drawing rendered from a description given by Lloyd truly resembled the countenance of brother Terry.

It was determined that Chino Brock had been in jail at LA PD Pacific Division on June 4 and was released at 9:05 p.m. This information ruled Chino out as a suspect.

Despite the hundreds of interviews conducted by police and Secret Service investigators, no new clues surfaced. The killers had literally gotten away with murder. We even went so far as to present the Julie Cross murder on the popular TV series *Unsolved Mysteries*. Because its format is a combination of "showbiz" and information, the script writers recreated one instance where Julie had phoned her good friend San Diego police officer Cheryl Meyer, who recounted that "Julie called me the day before she was to leave for Los Angeles. Julie sounded very distressed and scared. She said she felt something was going to happen to her in LA."

More than 5,000 tips from across the land were received at the show's 800 number. A team of four Secret Service agents worked the show to evaluate the calls. Many were bizarre. One tipster claimed that he knew Julie had been snuffed because she had uncovered information that linked Cuba to the assassination of President John F. Kennedy. Despite the apparent outlandishness of some of the assertions, every lead was followed up. And discounted. The case slowed to the pace of a glacial advance, although, as with all murder cases, it was never closed.

In 1989, nine years after Julie Cross' murder, Buck, a persistent, patient, intuitive, and insightful detective with the LAPD who cracked a triple murder case, became the man to bring the case to a close.

During Buck's investigation for a case of his, he interviewed a career criminal in Soledad Prison for the hopelessly hard-core in California, where Brock was also imprisoned. For whatever leniency he could arrange, the informant spilled his guts about various dealings with and "admissions" by Terry Brock.

"Who did he tell you he killed?"

"He told for sure, he tell me, he shot the woman, the policewoman, okay. With a shotgun."

A dogged detective with tentacles deep into "the hood," Buck gathered from a reliable source that Terry Brock along with another "crimey" named Andre Alexander had "talked real excited 'bout how they killed a White lady cop."

Buck re-interviewed Brock in prison, emphasizing that an unimpeachable source had fingered him and Alexander as the killers of Julie Cross. Brock readily admitted that he knew about the murder, but that it was committed by Alexander and his brother, Chino.

Besides being incarcerated in jail at the time of the murder, Chino couldn't be questioned about this homicide as he had overdosed and died a few months earlier. Buck was incessant in his questioning, his interviewing strategies. With witnesses present, he got Terry Brock to provide details that only a participant in the crime could have known—facts that never had been released from the files of the Secret Service and the LAPD.

His willingness to blame his dead brother did him in, and these two criminals were finally brought to trial. Both Terry Brock and Andre Alexander were convicted in 1996 of the murder of Julie Cross.

Julie died three years prior to the accidental deaths of three agents in Mariposa County during the Yosemite visit of Queen Elizabeth, and before then, the toughest moment of my career in the Secret Service was attending the funeral of Julie Cross. To this day, I find myself reflecting on her murder, remembering what a beautiful and dedicated person she was. And when I do, I must take several deep breaths before my fists unclench.

Chapter 19

Chase To Down Under

It was almost as if Rudolph Valentino had walked into the bank.

The murmurings of daily business noticeably hushed as one teller after another stopped her behind-the-cage dealings to visually drink in the man's uncommon handsomeness. And perhaps to fantasize just a little.

He stood just over six feet tall and had the perfect posture of an athlete with the practiced grace of a classical dancer. The light diffused almost halo-like off his ebony hair, which had to have been blended with a commercial sheen of some kind. His obviously well-toned body was packaged in a fine, I mean *fine*, Italian suit, faultlessly tailored so that every pinstripe intersected another stripe with engineered precision. A mapmaker could not have joined roads with better accuracy.

Fabio Veneziani dripped self-confidence and success, almost arrogance, yet was as outwardly friendly as a person could be, disarmingly so. He always waved to the women; even tried to remember their names. Without fail, Fabio always glided out of his way to shake hands with the bank manager, who believed that it was his job to make his valued clients feel as important as they doubtlessly were.

"God, he's gorgeous!" one teller whispered to her coworker. "I think I'd rob this bank for him," she joked.

"You don't have to. I've seen his balance," the other gal replied.

"Then he's even more gorgeous." She grinned.

"Mr. Williams, I believe we have a problem."

The call was from the bank's fraud investigator. "I have been in contact with another bank regarding a men's clothing business in Los Angeles, and we're sure that computer fraud has taken place in our DCS."

Law enforcement bureaucracy is a world of letters and acronyms—CIA, FBI, ATF, DEA, KKK, DC, AC/DC, ad infinitum. DCS is not a federal term but means "data capture system."

These two banks' management became alert to possible criminal activity when a flood of customers complained of unauthorized amounts appearing on their credit card statements. All of the charges were to Veneziani, Inc.

This company had showed deposits from August 1987 to November 1987 of just over $7,000. Suddenly, however, from November '87 to January 11, 1988, credit card deposits soared to over $300,000, all manually keyed into Veneziani, Inc.'s magnetic terminal. Likewise, the other bank had sustained $400,000 of charge loss. Again, all input had been done manually into the computer terminal.

All the cardholders confirmed that they still had their credit cards in their possession and not one had ever shopped at, or even heard of, Veneziani, Inc.

A brief review of Veneziani, Inc. accounts showed that the large sums of receivables no longer were in place and that only $3,000 remained. The personal accounts of Fabio Veneziani and his brother, Emanuele Veneziani, registered a total of minus $54.45.

As agent-in-charge of fraud and counterfeit investigations, I immediately authorized Secret Service involvement. We quickly learned that Fabio and Emanuele were in the United States on Italian passports. Emanuele, twelve years older than Fabio, was only 5'8" and weighed 145 pounds. Perhaps their mother had force-fed pasta to Fabio, giving him his attractive stature.

I dispatched two agents to visit the address of Veneziani, Inc., located in the ornate Cooper Building in the downtown garment district of Los Angeles. Five floors up, the investigators were greeted by a notice of eviction placed on the company door.

Five floors down, in the offices of the building administration, the facilities manager said that they had missed brother Fabio by one day. Fabio had told him that they were going to remodel their showroom and shut down their business for a few weeks. The manager said that in the four years the brothers had leased space there, he had never seen a single customer on the premises. The Venezianis were nearly four months in arrears for rent, so he served them with an eviction notice on January 11, 1988.

The agents next drove to a Beverly Hills apartment complex that the Venezianis had listed with the office building manager as their residence. The apartment manager reported that the Italian brothers no longer lived there, and that he had witnessed Fabio and Emanuele leaving quickly about three weeks earlier. A moving company had packed all the Veneziani belongings into crates used on sea-going vessels. He quite proudly remembered the name printed on the side of the crates was SeaLand Express.

Calling the shipping company, the freight manager confirmed and identified some of the freighted items: four brand-new motorcycles, a Porsche sportscar, two refrigerators, two brand-new television sets, boxes of brand-new electronic equipment, fine furniture, and other personal items.

The containers had been manifested aboard two Italian-flagged ships, and were addressed to Mr. Luigi Riccacione in Bari, Italy. The freighters were slated to dock in Naples, Italy, on or about January 31, 1988.

The apartment manager said that on January 11, Fabio and his wife attempted to get in their former apartment, but that he refused them access. The next morning, he entered the apartment to clean up for the next rental. He said the place was in total disarray. Clothes, cosmetics, and kitchenware were strewn over the place, and he found several boxes of brand-new clothes, plus a pile of discarded charge receipts.

The last that the apartment manager had heard was that the Venezianis had taken up residence at the ritzy Beverly Comstock Hotel on pricey Wilshire Boulevard, near Beverly Hills.

Our agents next visited the Beverly Comstock, learning that the brothers and their wives had stayed, and were gone, paying their $4,000 tab with an American Express card.

Further records tracked phone calls from their rooms. The most frequently called number was in the LA 213 area code, registered to a Bernardo Martinez. The Venezianis also called Bari, Italy, three times, possibly to "Mr. Riccacione"—the addressee on the cargo containers.

With such international connections—passports, names, and destinations—our agents contacted U.S. Customs agents who advised that Fabio and his wife had departed Los Angeles International Airport at 9 p.m. on January 13, 1988, en route to Tahiti.

Since the brothers had paid for their Beverly Comstock rooms with an American Express card, our agent called the credit card company and spoke to their investigator, who found that the Venezianis had applied and been approved for five different accounts predicated on the balance in their bank accounts at the two banks who had discovered the credit card fraud.

During the peak wire-transfer activity, the Venezianis had amassed more than $2 million, sufficient cash for credit approval. The American Express investigator also discovered that as of January 25, 1988, the Venezianis had spent lavishly on such items as clothing, china, bar bills, restaurants, hotels, and airline tickets. They owed American Express more than $150,000.

The charge records showed that they had purchased tickets on Qantas and Alitalia airlines, who were then contacted to discern their flight plans. Emanuele Veneziani had purchased tickets showing departure on January 8 to Sydney, Australia. Fabio's itinerary showed a January 13 departure to Papeete, Tahiti, and then to Sydney. Australian Federal Police also confirmed that visas had been granted to Emanuele and Fabio.

Our agents examined the bank records to determine how fraudulent monies had been withdrawn from the Veneziani accounts. It didn't take long to find dozens of merchant account checks on the Veneziani name made out to a person named George Pearl. All Pearl's checks had been signed by a Julian J. Garcia, whose moniker appeared on the approved signature list for writing Veneziani, Inc. checks at both banks.

Each bank had insisted that Garcia list his California driver's license number on the signature authorization cards. The agents immediately checked with the Department of Motor Vehicles to get Garcia's home address. They "galloped" to the site, an appropriate verb since the address was the Hollywood Park racetrack. Either Garcia lived on hay and oats, or he lied on the bank-verification forms.

The DMV clerk uncovered a second Garcia address in North Hollywood. The mailbox showed the apartment belonged to a Bernardo Garcia, not Julian Garcia.

During this investigation, we developed a confidential informant who claimed that she had worked with the Venezianis, and that she had been "stiffed" by them. No one makes a better underworld informant than a disgruntled associate. This woman admitted that the apartment was a "drop" address used by a man named Bernadru Olivares Martinez. We had Garcia's driver's license picture, which we immediately showed to our informant. Martinez and Garcia, she said, were one and the same.

Our informant ID'd George Pearl as a man referred to as "George the Gringo," a.k.a. George Kosth.

This done, we issued federal arrest warrants for Julian J. Garcia a.k.a. Bernardo Garcia a.k.a. Bernadru Olivares Martinez; and Pearl, a.k.a. "gringo," a.k.a. Kosth, for investigation of fraud.

Additionally, we arranged for the U.S. Magistrate in Los Angeles to issue arrest warrants for the Veneziani brothers for credit card fraud. These warrants were forwarded via all the proper channels to the Australian Federal Police.

On January 22, we obtained a search warrant for the seaborne crates upon their arrival in Italy and forwarded the warrant via the U.S. Attorney in LA to the Italian Customs Department.

Our snare—though still loose—had begun to tighten.

Then came the *snap*. The Australian Federal Police teletyped the words we wanted to hear: "Fabio and Emanuele Veneziani located and arrested January 29, in Cairns. Incarcerated pending your arrival."

When Fabio and Emanuele landed at Cairns, with their wives, Australian Federal Police officers arrested the two men immediately. They promptly threw these impeccably attired crooks into what amounted to a third-world jail, a cramped, steaming, non-air-conditioned cell already occupied by twenty-five alcoholic, unwashed Aborigines who hated the White establishment. It took but minutes for the brothers' tailored sports outfits to be fouled by smells that polluted the air, and by excretions of various kinds. The Veneziani wives, meanwhile, checked into a nearby luxury hotel and resumed their extravagant vacations on their counterfeit credit cards, but this time sans husbands.

Although I had been around the world many times in the line of duty, my assignments had been exclusively in the northern hemisphere. I was to make my first trip to the land down under, and frankly I was as anxious as a kid.

I contacted Honolulu-based agent Bob Twynham to request that he meet me in Honolulu, for the connection to Australia. Twynham was an excellent interrogator, and I wanted him along.

Dog-tired after the nonstop, nine-hour flight from Hawaii, in coach, we were greeted most heartily by two Australian Federal Police agents. They ignored our pleas to take us to our hotel, insisting that we start our Australian assignment in Australian fashion. Thus began a two-week-long attack on my liver by what has to be the most alcohol-tolerant society in the world. They took us to some of their favorite haunts in the notorious Kings Cross section of Sydney, a section devoted to strip joints, bars, restaurants, strip joints, bars, sex shops, and more bars. The pulse of Kings Cross doesn't crank up until well after dark, and then it races at an arrhythmic pace just until sun-up.

The evening began at the Beef and Stein, a bar whose denizens would have felt truly at home in a Fellini movie or in a *Star Wars* film. Outer space right here on Earth. The most bizarre apparition of the young night walked in, stopping Twynham and me in our tracks. We think she had a beautiful face, but frankly neither of us could take our eyes off her naked figure, which was fully and bountifully exposed beneath a clear plastic raincoat. I found this strange, and not just because it wasn't raining.

Ignoring our stares, the creature in the see-through "wrapper" ambled up to me and Twynham, ordered a Foster's beer, tossed it down in a couple of husky gulps, threw her money onto the bar, and swirled away through the door as easily as she had come in.

It *must* have been real, because both Twynham and I *saw* it. Or did we?

What do you say, or do, after *that*? Twynham and I just kept gazing around the room, hoping our transparent nymph would materialize again. But soon our now-revitalized eyes were transfixed by the prospect of another adventure in female anatomy. We had been staring at another buxom beauty who had caught our eye.

"What yer lookin' at, mate," she challenged us.

Twynham was first to respond: "Just trying to see your tits," he blared unabashedly.

Without so much as a beat, she unbuttoned her dress and laid bare what had to be one of the world's foremost matching sets of mammaries. At that, Twynham, ecstatic, took the proffered breasts in his hands and began to gently turn them as if trying to tune in the Super Bowl. Ms. Buxom accepted this action with a mixture of mild enjoyment and boredom. For whatever reason, she chose to speak to me during this interplay.

Without any kind of preamble, she said, "You know, women make better lovers…"

"Oh, are you a lesbian?" I countered.

"No, mate, I had a sex change operation six weeks ago."

Faster than a trigger pull, Twynham snapped back to reality from his reverie. I thought he was going to choke right there.

"That's right, mates," the bartender chimed in, "she's a bloke!" He laughed conspiratorially.

"If that's true, honey, I'll buy you a drink if you take off the rest of your clothes right here," I said.

She said nothing. Looking at me vacantly, he—she—just wandered away and melted into the crowd of freaks.

We refrained from conversing for several minutes after that, just nursing our drinks in a mist of cigarette smoke and fatigue. Then we became aware of the band starting to play and the crowd forming near the dance floor.

We looked up to see a dress flying above the heads of the now clapping patrons crowded around a dancing figure. Almost simultaneously, we recognized the dress as that belonging to the transsexual. We wove our way onto the parquet floor and wormed to the front of the crowd. There she was, naked except for the briefest of panties, gyrating with surprising grace and femininity. She saw Twynham. Surprising him with a strength that progesterone injections had failed to diminish, she grabbed Twynham and pulled him next to her on the dance floor, spinning and twirling him around as if he were an involuntary marionette.

The music built up its crescendo; the people were hooting and hollering encouragement. Twynham kept yelling at me, but I couldn't hear him. Finally, his words filtered through the fog: "Hey, Williams, see if she's got a dick!"

Frankly, I couldn't tell. The writhing, grinding transsexual wouldn't stand still long enough, and frankly, my eyes weren't focusing any too well. I grabbed Twynham off the stage, and we staggered back to the bar. The rest of the evening remains a blur, and from that point I only remember waking up with what had to be largest headache under the Southern Cross.

We had been scheduled for a meeting the next morning with one of the directors of the Australian Federal Police. I couldn't remember his name then; I don't remember it now. But I do recall that both Twynham and I reached his office about 10 a.m., feeling as if cotton had been shoved under our eyelids and our swollen tongues dipped in formaldehyde. The director greeted us: "You blokes want something to drink?"

"Coffee for us," I managed.

"No, mates, I mean beer!"

With that, he nearly sprinted to his private refrigerator, from which he grabbed a six-pack for each of us. Then he raced back to his desk to begin a two-hour, beer-punctuated chat with us and some of the other agents from the outer offices. He called it a "necessary case review."

At noon, the Australians took us to lunch—at another pub with six new faces from the Australian Federal Police. Again, the beer flowed 'til nearly 5 p.m. as we continued our "case review." In retrospect, I believe a "case review" is euphemistic for a case of Foster's. At five o'clock straight up, the police director stood officiously, looked at his pocket watch, and announced, "Well, mates, that's it for the day, but these two fellows here will take you to dinner."

"Only if we can pay," I insisted.

The Aussies chose the pub and the wine—five bottles between the four of us. They passed out. Twynham followed them into slumber land shortly thereafter. Somehow, by the grace of God, I stayed awake—barely. With every ounce of controllable strength left in me, I tried to rouse them, but to no avail. The restaurant staff helped us all into our car, and since I was the only one awake, they gave me the key.

Ever try to navigate in a foreign city, at night, with everyone driving on the wrong side of the road? With God as my copilot, I weaved through the city, and by sheer chance happened upon our hotel and a valued parking space. The parked cars in front and back surrendered obstinately to my efforts. I then tried, without success, to awaken our federal hosts. But I did manage to stir Twynham enough to get him out of the car. We left the feds in place and stumbled into the hotel. Thus, we concluded the second day of a very serious international investigation. Before I fell asleep, I swore that if day three ever arrived, and if it came anything close to days one and two, I was going to open the southern hemisphere branch of the Betty Ford Clinic.

Day three arrived abruptly and was most unwelcome. Not even a cold shower could chase the previous two days out of my system. But duty called, even 8,000 miles away from home. Twynham and I rendezvoused in the coffee shop for badly needed caffeine before we took a cab to the airport. We refused the offer of the feds to drive us, lest we get sidetracked to another grog shoppe.

We caught a domestic flight to Cairns (pronounced canes), vacation gateway to the Great Barrier Reef—truly one of the incredible wonders of our natural kingdom. Unfortunately, we were there to interrogate two denizens of a far different underworld. Even if we had the time, our heads wouldn't and couldn't have taken the additional pressure of a deep scuba dive.

Australian Federal Agents Barry Turner and Bruce Jacobs, who had made the arrest, greeted us at the comfortably small airport. Turner spoke first: "We had heard that two hard-drinking Yanks were on the way to Cairns, and we're here to claim you…" Our newly painted reputation had preceded us.

We were driven immediately to the Cairns jail, a dungeon of a place. The guards brought up brother Fabio first. Funny what a week in the hole will do to a man's appearance. Various crusty things adhered to his once splendid sports outfit. Five days of dark growth sprouted from his once-pampered face. In short, he looked like shit. He also looked as though he were glad to see us, just to get away from his unwanted cellmates, who chatted incessantly in a tongue that anthropologists have traced back nearly 50,000 years.

Twynham and I escorted Fabio to the local police station, where, after we advised him of his Constitutional rights per the Miranda Decision, we interrogated him most of the day. He denied knowing anything about a theft of funds. In a sworn statement, he placed all blame on Garcia, their influential bookkeeper since 1984, whom they promoted to general manager three years later. At that time, Garcia pleaded with the brothers to let him join their firm by offering to invest $120,000 in the business at a rate of $30,000 a month for four months.

"Of course, my brother and I accepted his generous proposal," Fabio said.

"Trusting him implicitly, we also followed Garcia's advice on how to set up our banking procedures," he added.

According to Fabio, Garcia had introduced George Pearl to the brothers, who named him marketing manager and assigned him the responsibility of liquidating excess clothing and conducting all outside sales. They paid Pearl's commissions in cash.

We hammered on brother Emanuele the next day. The sculptors of countenance were not as kind to Emanuele as they were to his brother with those movie star looks. After acknowledging his rights, and waiving those rights, he agreed to answer our questions.

Emanuele was a different kind of man—different from Fabio, and different, too, from most men we meet in these circumstances. He was quiet, almost serene, definitely an intellectual who, we were to discover, had earned a law degree. I had the uncomfortable feeling that I was interviewing a man of superior intellect and control, but one who lacked a certain street wisdom. Emanuele repeated much of what Fabio had said, but stated more eloquently that since he—Emanuele—traveled extensively on behalf of their business, he relinquished everyday operations to his younger brother, including banking and bookkeeping. He emphatically denied knowing anything about credit card fraud or any other dishonest practices by Veneziani, Inc., but added that since he had given signature authorization to Garcia, it was the accountant who had to be culpable.

If nothing else, their week in the Cairns slammer gave the brothers almost uninterrupted time to rehearse their stories. Neither brother broke, despite Twynham's and my stereotypical good guy/bad guy tactics. We turned questions inside out, backward and forward, and rephrased the same point countless ways. But the brothers did well. Our purpose in Australia had been completed, and we finally returned to our hotel to rest. We stayed an additional four days to wait for the extradition papers to arrive. In the meantime, Twynham and I finally jet-boated out to the Great Barrier Reef on a clear day with clear minds to drink in one of—if not the—greatest shows on earth. (Sorry, Mr. Barnum.) The rest of the wait we learned to do better what the Aussies seemed to do best: drink.

On the night before our departure, Turner, Jacobs, their wives, and a couple of other agents said they wanted to take us out to dinner. Of course, we agreed. En route to a quaint Italian eatery, we stopped at the "bottle shop" for some Italian wine. This restaurant did not serve alcoholic beverages, but it was acceptable to brown bag your own.

I came out with four bottles.

Turner objected, "You Yanks are awfully cheap!" So Twynham

and I went back into the shop to purchase two more bottles.

"That won't even last twenty minutes," Jacobs screamed.

So, we went back in again. Four trips and nineteen bottles of wine later, the Aussies finally admitted that we had "sufficient supplies to start dinner."

By midnight, every last drop of wine had been consumed. The word "pain" did not exist for the moment. As we lurched outside, the ladies contended that the night was far too young to call it an evening. They suggested dancing at a local club.

"Hear, hear!" the Aussies chimed.

Though the club was only a few blocks away, the wives insisted on taking tourist pedicabs, whose drivers obviously had transported inebriated customers before. But I'm not sure they were prepared to play *Ben Hur* Aussie style. The cops lined up the pedicabs and launched the great Cairns race. No chariot race in ancient Rome could have matched the glory of this race—Aussies vs. the Americans. Twynham stood throughout the race, "beating" the driver with his seat belt. Even Charlton Heston's sterling performance in *Ben Hur* paled in comparison.

We won. But Twynham lost—for at the front entrance, the rickshaw driver slammed on his brakes, ejecting Twynham from the cab, headfirst. Twynham landed face down, laid out in front of the pub like a welcome mat. At that moment in time, he could not have cared less who walked over him. So, we did. And went on into the pub to celebrate international relations until 4 a.m.

At seven the next morning, I was jolted awake by loud knocking. Rolling out of bed, still in my skivvy shorts, I dragged to the door and opened it. There, like an apparition from hell, stood the Aussie cops and their wives, apparently none the worse for wear, carrying fresh new bottles of champagne. They barged in, leaving the door wide open.

"Just want to wish you a *bon voyage*, mate," somebody chimed.

When Twynham refused to answer his door, another group of

cops "on urgent official business" got a pass key from the front desk manager and stormed into his room and carried Twynham, wrapped in a sheet, to my room. By noon, I thought I had died.

Consummate professionals, the Australian Federal Police somehow packed all our belongings and transported Twynham and me to the airport in time for our 3 p.m. flight. Then someone must have poured me onto the plane and strapped me in my seat, for the last thing I remember before waking up in Honolulu is that I had slumped off my seat in the boarding area.

I woke again in time to transfer planes back to the mainland; then I slept the entire five hours to Los Angeles. It was the quickest international flight of my life.

Infused with Alka Seltzer and aspirin, I reviewed the previous two weeks with our Aussie friends, and I realized that I hadn't drunk that much alcohol since I streaked bare-assed with eight of my teenage army-brat buddies down some *Strasse* in Germany more than twenty years earlier.

Then a little luck began to play along in this investigation. On February 15, George Kosth was arrested while driving across the border from Juarez, into El Paso, Texas, in a sparkling new Mercedes. Responding to an alert issued by our office, U.S. Customs found that he was traveling under the name George Pearl. But perhaps worse for him, a Customs canine sniffed out two small bags of cocaine in the trunk of his car. He became ours to "work." And work him we did. I sent our agents to El Paso, to question Kosth. With the added threat of drug smuggling hanging over him, Kosth decided to cooperate with us. He implicated the Veneziani brothers and revealed that Martinez had fled to the Dominican Republic. That was the bad news. The good news was that Kosth had Martinez' telephone number.

As ordered, Kosth contacted Martinez at a bar hangout, and enticingly described a new credit card scam.

"I ain't comin' to Los Angeles, man," Martinez said.

"Then meet me in Miami," Kosth was instructed to say.

Kosth/Pearl and our two agents flew to Miami to await Martinez' arrival. Finally, he called and Kosth said he would pick him up at the airport.

"When you see Martinez, run up and give 'im the ol' Latin *abrazo*. Then hold him," Kosth was told.

Kosth played the part beautifully. His "salary" for this acting job was erasure of his recent drug smuggling charge, so he wasn't about to let Martinez loose.

As the Secret Service agents, guns pointed, encircled the two friends hugging, Martinez dropped his hands, looked murderously at Kosth, and seethed out a single word in Spanish. Translation: Asshole!

Meanwhile, in Rome, Italy, U.S. Secret Service received notification from Italian Customs that the Venezianis' shipborne containers had arrived and had been seized by their agents on the waterfront.

As expected, the containers held enough television sets and other electronics to stock a Circuit City outlet; sufficient mink coats to sicken Greenpeace and other anti-fur activists; a new Porsche and four Harley-Davidson motorcycles, plus a variety of modern electronic kitchen appliances that would most assuredly seduce Betty Crocker into a pantry-sized orgasm.

In comparing the bills of lading with the contents of the containers, our agents discovered that the numbers didn't jibe, leading us to believe that the wives of several customs officials might be wearing the latest fur fashions to Sunday church services. Despite the discrepancies, the containers were padlocked for their shipment back to U.S. warehouses.

Jeff, the case agent, continued his investigation of the Veneziani machinations. A consummate, detail-oriented, and patient investigator, Jeff left no pieces of paper unread. From the mess gathered up from the floor of the Venezianis' Beverly Hills apartment, he uncrumpled a small slip that indicated Emanuele had visited a bank in Lugano, Switzerland, just prior to the brothers' Australian escapade.

From later interviews, Jeff uncovered the fact that Emanuele had stuffed $1.5 million in cash inside a custom-made money belt and had then deposited it in Lugano. Wearing that kind of money under his clothes, he had to have resembled Humpty Dumpty, and Jeff was now putting all the Veneziani pieces together, and the total egg smelled like organized crime.

Another piece of information Jeff ferreted out tied the Venezianis to a number of truck heists of fine suits. Via a labyrinth of national roads, the suits, which sported well-known labels, had been delivered to the home of Bernadru Martinez and his wife. Together, they would sew in new labels so that these pinstriped, fine-wool ensembles could then be wholesaled to other men's stores. Distribution of the re-labeled suits became Kosth's responsibility as outside marketing director for the Veneziani clothing operation.

Jeff's extensive follow-up of leads found further evidence of mob connections, one of which revolved around a woman who identified herself as being a member of the Italian Trade Commission. He arranged an interview with her to ascertain her involvement with the Veneziani brothers and to learn more about her self-representation as a member of the Italian Trade Commission, in which she used her position to make bribes. She said that she'd come to his office the next day. However, within a few hours of that conversation, Jeff received a phone call from an attorney who demanded to know the details of the Secret Service's interest and if she was under investigation.

"Do you represent her?" Jeff asked.

"No."

"Then I intend to reserve my conversations exclusively with her," Jeff said.

Minutes later, Jeff answered another call from an attorney who said that he was now representing this woman and that he had "advised her to refrain from any contact with law enforcement."

This attorney had been a DEA agent who had resigned while under an indictment which accused him of selling operational information about the Drug Enforcement Agency and DEA informants to drug dealers. He was never brought to trial. Instead, he subsequently attended law school and was admitted to the bar.

Jeff then learned of other transactions via different sources, but because of fear for their safety, they would not testify.

Emanuele Veneziani had hired an attorney, the son of a well-known Los Angeles mob figurehead. According to a background check with the Los Angeles Police Department's organized crime unit, he reportedly had maintained connections with organized crime, and at that time was being "reviewed" for his representation of South American drug dealers. The Veneziani brothers remained in custody in the Terminal Island Federal Penitentiary, Long Beach.

Barry Turner and Bruce Jacobs, the Aussies who arrested the Venezianis, flew to our side of the world to testify in federal court. The court convicted Fabio Veneziani on thirty counts of credit card and mail fraud. The jury acquitted Emanuele on twenty-nine of the same charges and was hung on the thirtieth charge. Evidently, they believed that Fabio had been the schemer and perpetrator.

Still, we sent both back to the Federal Penitentiary, for the government wished to retry Emanuele on the undecided charge. Ultimately, Emanuele pleaded guilty to the thirtieth charge (we believe at the behest of his organized crime people, for we were getting close to connecting others to a clothing bust-out scheme), and he received thirty months in federal prison. Fabio received a twenty-four-month prison term.

Both brothers were fined an additional $250,000, and they were ordered to return more than $150,000 in illegally obtained merchandise, in addition to $54,000 worth of clothing acquired through the clothing bust-out scheme.

Martinez got twenty-four months. And Kosth weaseled a probation. In all, very light sentences for these first-time offenders.

What did *we* get? Frustrated.

Except for an amazing time with our mates down under.

Chapter 20

Bad Pennies Always Turn Up

We received a bulletin from the Denver Colorado Police Department that they had arrested three men using counterfeit credit cards and phony California drivers' licenses in a cash advance scam. The numbers embossed on plastic were all traced to the Bank of America Credit Card Center in Pasadena, California.

Bank of America's chief investigator reported that the counterfeit cards were individually silk-screened and embossed, and "rather fine pieces of work." The numbers all had been stolen from the Pasadena facility.

One of the suspects, Michael Smith, agreed to cooperate. He saw squealing as the avenue to a reduced sentence. Smith fingered his source, a man named Rashaad Ali, who currently was out on parole for bank robbery. He told us where Ali lived, and that he kept his counterfeit supplies and printing operation in a nearby storage locker. Smith also set us up with someone in the records section of the Bank of America who sold stolen microfiche to Ali.

Smith arranged the meetup a couple of days later. I assigned

Agent Marcus to accompany Smith, to meet the inside guy, Pincus "Big Man" Franklin. Big Man suggested they meet in the parking lot outside the bank processing center.

"Hey, man, what's shakin'?" Smith greeted Big Man. They performed a little handshake ritual that Marcus thought was patently stereotypical. But for the life of him, Marcus, who grew up in the ghettoes of Chicago, where drug dealers and pimps blatantly sported outrageous jewelry combinations and clothing, still stood amazed at Big Man's attire.

Despite the sweltering, humid temperature of this July afternoon, Big Man wore a full-length mink coat. It made his royal hugeness look even more elephantine. Perspiration cascaded down the overweight man's temples. God knows where it had to have pooled.

"My man here wants to buy some names. Can you fix 'im up?" Smith asked.

"Just lay on the green," Big Man answered confidently.

Agent Marcus reached into his pocket and pulled out a $1,000 roll of hundred-dollar bills.

"Lemme see the names, man," Marcus said.

Big Man slipped his hand inside the fur coat at just about shoulder-holster level, fumbled for an instant, and Marcus expected to see a .45 pop out. Instead, Big Man produced a sweat-soggy envelope.

"What you want is right in here, man. Riches beyond your dreams. You gimme the green. I give you the film."

"Better be good stuff," Marcus muttered as he handed the marked money to Big Man and took the envelope.

The exchange was the signal. Agents dressed like ordinary white-collar workers heading to their cars at the end of a workday closed in quickly, their guns drawn. At the same time, Marcus shouted, "Secret Service! You're both under arrest."

"Don't shoot…don't shoot," Big Man pleaded, hands raised.

We pushed the pair against the car for a pat-down. As agent in charge, I asked Marcus to frisk Big Man. An expression of disgust crossed his face as he began probing the sopping wet fat folds hanging down Big Man's body. I wondered whether my unhappy agent was reminding himself that the Secret Service never promised that the job would always be pleasant.

A computer check revealed that Big Man was on parole after having spent three years of a five-year sentence in state prison for armed robbery. That didn't surprise me. What blew me away was that the Parole Department had allowed him to be in such a sensitive post—what amounted to a candy store for a sweet-toothed larcenist.

Afraid of a long sentence, Big Man, like Smith, agreed to cooperate. He identified Ali as his major client and confirmed that Ali made counterfeit credit cards. We immediately began twenty-four-hour surveillance of Ali's home. Each day, we followed him to his rental garage, Bldg. F, Locker 141, where the resident manager identified his tenant as "Mr. Malcolm Nodkoff."

Ali-Nodkoff elected to drive either a gray Mazda or straddle a blue Harley-Davidson motorcycle on his daily rounds. A DMV check of the license plates showed that both vehicles were registered to a Rashaad Picot. So now we were watching a man with *three* names.

We obtained a search warrant for both locations. Not surprisingly, at our first stop, the storage facility, we uncovered a complete counterfeit factory. We confiscated newly forged credit cards, credit card blanks by the thousands, phony drivers' licenses, photo equipment, silk-screening apparatus, Bank of America microfiche, a microfilm reader, State of California and County of Los Angeles seals, and photographs of various future recipients of Ali's handiwork.

Included in the collection of IDs was our very own informant, Michael Smith, who had used the moniker Robert Robbins when he was arrested by the Denver Police Department.

Next, we paid an uninvited visit to Ali's home. We arrested him and his girlfriend without incident. This proved doubly fortuitous.

There was an active arrest warrant out for the well-manicured and stylishly clothed lady friend who had been on a magnificent shopping spree using two stolen credit cards.

A search of Ali's home turned up more incriminating evidence, and the two were arraigned and assigned bail. We had accumulated so much evidence that we celebrated Ali's removal from society. Our investigation had cleared up a massive nationwide distribution. However, to our chagrin, the U.S. Attorney rejected our rock-solid case. Why? Because credit card fraud had just recently become a federal offense, and the gears of the federal judiciary hadn't been well enough oiled to fully prosecute the crime.

But we weren't about to let Ali get away. I talked the County District Attorney's office into charging Ali with credit card fraud. Satisfied, the Secret Service stepped aside.

Nearly two years later, we arrested a suspect named Christopher Cross for passing newly printed counterfeit twenties. Traces of green ink still tinted his fingers.

Generally speaking, passers of counterfeit money are nonviolent. They're "quiet" criminals. Rather than suffer through countless and seemingly endless interrogations, they'll often cooperate. Christopher Cross willingly identified his source as a "guy who's out on parole for bank robbery and on bond for credit card fraud."

My radar immediately began to ping.

"His name wouldn't be Ali, would it?" I asked.

Cross nodded his head "yes," somewhat surprised. And I shook my head in disgust. It had been two years since I had turned Ali over to the state, time enough to have brought him to trial. Obviously, the wheels of justice had flat tires.

As with Smith, Cross agreed to help us. Right then, he phoned Ali from my office and told him that he had scored "a big package" and wanted to introduce him to a guy "who wants to buy counterfeit."

I assigned Agent Steve to the undercover buy. Though one of

the nicest, most gentle persons you'd ever meet, Steve also was one of the world's meanest-looking men. In comparison, he made now-deceased heavyweight champion Sonny Liston look like Peewee Herman. Steve's head was huge, and it rested on a tree-stump neck connected to an ultra-thick body after which God probably designed the bulldog. Getting hit by this man's hands would be tantamount to being whupped alongside the head by an iron frying pan. To see him was to never forget him.

By 4:30 p.m., Agent Steve and Cross were waiting in Steve's car behind the agreed upon meeting spot when Cross spotted Ali near the side entrance to the restaurant.

Oh my God, Steve thought when he saw Ali. *This isn't going to work.* Ten years earlier and 3,000 miles to the east, Ali had been one of Steve's prized informants. At that time, he was using his real name, Eric Picot. He had helped Steve set up a successful counterfeit sting.

However, not showing his dismay, Steve ordered Cross to start the deal. Cross left the car, met Ali by the side entrance to the restaurant, then disappeared. Five minutes later, Ali—with Cross in his car—drove up next to Steve's car. Ali kept the motor idling.

"Why were you late?" Steve barked, taking the initiative.

"I was going to get the stuff," Ali answered.

Cross left Ali's car, walked over to the passenger side of Steve's auto, and got in. He handed Steve an envelope that contained $10,000 in counterfeit hundreds.

Steve leaned out of the car window slightly and shouted, "Is it all there?"

"You don't have to count it," Ali assured him. "It's all there."

"Well, I'm going to count it, because I don't intend to get stiffed. Got any problems with that?" Steve glared at Ali.

"No, man, take your time. Take…your…time."

Steve did take his time. He could see Ali twitching nervously behind the wheel of his car.

"Okay, it's there. Did Cross tell you I want to do a larger package?" Steve called across to Ali.

"No, but we can do one after *this* deal."

Steve passed to Cross an envelope containing $2,000 cash, all prerecorded for evidence, and told Cross to hoof it over to Ali. Ali took possession of the legal tender, then immediately backed out of the parking space. Just as he was clear of the stall and about to turn in to the street, a Secret Service backup team nosed in front of him, forcing him to slam on his brakes. Steve backed out and jammed Ali between the two government cars. For the second time in two years, Ali was fingered by two snitches and collared by the Secret Service.

Amazingly, he hadn't recognized the man with the face that people never forgot.

"Okay, okay, I'll cooperate," Ali surrendered while being interrogated. "I get the cash from an Oakland gal, Jackie Wilson."

"Does she print it?"

"No, she buys it from a brown honey named June Mook who's from Sacramento."

The agents confirmed Wilson's number in Oakland and verified that Mook managed a shabby Sacramento complex.

"Did you guys search Ali's house?" I asked my agents.

"Ali told us he had hidden three thousand dollars in a garbage can outside his house. But he said if we searched his house, his roommates would find out about him and they'd notify everyone of his arrest. We confiscated the cash he told us about."

That was a long-winded way of saying "no, we didn't search the house." And that had been a minor mistake. Although my agents reclaimed three grand in counterfeit hundreds from the trash can, they had believed Ali and left his premises unchecked.

Ali agreed that it would go easier on him if he cooperated. He picked up the office phone and dialed Mook.

"Honey babe, I need a hundred thou… Can you get it for me?"

"Fine, no problem. When you comin' up?"

Ali looked at me. I whispered, "Tomorrow."

"Tomorrow, babe…call you when we get in."

Ali and I, along with Agent Luther Ivory, caught a 4 p.m. flight to Sacramento. Ivory was superhuman—a former Mr. California body builder. There wasn't a suit fabric woven that could hide his physique. The man was the definition of Awesome.

We were met at the airport by a couple of our guys from Sacramento who ferried us to a nondescript motel. Ali played his role to the hilt, insisting that he get his own room and that we buy him a steak dinner. We did.

The next morning, we had Ali call Mook to arrange a meeting at 7:30 that evening. Ali wore a wire so that their conversation could be monitored. Ali and Ivory met Mook in the coffee shop. The exchange seemed to take forever. Mook bragged incessantly about her sophisticated, "foolproof" scam, which involved a girlfriend who was a bank teller. Her friend would surreptitiously remove real greenbacks, then replace them with counterfeit hundred-dollar bills.

"It's foolproof, babe," Mook enthused.

Ivory just shined her on.

While waiting for dessert, Mook finally turned over a brown paper sack containing the $100,000 Ali had requested.

"Got the real cash in the car, baby," Ivory said. "Let's go get it."

Outside, Ivory removed his hat—the signal. Five agents efficiently surrounded the trio of counterfeiters and cuffed them all. Ali and Ivory went with the Sacramento agents. My associate, Bob, and I somehow got the pleasure of transporting June Mook—all 5'1" and 265 pounds of her.

This may have been one of the most challenging arrests of my career. How do we stuff a woman of her girth, hands cuffed behind her, into the back seat of a two-door Plymouth? As junior agent, Bob got the backseat assignment. He climbed in first. Then, as he pulled, I shoved. Somehow, Mook squeezed in. We hadn't even begun to think how we were going to get her out.

Apparently, the only words this woman knew were "you muthafuckers." Throughout the short trip, she kept up a nonstop fusillade of "you muthafuckers" until I had had it. I slammed on the brakes in the middle of the road, turned in my seat, and leaned toward her until I was a nose hair away from her fat face. Then I bellowed, "Shut the fuck up!"

Mook was shocked into lip-quivering silence. I couldn't remember silence ever being more golden.

But I must admit, Mook might've had the last laugh. She sat back there smirking and whispering to herself. "If you muthafuckers think you had trouble getting me *in* here, just wait till you suckas have to get me out."

"Everybody out," I said matter-of-factly at the entrance to the Federal Building. Sowers climbed out easily enough, and we both walked around to the right side of the car, waiting for Mook's first move. And we waited. And waited.

"I can't get out by myself, honey," Mook said smugly, still with hands cuffed behind her. She just sat there smiling, knowing that this was *our* problem, not hers. She leaned so heavily against the back rest, we couldn't even budge her forward enough to unlock the handcuffs so that she could help us help her.

Oh, for an engineering degree, a block and tackle, a steam shovel, Ivory's incredible strength. The jaws of life.

I finally ordered Sowers back into the car and told him to shove Mook toward me, while I grabbed what I could and pulled her toward fresh air—she screaming and swearing all the while. Sowers grunted and I damn near herniated as we inched her closer and closer to freedom.

Then as she tried to squeeze between the doorframe and the front seat, which we had slid as close to the dash panel as possible, Mook jammed in place. In desperation, Sowers coiled up, planted his feet on her Rock of Gibraltar-sized backside, and pushed her hard toward the door while I grabbed her beefy arms and pulled with all my might.

Inch by inch Mook shifted outward. Finally, she was expelled with one last heave from Sowers. I wasn't prepared for this sudden explosion, so Mook landed right on top of me, and we both tumbled to the ground.

When I opened my eyes, all I could see was this creature on top of me and Sowers laughing hysterically. I rolled out from underneath Mook, and Sowers and I promptly strained ourselves trying to help her stand up.

In the interrogation room, Mook waived her rights and agreed to answer all of our questions. She stated that she received counterfeit 100s from Jackie Wilson in Oakland, but it was Jackie who traveled to San Bernardino to pick up the money from Ali, "who prints the money."

This story, of course, contradicted Ali's alibi, which claimed he got his money from Mook.

Our questioning lasted into the early hours, and we were getting nowhere. Each suspect had been identifying the other as the source of the counterfeit money. At 5 a.m., I finally decided to try using a lie detector. Both Mook and Ali agreed to undergo the test. It takes an expert to read the graphs recorded during interrogation, and the results are not admissible in court. Several hours later, our polygraph agent walked in with coils of graph paper rolled in each hand.

"Well…?" I asked.

"Ali was deceptive in *all* areas of questioning," the specialist reported.

I went back into the room where Ali was lounging around, walked up to him, lifted him by the shirt, and said, "You were lying, man. I want this cleared up right now!" I dropped him back into his seat.

Just then, Ivory came into the room and Ali bawled to him, "Hey, brother, this pig agent is pickin' on me, man."

Ivory looked at me, and I said "no" to him with an almost imperceptible shake of my head.

"The polygraph test says Ali is lying through his teeth, Ivory."

Ivory, all 225 championship pounds of him, strode over to his "brother" and nearly bench-pressed him out of his "cool dude" attitude.

"You'd better talk…" he paused for effect… "cuz you've made me miss my workout, and I just might use you to break a sweat."

And Ali did talk. He admitted to printing the money in his home—the home he convinced my agents they shouldn't search—then giving the bills to Mook to distribute.

Agents raided his home and storage locker, seizing all of Ali's printing equipment and supplies, plus his Mazda (used to transport illegal goods).

At the time of this most recent arrest, Ali was still on parole for bank robbery and out on bond awaiting sentencing for his counterfeit card scheme of two years ago. He now pleaded guilty in Los Angeles Federal Court to one count of counterfeiting. With his past record, we thought he'd surely get ten years. His sentencing was slated for July. Meanwhile, he whiled away the hours at Terminal Island Federal Prison in San Pedro.

Even during Ali's early imprisonment, his counterfeit product had kept pouring into our offices. He must have passed tons of it. Knowing that he was going to be sentenced soon, I went to the prison to interview him again. Resigned to his fate for the next decade, Ali spoke freely.

The interview was going well, when I received a phone call from the assistant U.S. attorney, who was absolutely irate that I had spoken to Ali in prison, even though Ali had admitted guilt. The attorney accused me of "violating Ali's rights of due process," and I was forced to write a letter to the U.S. Attorney's office explaining why I had chosen to interview this convicted felon in prison.

As a result, a federal judge decided that "…agents had acted unethically." Instead of the ten years I expected, Ali the convicted bank robber/cum counterfeiter received only four.

I violated *his* rights? What a joke!

But I bet the only one laughing was Ali.

Chapter 21

Juan and John— The Robertson Coincidence

Juan Robertson and John Robertson were both U.S. attorneys. They have no connection or relation, just the same last name and my eternal frustration with both of them.

I first met Deputy U.S. Attorney Juan P. Robertson in October 1977, when I went to his Los Angeles office to request prosecution proceedings against a confessed thief and forger. Hardly a sterling character, Jay Kline had prior felony convictions for armed robbery.

I presented substantial evidence, namely a signed and sworn statement from Kline admitting to stealing, forging, and cashing a U.S. Treasury check in the amount of $1,500. Additionally, we found Kline's fingerprints all over the check, plus an endorsement on the back that matched Kline's handwriting. We obtained even more incontrovertible evidence when the owner of the convenience store where Kline cashed the check positively identified our suspect.

"I've got a sure one here," I told Robertson confidently.

"Well, I don't think I feel like wasting time prosecuting a case like this," he said.

I stood there absolutely incredulous. "I thought that's what you got paid to do," I said.

Robertson gazed at me from behind the security of his large desk.

"There's more than substantial evidence to convict, plus Kline has a criminal history," I argued. Perhaps it was my youth, but I couldn't hide my disgust at his cavalier attitude. "I don't know why, but you're not taking this violation seriously enough," I charged.

Then without provocation…maybe he just didn't like my looks…he launched into a shrill tirade about how "Secret Service agents are a bunch of cowboys who think that everyone ought to be prosecuted for something."

That did it. I blasted back, "Most U.S. attorneys are a bunch of gutless wonders who want to prosecute big-time cases only so they can make names for themselves and earn big money in private practice!"

Robertson ordered me to leave his office, throwing in a few stereotypical insults aimed at federal law enforcement officers in general.

I almost lost it right there, but in a tightly controlled tone I said, "You know, Robertson, I'd throw you out the window if I thought I could get away with it."

Without waiting for his reaction, I turned and walked out of the office, slamming the heavy door behind me with all my strength. If that didn't register on the Richter scale, it certainly had rattled Robertson. When I returned to the Secret Service office, I was met instantly by my boss.

A career Secret Service officer, Bob Powis was a tough but fair administrator who demanded 150 percent blood and effort from his charges. But if you performed, he backed you all the way. With a simple index finger summons, Powis ordered me into his private office. I knew I was going to be chastised soundly for saying things in a fit of anger to a U.S. attorney.

Looking over his half-glasses, Powis in a quiet, even tone said, "I just got a call from Robertson. He said you threatened to kill him."

When I told him what had occurred in Robertson's office, Powis said nothing. He simply looked at me. Then he picked up the phone, dialed a number, and asked for Robertson.

"Robertson? Powis. You just told me my agent threatened to kill you. You're lucky you were talking to him rather than to me, because I *would* have thrown you out the window. Don't you *ever* talk to one of my agents like that again. And by the way, I'm personally calling the U.S. attorney, and we will have this asshole prosecuted."

Powis slammed down the receiver and glared at me. "Now get out of my office and get back to work."

I felt like a little boy whose stern but fair father had come to his defense and supported him fully after hearing the facts. I left Powis's office wearing a giant smile across my "boy" face.

Much later—in 1990—while scanning the Orange County Register newspaper as I pedaled an exercise bike at the local health club, I saw a headline that captured my attention: "Former Federal Prosecutor Faces Charges He Distributed Cocaine." The story beneath the headline told me that "Juan P. Robertson, a Los Angeles attorney who is a former federal prosecutor, was arrested on charges that he distributed cocaine and invested the profits in an Alaskan gold mine."

I hadn't thought about Juan P. Robertson since 1977, but upon reading this news item, I remembered how Powis had chewed Robertson out, and I wore a giant smile across my now middle-aged face.

Meanwhile, in August 1978, I received a phone call from the security office at Disneyland. Their guys had arrested two Colombian nationals for passing counterfeit money. The two suspects had been collared in the parking lot outside the Anaheim amusement park after they had decided to call it a day—a profitable day.

When my partner, Jim, and I arrived at the Disneyland security office and began our questioning, we learned that the two men had been transported back to the security headquarters *un*handcuffed, and that a pat down revealed no more counterfeit cash. Upon hearing that, Jim immediately went out to the unmarked security car and searched the rear passenger compartment. It didn't take long for him to find thousands of dollars in counterfeit bills stuffed beneath the seat.

After the newly found evidence was presented to them, both suspects readily admitted they had passed the bogus money. They squealed on a man named Eduardo Belachur, who they said was currently in Bogota, Colombia, South America, obtaining more counterfeit currency as well as drugs.

Once these two starting "singing," we couldn't stop them. They both agreed to cooperate on the understanding that if they double-crossed us, they'd be given more severe sentences, and that word would be leaked that they were government snitches. The "word" scared them more than the threat of prison. They said that Belachur, his wife, and small child lived in the glitzy Malibu Colony home of Hollywood actor James Whitmore, where Belachur and his wife served as handyman and house maid respectively.

A telephone call to a bar in Bogota reached Belachur on the first try. A great Latin beat in the background accompanied the conversation. With one of our Spanish-speaking agents monitoring the call, it was evident that Belachur was excited to be hooked up with a new buyer for the counterfeit dough and that they would get together as soon as Belachur returned.

The following day, Jim and I drove north along Pacific Coast Highway to Whitmore's seaside estate, where we were about to cast the actor in perhaps one of his more demanding roles. Whitmore agreed to participate in this real-life drama and promised to inform us when Belachur returned. Two days later we got the call.

Whitmore knew only that his handyman passed funny money. We hadn't informed him that Belachur was wanted internationally—a fugitive dope dealer who was outrunning Interpol arrest warrants for crimes committed in Argentina.

Our informants arranged a meeting for Belachur to meet an "Anglo" who had done some dope business and who wanted to buy counterfeit. They agreed to meet in the parking lot of a shopping center at 11 p.m.

The story our undercover agent was prepared to share was that he wanted to stiff a dealer who had stiffed him with some bad coke. Sounded plausible to us. It must have impressed Belachur too, for the deal went down as smoothly as any we had produced.

The signal for us to swoop down and arrest Belachur was simple: The undercover agent was to pop open the trunk of his car and place the counterfeit money in it. This, too, went without a hitch until…

From concealment in the parking lot, Jim and I sped to the crime site from one direction, while a novice agent driving his own car raced—truly raced—from another. In his eagerness to participate in the arrest, the young agent slammed on the brakes and spun. He threw open the door while simultaneously transferring his .357 magnum to his left hand. Somehow, the gun fired accidentally as he got out of the car.

Time stopped. Everyone—good guys and bad guys—froze. Nobody knew from which direction the shot was fired. We thought we were set up. Belachur thought he was being hit.

With no more shots, Jim and I proceeded to move in. A local resident, however, had called the Los Angeles County Sheriff's Department, and a patrol car pulled up just as we were cuffing Belachur and our undercover agent. The officer on the passenger side of the sheriff's car jumped out of the cruiser, took cover behind the door, pulled out his revolver, cocked it, and pointed it directly at me. Even in the low light, I could see that the officer's hand was shaking dangerously. His finger tensed against the trigger.

"Put down your gun!" he ordered.

Time stopped again. I did as he commanded, at the same time trying to explain that we were Secret Service. This didn't mollify the nervous and suspicious sheriff's deputy, who kept his finger snugged against the trigger. The shaking gun glistened in the reflection of neon lights from the stores in the shopping center.

Finally, another voice broke the tension, a calm, but firm voice: "Uncock your weapon, Sheriff."

"Thank God," I mumbled to myself.

The voice belonged to the driver of the patrol car, a full-time sergeant who commanded his reserve officer to stand down. We finished our arrest amidst the apologies of the sergeant, who sat in his car for the next ten minutes, calming down his twitching partner. Jim and I also took ten.

The next morning we drove up the coast to Whitmore's home, where we searched Belachur's quarters. We found nothing until Maria Belachur pointed us to a stack of children's books.

"Een there," she managed softly. We opened the books to find nothing but beautiful little renderings of ducks and dogs, kittens, and cherubic children scrambling on grassy fields. Perhaps a wealth of fun for a child, but certainly not a cache of cash.

The helpful wife grabbed one of the books and peeled back the inside cover. There, in this and the other books, in some of the most ingeniously camouflaged compartments I've ever seen, lay excellent quality counterfeit bills totaling $8,000. Had it not been for Maria Belachur, motivated more by fear than altruism, this additional evidence probably would have been stashed on some child's library shelf, ready for use when Belachur got out of the federal pen.

The Belachurs were booked, and a further check revealed that the couple were illegal aliens from Argentina. It was then I met John D. Robertson, assistant U.S. attorney assigned to the case. We presented all of our evidence, underscoring the fact that Belachur was an international drug smuggler wanted by Argentina. We also had evidence suggesting that while out on bail, Belachur had distributed counterfeit money from Salt Lake City to Anchorage.

Despite all the information I supplied to the U.S. Attorney's office and to Robertson specifically, none of this was entered at Belachur's sentencing. The Public Defender's office urged probation for Belachur. Attorney Robertson did not object in any way; rather, he supported the recommendation that Belachur be placed on probation in complete contradiction of the recommendation of incarceration by the U.S. Probation Department.

The judge sentenced this career criminal to three years' *probation*. Both Jim and I were so upset that we complained stridently to our boss, asking that he do something about what we perceived to be a total miscarriage of justice. To his credit, our boss wrote a letter—rather formal and benign though—voicing his and our consternation at the withholding of support by Robertson for the probation officer's recommendation that Belachur do some real hard time.

Robertson responded with a three-and-a-half-page treatise of self-defense, denying that I ever informed him of Belachur's sordid history.

Bullshit!

His letter is a classic example of bureaucracy at work. He rambled on, spouting his expertise, and concluded: "After considered reflection, I am indeed satisfied that I handled this particular case in an acceptable manner."

I say it again: Bullshit!

This case clearly reveals the frustration an agent goes through when he knows how guilty a person is. But as much as I hate to say, it is part of the job.

Chapter 22

Lady Luck

"**Hurry it up!**" the greasy-haired young surfer screamed at the ticket agent as she counted the five crisp $100 bills he had handed her.

"Don't worry, the plane won't leave without you," she responded serenely, while apparently tapping out ticketing instructions on the reservations computer before her.

As she continued her digital dialogue with the computer screen, a large, uniformed officer quietly approached the impatient traveler, placed a frying-pan sized hand on his shoulder, and said, "Excuse me, sir, would you mind accompanying me to my office? Quietly!"

After about a two-hour wait, the fidgety surfer, who was only nineteen years old, met the Secret Service for the first time in his life.

"Where did you get these counterfeit hundreds?"

"What? Counterfeit?" the boy retorted, obviously shocked at the revelation. He was either a great actor or truly ignorant of what he had been carrying around in his battered nylon wallet.

"I'm going to ask you again. Where did you get these hundreds?"

"I got 'em in a poker game. Honest, man! I didn't know they

were no good, honest, man!"

Convinced that this scummy kid was too stupid to lie, the agent let him go, but kept the bogus bills and showed them to me the next morning.

I took the bank notes and studied them under a magnifying glass. All were of the same circular number, had the same identifiers and markings. All obviously had come off the same photo offset press and were printed on the same paper stock, were of the same quality and family. In my estimation, the chances of receiving five such bills in one poker game were too great to accept. The kid had lied through his yellowed teeth.

I ran the C-notes through our computer. My instincts had been correct. *In active U.S. circulation for about nine months. Originally traced to and believed to have originated in Marseilles, France.*

"Let's find the surfer boy," I said to Jim, my partner for this investigation.

If I had wanted to blend into a crowd, Jim would not have been my choice for undercover work. A former lineman for Oregon State University, Jim stood nearly 6'5" and ruptured scales at more than 240 pounds. Not wanting to look "too government," we signed out an old van from our motor pool and began the tedious freeway trip from downtown Los Angeles to the surfer's paradise of Huntington Beach.

From the address the kid gave at the airport, we tracked him to a rented house near the beach. The house, set among well-kept homes and neat gardens, had become a flop joint for surfers and druggies—an address well-known to the patrol cops of the area.

After a stern request at the front door, one of his brotherhood roused our suspect out of bed, and our surfer stumbled out, his eyes bloodshot and bleary. But it didn't take long for his eyes to pop open when he saw 450 pounds of Secret Service confronting him. With both of us grabbing and squeezing his needle-pricked arms, the 140-pound surfer required very little persuasion to join us in our van.

"Where'd you get the bad cash?" I asked.

He was shaking so badly, both Jim and I thought he was going through withdrawal.

"Don't hurt me, man," he whined. We repeated the question, hinting that there were some bad guys in the federal penitentiary who spent lots of time fantasizing over young surfer types. This really shook him.

The kid blurted that he received ten $100 counterfeit bills as change for dope he had purchased from a guy named Wayne Brown, who lived in a fancy Newport Beach condo. The druggie surfer hadn't realized the money was bad until he was caught at the airport.

Since Newport Beach was only about five miles farther down the coast, we "asked" the dude to show us where the source lived. When we got there, he was home, Surfer said, because his glistening black Stutz Bearcat was parked under the carport.

We ran a quick check on Brown and received a rapid reply: He had been out of Soledad State Prison about a year after having served for drug distribution. Next we had the kid call Brown from a pay phone at a nearby mini mall. Brown answered, sounding as though he might have been inhaling some of his own stuff.

"Hey, man, you stiffed me with counterfeits," the kid charged.

Brown seemed to sober up. "How do you know they're counterfeit?"

I'll give the kid this—he responded creatively. "Because I looked at the bills, and they all had the same markings. Plus, some lady at the 7-Eleven challenged me, and I had to sweet talk her into taking it."

"Get lost, kid!" Brown snarled. "Take a hike!"

"Look, man, I'm comin' up to the house for more money, and you'd better give it to me," the surfer boy said. He thought that if he didn't get Brown to cough up some counterfeit money as proof for us agents, he'd be sent to the carnivores at the federal pen.

We were happy with Brown's response to the surfer, for inadvertently he had admitted to "culpable knowledge."

At that point, we put the kid back in the van, cuffed him to the seat, and went to Wayne Brown's condo. As we walked up to the front door, we saw the curtains move slightly. No one responded to our knock on the door as we had suspected might happen.

"Wayne Brown, we know you're in there. Open up…we want to talk to you!"

We waited. And waited. And waited.

Finally, Jim picked up a metal lawn chair and smashed it through the glass storm door guarding the main wooden door. Glass shattered all over the patio area.

Brown, who was surprisingly large—obviously from months of pumping iron in Soledad—swung open the door and trumpeted, "What the fuck you doin'?" As he cocked his beefy arm to swing, Jim and I tackled him simultaneously. Despite his size, we just about broke him in two as we drove him back into his living room. His girlfriend, shocked out of a semi-stupor, started screaming.

While my partner held Brown down by the throat, I identified ourselves and told him we were interested in the counterfeit money he had given to the surfer. Realizing that she wasn't going to be murdered, the girlfriend settled down to whimper in the corner.

The shock on Brown's mustachioed face began to wane as we hoisted him up. Obviously, his contact with law enforcement to this date had been somewhat more sedate. However, as we questioned him about the counterfeit bills, he played stupid.

"Search my home," he challenged. "You ain't gonna find nothin'."

He was right. We didn't find anything related to counterfeit money. But my quite tall partner did spy substance of a suspicious nature resting atop the refrigerator: a layer of white powder spread across the entire length and breadth of a one-half-inch-deep, twelve-by-eighteen-inch cookie pan.

"What have we here?" Jim asked, as he carefully lifted the pan down from the icebox.

Brown's confidence evaporated faster than a cokehead could inhale a line.

"You *did* tell us to search your home," I said.

"Okay, okay," Brown sputtered. "I did have some funny money, but I got it from some guys I sold some dope to in Vegas."

"Who gave you the money?" I asked.

"There were these guys, an Israeli and a Frenchman. After Vegas, they met me at a motel near here. They said they had a hundred thousand dollars in counterfeit money, and that they wanted to trade for some good dope. They showed me the cash, and I pulled a gun on 'em. And slapped 'em around a bit too. Then I took their suitcase and split."

Brown said that he had dealt off most of the cash in Mexican dope deals. He offered us a deal. "If you guys don't take me in on the dope, I'll help track down the Jew and the Frog. They said they had two million dollars more."

We knew that because of the way we had obtained the information from Brown, we couldn't successfully prosecute him. So, we meted out our own justice. Jim took the pan of cocaine and flung the powder into the air. Both Brown and his girlfriend stood in frozen disbelief as probably a million dollars spread, sifted, and settled its way into the deep and dusty shag carpet.

My voice jolted them back from near catatonia: "Find them," I ordered.

Brown said the Israeli was named Mordehay Ben Hamo and that he hung out at Caesar's Palace, one of Las Vegas' more elegant casinos at the time. Obviously, Ben Hamo was known at Caesar's, as the operator put the call directly through to the health spa. Ben Hamo wasn't there, but we were told he was expected back that evening.

The call corroborated Brown's claim, so we told him that if he wanted to stay out of Soledad, he'd better accompany us to Vegas that night. He agreed.

Jim then went outside and uncuffed the surfer, who was sitting quietly in the van, told him to beat it, and reminded him that the "big house" was his next stop if he didn't clean up his act. Then we drove Brown to LA, got three tickets to Las Vegas, and were booked into the MGM Grand by eight that night.

En route, Brown decided that he liked us. He hadn't ever dealt with law enforcement people quite like us. As he explained, "I like your ballsy approach."

For the purpose of cover, we each checked into separate rooms. Neither Jim nor I was concerned about Brown escaping. We told him that in addition to our round-trip ticket to Vegas, we had purchased a one-way ticket back to the state pen. But as it turned out, we needn't have threatened him, for he began to feel strangely chauvinistic. He simply became pissed off that these foreigners were in *his* country taking *his* business away from him.

That night, we went to Caesar's Palace and played the slots, dropping who knows how many of Uncle Sam's dimes while waiting for Ben Hamo to make his appearance. About midnight, Brown nudged me and identified Ben Hamo.

"Go get him," I said.

When Ben Hamo saw the imposing figure of Brown approaching, his mouth dropped so far you could have dumped a cup of nickels in and still had room for a cup of dimes.

"Calm down, man," Brown said. "I got a deal for you and I got someone I want you to meet."

Brown beckoned me over and identified me as a cellmate of his in Soledad. "Ron here wants some of your cash," Brown explained as we walked to a table in the bar, "'cause he wants to score on some Mexican stuff."

"You look like a cop to me," Ben Hamo said accusingly.

I reached across the table and swept the ashtrays onto the floor as I pulled Ben Hamo across to me so that we faced eye-to-eye.

"Look, asshole," I whispered menacingly, "I don't care what you think or if you deal with me or not, but it's in *your* best interest, 'cause there's dope in it for you at the end." I threw him back into his chair. As he rocked backward from the force of my shove, Brown began laughing almost uncontrollably.

"What's so fucking funny?" Ben Hamo hissed.

"That's what you looked like the last time I saw you. Seems like you're always getting smacked around," Brown teased.

Composing himself, Ben Hamo said that he'd discuss the matter with his partners. Then he got up, tucked in his shirt, and walked all the way across the casino. Still within our sight, he met with another person, whom Brown identified as being the Frenchman with the counterfeit money. So, this was the Marseille connection.

Twenty minutes later, Ben Hamo returned to report that he could arrange something. "How long will you be in Las Vegas?" he asked.

"I leave town in the morning for a couple of days, but I'll be back. If you're really interested in doing a deal, you can leave me a message at this number," I replied. The Vegas number I gave fed into a special phone at the Las Vegas office of the Secret Service, and the secretary had been coached to act as our girlfriend should any calls come in. Actually, Sherry was so beautiful that every agent who worked Vegas wished that she really would become his girlfriend.

In reality, neither Jim nor I were leaving town. We had been assigned to protect Vice President Walter Mondale during a two-day Vegas stopover. If Ben Hamo or the Frenchman bothered to catch the evening news, our cover could be busted.

For the next two days, I never took off my dark glasses when outside my hotel room, and I combed my hair differently each time I knew there were going to be cameras pointing in the veep's direction.

During my protection duties, Ben Hamo made a smart move in checking me out. The secretary in the Vegas office played her part perfectly—that of my girlfriend. She said that I had gone back to

LA to do a deal there.

At midnight on the second day of Mondale's visit, the veep left town in Air Force II, and I returned to the MGM Grand to continue the undercover work. I immediately called Ben Hamo and told him that I had just returned and that I wanted to get together.

Festooned in gold chains, wearing a garish, satiny blue shirt with the buttons open down to mid-chest, I sought him out at Caesar's.

"I can get you two million," Ben Hamo promised, "but I can only get my hands on eighty thousand dollars by tomorrow."

"Bullshit, man," I said.

Backing up defensively—obviously by now he thought he was everybody's favorite punching bag—he said he could have it within the week.

"How much is the eighty grand gonna cost me?" I asked.

"Twenty thousand real money," Ben Hamo replied.

"We'll do the deal tomorrow night," I said firmly.

"Okay, here at Caesar's, ten o'clock."

"You'd be real stupid to do dirt in your own backyard. We'll meet at the MGM Grand."

Upon returning to my room that night, I called my boss and requisitioned $20,000 to be wired to the cash cage at the Grand as show money. Early the next day, a bellboy brought a note of confirmation to my room that twenty Gs awaited my signature in the casino.

That night, right on time, Ben Hamo met me in the lobby and asked me to show him the cash. I escorted him to the cash cage, gave them the phony ID that I always used in undercover work, and watched as a guard wheeled within view a cart stacked with money.

"Okay, dickhead, let's see your stuff!" I demanded.

Ben Hamo reached into the inside breast pocket of his coat, and I immediately stiffened, expecting to see him produce a pistol, but he brought out only a hard pack of Marlboros.

"Take this to the bathroom and peek inside," Ben Hamo

instructed. I walked slowly and coolly to the nearest men's room, entered a toilet stall, opened the pack, and extracted five virginal $100 bills. Eureka! Each had the same markings as found on those we confiscated from the surfer. I rushed back to Ben Hamo and told him, "Beautiful, man, I'm ready to deal."

But Ben Hamo's antennae were always tuned to conspiracy and double cross. He asked, "Where's Wayne at?"

I said that Brown went back to Orange County, that we didn't need him anymore, but he didn't buy that. "I want to talk to him… NOW!" he insisted. It was obvious that Ben Hamo was still suspicious of me when he added, "How do I know that Brown's not in jail and you're not a cop?"

"Okay, let's call him," I countered confidently.

I called Brown. "This fuckin' mutt won't do the deal unless you give him the go ahead… Straighten the asshole out," I ordered.

After just a few seconds on the phone, Ben Hamo hung up and said, "Okay, let's deal. We want five thousand tonight for twenty thousand phony. We'll do the rest tomorrow."

At that, I grabbed him again, pulled him up by the shirt so he was standing on tiptoes face-to-face, and said, "What are you trying to do, set me up?"

Again, Ben Hamo exhibited the kind of nervousness a smaller man shows when he's sure he's going to have the shit kicked out of him by a larger adversary.

He stuttered, "I'm not the one with the money. My partner has it, and this is the only way he'll do it. Only in two separate buys."

I knew we were going to take him down anyway. So, I went to the cash cage, checked out $5,000 of my marked money, stuffed it in a flight bag, and went back to the bar where Ben Hamo was trying to calm down with a drink. I flashed the cash.

"Okay, give me the money and I'll go get the twenty thou…"

"Fuck you! Do you think I was born yesterday?" I spat. "You get the good stuff when I see the twenty Gs."

We argued for the better part of an hour. Finally, I came up with a solution: "Look, if we're gonna do the deal, let's walk to the empty table over there and tear the five K in half. You get the twenty thousand to me, and we'll exchange hand to hand. You can tape the bills back together because both ends have the same serial number."

He hesitated again, and that's when I really got agitated. I blurted, "If you don't agree to this now after all the fuckin' time I've put in here, I'm gonna kick your ass so badly that you'll be lying face-down on a stretcher all the way back to the Wailing Wall." Then I added calmly, "And if you want any dope out of this, I suggest you consider doing it my way."

He gulped his agreement.

Instead of tearing up the money at a table in full view of other patrons, we walked over to the unmanned counter of the in-hotel car rental company. As we began tearing up the money, a cleaning attendant nearby stopped swabbing the floor and stood there gaping.

"Get outta here!" I barked. She did.

One of the agents who had been assigned to watch us throughout the evening from a nearby post put his hands over his face and just shook his head in disbelief as we shredded the money. Actually, I had a hard time containing myself.

Ben Hamo complained nervously, "Hurry, man, I think we're being followed."

"What's the guy look like?" I asked quietly, not taking my eyes off the bills we were ripping in two.

"Some big Black dude with an Afro," Ben Hamo answered.

Ben Hamo's radar was right, of course. The Afro belonged to an agent from the San Francisco office of the Secret Service.

After we finished tearing the money apart, Ben Hamo took his half and stuffed it into his pockets. "I'll be right back," he promised enthusiastically.

I wanted someone on stake-out to follow Ben Hamo as he

walked away, but none of the other agents understood my signal. They simply remained in place, keeping their eyes protectively on me. Within a few moments, however, Ben Hamo returned with a brown paper sack stuffed with the counterfeit hundreds.

As the agreed-upon signal for the agents to appear and arrest Ben Hamo, I was to light a cigarette. Not too creative, but certainly an unmistakable message, considering that I never smoked. However, this proved to be more difficult than I thought. I had trouble striking the match because I also had a fistful of dollars.

I tried to catch the eye of the agent closest to me, but he wasn't paying attention to me right then. An incredibly gorgeous girl had sat down next to him. As assuredly as a compass needle seeks the magnetic North, his eyes responded to her face and her cleavage with equal speed. I kept trying to light my cigarette.

Finally…finally…the agent sauntered nonchalantly toward us. Once past us, he did an about-face, walked up quietly behind Ben Hamo, and shoved the cold muzzle of his revolver into the man's ear.

Ben Hamo was so surprised that he overreacted. He jerked the money out of my hand and sent it flying all over our part of the casino. Like frenzied sharks, nearby casino customers jumped on the confetti of cash. Six Secret Service agents posted in the place had a near riot on their hands as they tried to keep the patrons from grabbing the cash.

"*Asshole! Asshole!*" I yelled at Ben Hamo. "You set me up, you bastard!"

Two of the agents cuffed both me and Ben Hamo and made a show of holding me back as I tried to kick the Israeli. When the agents separated us, I asked, *sotto voce,* if they had collared the Frenchman.

"No, all the guys stayed on you." I got angry at my backup guys for this. I felt frustrated that we hadn't nabbed the guy I suspected of being the brains of the operation.

But somehow, Lady Luck was riding on our shoulders, for just at that moment, the Frenchman came running balls-to-the-wall around the corner toward us, as if tipped off to the bust.

"That's him," I said calmly.

The Frenchman never even saw us. A Secret Service agent simply clotheslined him as he dashed by and took him out faster than Hulk Hogan dispatched the bad guys on TV wrestling back then.

I did not confront the two unhappy prisoners that day, but during interrogation by other agents, Ben Hamo admitted that he was only the middleman, that the Frenchman was the one who had access to the $2 million. The Frenchman admitted only to the $80,000, refusing to say more for fear of being killed if he talked. He preferred jail to the more permanent sentence.

When I appeared in court the next day, Ben Hamo's smile blew off his face when he realized that I was the one swearing to the affidavit of arrest.

"I knew it," he mumbled under his breath.

The Frenchman received six years and deportation; Ben Hamo got four and deportation to Israel.

What happened after that? My guess is that probably both returned to the United States with new identities and appearances, and became lounge lizards, sunning themselves under the neon sunlight of the Las Vegas Strip while scamming innocent people out of their hard-earned vacation money. I hope I'm wrong.

Chapter 23

The Sparrow Has Landed

"Williams, got a guy who says he knows something about a counterfeit money operation." The duty desk officer gave me the name and number. "Call him after eight this evening."

At eight promptly, I called the number and a man picked up the phone before I heard even one ring on my side of the headset. The call got interesting right away.

"I'm a Realtor, Gerald Walhberg, here in Mission Viejo, and in conversation with a colleague, another Realtor, I told him that I was from Las Vegas, that my brother had several successful businesses there, and that he actually knew members of organized crime. This Realtor, George Minka, gets really close to me and in a low voice says, 'You think anyone there in Vegas would be interested in counterfeit money?' George tells me he has a friend who can print real good counterfeit money and already has several thousand dollars of it, and they're looking for buyers. So, I got to thinking that maybe you guys, the Secret Service, might want to know about this, right?"

"Absolutely. Where can I meet you tonight?" I replied.

One of the first considerations on starting a new case with an unproven informant is that he or she might just be blowing smoke. As a matter of practice, the Service requires that we corroborate the information, so my partner, Jim, and I drove the hour-and-a-half trip to Mission Viejo, to an address suggested by our caller.

From a "For Sale" sign posted on the front lawn, we learned that we had arrived at "the home of our dreams." Wahlberg had suggested this house as the meeting place because it was unoccupied and neighbors had grown to expect strangers on the premises. While checking the place inside and out, we stumbled on a bit of luck: the phones were still connected.

We had Wahlberg call George Minka after Jim had attached a tape recorder microphone to the phone to capture their conversation. We fed him the key questions.

"George, listen, I talked to some of my people in Vegas, and they said they're interested. What denominations do you have?"

"I've got twenties, fifties, and hundreds, but I only have several thousand right now. I'd love to meet your people. We'll print to order," Minka gushed, adding, "I'll print up whatever they want!"

They set up a meeting for Tuesday night with Minka promising to bring samples. I decided the perfect undercover agent for this investigation would be John Pavlick posing as Johnny Paladino. Central casting could not have found a better man for the part. Of Croatian heritage, Paladino looked like the stereotypical little hood portrayed by Hollywood. He was short and muscular, with a swarthy complexion, and even wore a diamond pinky ring.

We ran a check on Minka and found that he and his wife, also a real estate agent, lived in a $300,000 lakefront home in Mission Viejo, an extremely expensive property at that time. On Tuesday afternoon, our Realtor informant met with Paladino to set up their story. In short, the story was that Paladino had purchased a bunch of suits from Wahlberg's brother and had recommended other "associates" to the haberdasher.

In undercover work, the idea is to get in and get out. The longer one plays the game, the greater the chance of being found out. And *rubbed* out. Some agents enjoyed that tension more than others. No Academy Award-winning actor or actress has ever played a part better than the agents whose lives—and livelihood—regularly depend on their convincing performances to the sleaziest audiences in the world.

Paladino was to play such a part. And for that matter, Wahlberg, too, had to muster up his thespian skills in order for this minidrama to play out.

Wahlberg and Minka arrived early at the designated restaurant. They were ushered to a reserved table, under the watchful gaze of two agents who were convincingly wolfing down some sirloin steaks on their government expense account. Paladino arrived precisely at 7:30, and appeared friendly but reserved, interested but cautious as Wahlberg introduced him to Minka.

After some small talk, Paladino interrupted, "Enough bullshit! Let me have the stuff."

Minka quickly pulled out an envelope and slid it across the table. Paladino didn't bother to open it but slipped it nonchalantly into his breast pocket. He took several bites of his steak, wiped his mouth, looked at Minka, and said, "I'll show it to my people and then I'll get back to you." Paladino intended to finish his meal, but it was obvious that the dinner meeting was over. Minka understood, got up from the table, and left the restaurant.

We made no attempt to follow Minka as he drove out of the parking lot. If he made the tail this early in the investigation, the case would have been blown right there, and we probably would never have discovered the printing source.

Shortly after Minka left, Paladino and Wahlberg left the restaurant and began a series of evasive maneuvers in case Minka thought to have them trailed. He didn't.

Thirty minutes later, we rendezvoused with Paladino, who

handed over the counterfeit money. That evidence included $20s, $50s and $100s of surprisingly good quality.

I phoned in the description of the money to our duty agent, who ran an immediate check. None of the bills had been listed on the computer index, a data base that catalogued known "identifiers" which had been passed anywhere in the world within the previous twenty-four hours.

We shipped the notes to our lab in DC to ascertain the kind of paper, what watermarks there might be, the printing technique used, the degree of quality control in the printing process, the composition of the inks, and whatever other information could be determined chemically and microscopically.

There are dozens of counterfeit investigations being conducted simultaneously throughout the United States. There just happened to be a similar case unraveling in Las Vegas at that time, so we decided that since Minka believed Paladino to hail from the gambling mecca, we would send Paladino there to work that one as well. Additionally, Las Vegas provided a better cover for Paladino should we feel it necessary for Minka to contact him.

Meanwhile, we started to surveil Minka, hoping he would lead us to his printing plant. Late one night—or was it early one morning (1 a.m.)—I drove to Minka's mansion to scope out his residence. He had conveniently left his Cadillac in the driveway, so we planted a magnetized electronic tracking device up in the rear left wheel well.

Such a transmitter back then was larger than the movies lead most of us to believe. The device was about the size of a quart-sized milk carton and really couldn't be entirely hidden, so an important part of our sophisticated sleuthing technique was called "prayer." We prayed that our prey didn't suspect they were being tailed.

A sensitive receiver in the tracking car indicates the direction the target car turns by a needle that points left, right, or straight ahead. So simple—even a Secret Service agent could understand the directions.

So it was that two of our younger agents followed Minka early one morning along the maze of freeways that connect all of Orange County's contiguous communities. The agents trailed Minka into the vicinity of Anaheim Hills, where the signal abruptly went silent. No number of pattern checks along major roads and labyrinthine neighborhood streets picked up the telltale beep of the subject's vehicle. We had lost him.

Later that night, we sneaked back to Minka's home to retrieve the tracking device from his car, which was parked in the driveway, but the device was gone. Minka probably had bounced over some potholes or railroad tracks, thereby dislodging the transmitter. As far as we know, it was never found. And had it been, for obvious reasons there was no forwarding address stenciled on it. We put a new tracking device on Minka's car that night.

Several days passed with no communication between Paladino and Minka. We wanted to keep Minka nervous. Finally, Paladino called Minka.

"The bosses like the quality of printing, but they don't like the paper your guy is using. I'm going to bring over a ream of really good quality paper, and we want you to print up a sample package for us. I'll arrive at LAX tomorrow at 8 p.m. and deliver the paper to you personally."

This part of the surveillance was our "paper chase" strategy, for we would now follow Minka and his ream of paper directly to the printing source. Paladino and Minka agreed to meet at a hotel bar. Naturally, we had agents positioned around the hotel to scan for any countersurveillance Minka might have arranged. We also arranged for a chase car equipped with an electronic monitor to follow the beeper we had reaffixed to Minka's car the night before. As bad luck would have it, Minka chose to drive his wife's car, a Mercedes sedan.

While Minka and Paladino made small talk inside the bar, I had one of our sneaky techies attach another beeper under Minka's Mercedes, tethering it electronically once more to our chase team's car. We also parked an undercover van next to Paladino's rented sedan so that when he and Minka came out to exchange the paper, we could photograph them in the act.

Just as we planned, Paladino led Minka to his car, where he retrieved the ream of paper and presented it to Minka. From inside the van, the whine and click of the single reflex camera's automatic shutter and film advance seemed to us to be loud enough to betray our existence. But our engineers assured us that Minka had a better chance of hearing a flea fart under a shaggy dog's fur coat than he did of detecting the grinding electro-mechanics of our Nikon. In retrospect, I might add that our pictures developed prosecution-perfect!

Paladino and Minka shook hands, and Paladino said, "Listen, here's my number in Vegas. Call me when you've got the samples."

Minka always seemed nervous. He looked around frequently during his verbal and paper exchanges with Paladino in the parking lot. When he left, he drove evasively—in and out of parking lots, reversing his direction several times, pulling in and out of driveways and making 180-degree turns. He seemed to be scanning for tails. Sometimes he'd slow to a speed well below the posted limit; then he'd accelerate to twice as fast and whip around corners as if he were trying to emulate the driving exhibitions in car chase movies.

Despite his best attempts, we were all over him, literally—we also had a cooperating California Highway Patrol helicopter shadowing his every twist and turn. However, Minka maneuvered himself into some heavy traffic on the San Diego Freeway, and our chase car couldn't catch up. Ultimately, signals from the wheel-well transmitter faded out of range, and the air team lost him too. The copter began an immediate crossing pattern search and was about to call it quits when Minka's car popped off the freeway onto a little-used offramp into an industrial area.

"I've got 'im," the "chippie" (CHP) crackled over the two-way radio. My agents on tail followed the radio directions given by the sky cops and caught sight of Minka's taillights just as he made a fast turn onto a street of nondescript, slab-sided buildings zoned for light industry. The agent's radio receiver jumped to life again, its needle unerringly guiding them down the darkened streets. They caught one more fleeting glimpse of Minka's car just as he turned off his lights in the side driveway of a building that read "OCR Business Forms."

A quick check revealed that OCR was a printing business registered to an individual named Guy Sparrow. Minka stayed at the printing business for nearly four hours before he drove home at 1 a.m. This time, he wasn't particularly cautious, so our agents enjoyed an easy tail, keeping him in sight and sound from a discreet distance back. Meanwhile, I assigned agents to keep a twenty-four-hour watch on OCR.

The next day, Paladino received an uncommonly early phone call in Las Vegas.

"Your bosses are really stupid!" Minka barked.

Perplexed and defensive, Paladino asked, "What are you talking about?"

"You said you didn't like the paper we printed on. Well, your stupid bosses gave me a ream of the exact same paper."

Minka's people had printed their samples on an extraordinarily fine grade of paper called Crane's Crest, manufactured by the same company that creates the stock used exclusively by the U.S. Bureau of Engraving.

"Okay, okay," Paladino said, "print up another run and we'll take a second look at it."

We inquired with the local major paper distributor to see if anyone had ordered Crane's Crest. The manager simply stated, "If they did, I'd have notified you guys."

Crane's Crest is so close in quality to the paper used for currency that paper distributors make it a point to tell the Service when any is sold and to whom it's sold. And in case they forget, we routinely visit the paper sellers.

As I was about to drive away from the warehouse, the manager ran up to the side of my car, pounded on the top, and sputtered, "Mr. Williams…I just remembered…we didn't sell any, but I did give four reams to a man named Guy Sparrow about a month or two ago."

Over the next several days, our agents recorded on infrared film the late-night comings and goings of both Minka and Sparrow. On the fourth day, Minka called Paladino at the Las Vegas number and announced that the $10,000 package was ready for delivery and that he wanted to meet some of his higher-ups.

"I've got to protect our people. I'm the only one you'll ever meet," Paladino stressed, adding, "…just in case you're setting me up…"

They agreed to exchange cash for "cash" the next evening. That established, I had to decide whether to arrest Minka at the time of the trade or to play it all the way out, hoping to trap Sparrow as well. After an office confab, I decided that even though we'd have Minka "real dirty," we should cut Sparrow's wings in the process. We'd let the buy go through and order up a package of $10 million in the process.

Again, the two joined up at the hotel bar. After a couple of drinks, Minka insisted that Paladino accompany him to his car.

Minka challenged Paladino, "How do I know you're not a cop and that you're not wearing a wire?"

"You petty asshole," Paladino retorted. Paladino agreed to a pat down on one condition: "that I check *you* out, because frankly I don't trust you, either."

Paladino slid out of his coat, undid his tie, and unbuttoned his shirt.

"Take it off," Minka ordered. Paladino complied. He was not wired.

"Now it's your turn," Paladino said. Minka began to undo his shirt when Paladino commanded, "Not here, outside the car!"

"Up yours!" Minka shouted.

"The deal's off then, asshole!" Paladino threatened.

Minka got out and looked around to make sure there weren't any curious hotel guests around before he complied. He wasn't wired either.

"Satisfied?" Minka growled.

"Not quite. Against the car!"

Minka stood there, at first incredulous, then angry, glaring at Paladino. Nevertheless, greed overcame pride, and he turned to lean against the car for the embarrassing pat down. Paladino began the frisk, reaching between his legs and jamming his open hand against Minka's genitals. Minka grimaced in pain.

"Just making sure you don't have one of those new miniature radio transmitters," Paladino explained.

By now, a few patrons had gathered at a cautious distance to watch, though the scene wasn't terribly uncommon in this area known for narcotics. Paladino flashed a huge smile of victory toward the surveillance van. You couldn't hear either the shutter or film advance of the Nikon recording the strip search, and of course not the stomach-aching laughter from the agents inside.

Minka handed over the new "money," and Paladino reciprocated with four $1,000 bundles of real hundreds. After a cursory review of the counterfeit, Paladino nodded his head and told Minka to wait while he retrieved twenty reams of Crane's Crest—enough for $10 million.

They shook hands. As they turned away to go to their respective cars, Paladino turned and yelled to Minka, "By the way…you've got great legs."

"May I speak to Mrs. Minka, please," I said to the receptionist who answered the telephone at the realty office.

"This is Mrs. Minka. May I help you?"

"My name is Ron Snow," I said. "A business associate gave me your card. I've just moved here from Kansas City—new sales territory—and I was wondering if you could show me some homes this afternoon?"

"Why, yes, Mr. Snow. Of course."

I drove to her office hoping she would be able to ferry me around Mission Viejo in the Cadillac so that two agents who were shadowing me could remove the beeper, whose batteries had gone dead. But my plan went slightly awry, for she was now accompanied by her husband.

He looked at me suspiciously from the first moment.

"Glad to meet you, Mr. Minka," I said. "Kind of unusual to have a husband and wife team show you around, isn't it?"

He didn't answer, but immediately and quite aggressively began a rat-a-tat-tat line of questioning.

"Where you from, Mr. Snow?"

"Kansas City."

"How long have you been out here now?"

"Couple o' days."

"Where are your offices?"

"Gonna work out of my home to start with. I'm on the road a lot."

"Who d'ya work for?"

"Mobil Oil Company."

"What's the address there in Kansas City?"

"It's 210 West Tenth," I said, having remembered the number from my year's employment there before I joined the Secret Service.

"Do you have a card?"

"No, I don't!" I was beginning to show some annoyance.

"Isn't it unusual for a businessman not to have any cards?"

At that point, I got just a little short of pissed. I said, "I have cards, but you're not getting one!"

"Why not?" he asked condescendingly.

"Cuz, Mr. Minka, I don't think I like you very much, and you are not one of my customers or leads."

Mrs. Minka intervened. "Let's all get into my car and go look for suitable homes for Mr. Snow."

I got into the front seat. George Minka slithered into the back seat of the Cadillac. He kept up his interrogatory bombardment between questions posed by his wife about my desires in a home. He asked about my family, my education, whether I'd ever been in California before, about the oil business. I felt that his instincts about me were accurate. I answered him evasively and tried to describe to Mrs. Minka the type of home my wife and I would love.

Throughout the tour of available Mission Viejo homes, I asked many demographic questions about California, letting them know that I knew nothing about this reputed land of "fruits and nuts."

Minka kept peppering me suspiciously. Finally, I turned around in the seat and fired, "Hey, what's with you? I'm trying to buy a house, and you're playing cop with me. I don't appreciate it!"

He flat-out said, "I don't think you work for Mobil Oil."

"And I don't care what you think. Take me back to my car!"

"I'm sorry, Mr. Williams. My husband isn't usually like this. I'm so sorry."

Back at her office, I shook hands with Mrs. Minka and left. I immediately called the Secret Service office in Kansas City. "Listen. Talk to security at Mobil Oil right away. I'm in a counterfeit investigation here and I have the feeling the suspect is going to call to confirm my story. I'm Ron Snow, marketing manager, and I've been transferred out to Southern California. Tell them what I look like and be ready for a call."

Not more than ten minutes later, the Mobil operator received a phone call for Mr. Ron Snow. Upon a minutes-old directive, she forwarded the call to the on-duty director of security.

"I'm sorry, Mr. Snow isn't here. He's in California on business."

Minka began a series of questions, including some about Snow's physical appearance. The security man answered Minka patiently. Then he turned the tables.

"Why are you asking all of these questions? I'm afraid that without authorization from Mr. Snow, I can't answer any more of your inquiries."

Apparently convinced that "Snow" was a real house-buying prospect, Minka said, "If Mr. Snow calls, please tell him that Mr. Minka apologizes. I just haven't been myself lately. Thank you."

What an ass!

Paladino was in the Las Vegas office a few days later when the undercover phone rang.

"It's George Minka. I'm in Vegas with my wife. Maybe you want to show us around town? Get us some show tickets?"

"No, I would not," Paladino replied. "How's the money comin'?"

"It'll be done in a couple of days," Minka assured him. That told us just how far along Minka and Sparrow were. This was information we needed to plan the legal steps we had to initiate. I had obtained search warrants for the printing plant, for the homes of both Minka and Sparrow as well as the real estate office where "Team Minka" rented their desk space

Minka insisted on meeting Paladino at Caesar's Palace for a drink. After a few cocktails, Paladino accompanied Minka to the crap tables and watched as Minka bet the genuine $100 bills he had given to Minka several nights before.

I admit I had fantasized about how we were going to take Minka down. I wanted this to be a truly stylish arrest. I would have Paladino sweep up in a Rolls-Royce or a limo to effect the exchange. However, my dream plan went the way of most novels when I received a radio call from my surveillance team, reporting that both Sparrow and Minka were observed loading boxes into the trunk of Sparrow's car.

As much as I wanted to play Cecil B. DeMille, I couldn't let them leave. If they got away, we might blow the case.

I said, "Let's take them."

Our agents stopped Sparrow before he made it to the freeway. He was alone. As the agents approached with guns drawn from both sides of his car, Sparrow slumped dejectedly in his seat. In a whisper, he admitted that the agents would find some counterfeit money in the trunk of his car. But that was an understatement. He had more than $700,000 hugging the spare tire in the trunk. Three-quarters of a million dollars of very good quality reproductions.

When Minka saw the flashing red lights behind him, he pulled over to the side of the freeway. I sped with my own red lights flashing to the site. By the time I arrived, Minka had been cuffed and stowed to the stained back seat of our government car—quite a comedown from the pleated upholstery of his luxury car.

Minka didn't see me approach from the rear. I stuck my head in the door, close to his face, and identified myself: "Ron Snow, Mobil Oil. Can I sell you some gas?" I could tell he didn't like the smirk on my face one bit.

With him in custody, I advised him, "It will go easier on you if you cooperate with us, Mr. Minka."

His reply was sincere: "Go fuck yourself."

We drove Minka to the Los Angeles County Jail, where he was tucked away in a special cell, for which the U.S. government pays a monthly rent.

Sparrow admitted that he had more counterfeit money at home. He gave us signed permission to search, so a warrant wasn't necessary. We escorted him into his spacious home and into the bedroom, where his wife was sleeping. It was a sad sight for me. A giant of a man standing more than 6'7" in height and weighing 270 pounds, crying like a baby as he told his beautiful young wife that he would have to go to jail.

I sat with Sparrow and his wife during their tearful goodbye while other agents searched the home and garage. They struck a mother lode in the garage, where they unearthed another $300,000.

Meanwhile, a second team of agents visited the Minka household.

Their greeting wasn't so benign as the one at the Sparrows'. Hurling a barrage of profanities through the front door, Mrs. Minka refused to let them in—that is, until they threatened to kick the door down. Grudgingly, she opened up, but she was so abusive—calling the agents robbers, thieves, and assholes, and worse—that finally, in desperation, one agent threatened to arrest her on obstruction of justice charges if she didn't shut up. She finally did.

Going from room to room, the agents uncovered roughly $2,000 in marked government money that Paladino had paid to Minka in exchange for the first batch of counterfeit bills.

The next morning, we went to the real estate office and searched the Minkas' desks. And I mean *search*. Every paper clip and dust ball in the place was piled atop the oak furniture by the time we finished. And when we left, there was no question in anybody's mind that Minka had been a bad boy. We informed the manager in a very loud voice that George Minka was under arrest on counterfeit charges.

Ultimately, both Minka and Sparrow pleaded guilty to the counterfeiting charges. And the real estate associate who started this investigation with his informant call? Over a fine steak dinner at the lakeside restaurant, where Paladino first met Minka, I presented him with a $2,500 reward, compliments of the people of the United States of America.

Chapter 24

Marcos

Secret Service agents aren't paid to pass judgment on the people whom they are assigned to protect; so, let it be known that I will try to be objective and not refer to Ferdinand and Imelda Marcos of the Philippines and their chief henchman, General Ver, in anatomical terms.

In 1979, I had been part of a contingent assigned to protect "his and her royal highnesses," who were to visit friends and properties in Honolulu, Hawaii.

Immediately upon our arrival, the local Secret Service office and the U.S. State Department gave us an intelligence briefing indicating that we could expect almost anything from the large faction of anti-Marcos dissenters who either lived in Honolulu or were planning to fly in for protest purposes. Additionally, we were told of CIA-sourced information regarding Filipino Communist cells that might try to infiltrate and assassinate. In short, the Marcoses were known in Secret Service parlance as "high risk protectees."

Their sizable party was to occupy an entire floor of a swanky hotel on Waikiki Beach. Prior to their arrival, we checked out the entire facility from a security standpoint in cooperation with both the Honolulu Police Department and the Philippine presidential protective service. We made it unmistakably clear to both the police department and the Filipinos that the Secret Service was in charge of the operation.

In most cases, the police departments with whom we work are thoroughly professional and anxious to cooperate with us. We value their involvement as they are an integral part of our protection duty. The Honolulu PD certainly fit that assessment, and they provided their crack FART professionals as a critical part of our protection plan. FART is a humorously coined acronym for Fast Action Response Team. Similarly, we have CAT—short for Counter Assault Team—an antiterrorist specialty group within the Secret Service. I was a member of CAT.

In preparation for the Marcos' arrival, we prepared the president's suite with a dual alarm system that consisted of both a touch pad and a motion detector on the patio outside of his spacious suite. Today, of course, we utilize much more sophisticated electronic and infrared systems that are virtually penetration proof and power-source autonomous. However, back then, our system had an inherent weakness in that it tied into the hotel's electrical grid.

Our personnel were spread throughout the hotel grounds, with a Secret Service agent, a local policeman. and a Filipino security guard posted to the president's hotel suite door. Additionally, more guards were placed at the elevators.

We were ready for the "royal" visit.

I was the shift leader, the agent in charge of the midnight-to-8 a.m. detail. The second night of my watch, the hotel lights blinked off without so much as a warning flicker. And they stayed off. A quick glance at our alarm system revealed that our electronic "wall" had been compromised. Immediately, I ran to the window to see if the lights of Honolulu had also been blacked out. But in the clearness of the Hawaiian night, they were twinkling almost as brightly as the constellations above us. Remembering the security briefing we had the day before, I could only think that there was now an anti-Marcos operation in swing.

I grabbed a flashlight and snatched up an Uzi—yes, the compact, fully automatic assault weapon of Israeli manufacture—and ran down the darkened hall to the Marcos' suite. The guards were still there, somewhat puzzled, but attentive to any movement in the hall.

When I got to the door, I reached for the key that we always keep in the lock in case of emergency and was shocked to discover that the key was missing.

"Where's the key!" I screamed.

"He has it," said the American agent on duty, pointing to the Filipino guard.

"Give me the key!" I commanded.

"No, no, no, we can't go in!" the Filipino guard protested, explaining that we would have to wake up General Ver.

The Filipino guard had legitimate concern about his own longevity when it came to his boss. General Ver, whose brutal nature and manipulative history is well documented, had become chief of Philippine armed forces and director general of the National Intelligence and Security Authority under Marcos. Amnesty International in 1983 concluded that under Ver's command, "torture was so prevalent as to amount to standard operating procedure for security and intelligence."

Interestingly, early in his sordid career, Ver had been sent to the U.S. by Marcos to train with the U.S. Secret Service and police academies. Soon after his return to the Philippines in the mid-sixties, he became Ferdinand's security chief, bodyguard, and chauffeur.

Perhaps it was due to some of our Secret Service training that Ver successfully saved his president and first lady during a riot in 1970, when 20,000 students in Manila surrounded their entourage and threatened their safety. When the crowd pressed dangerously close, Ver took Marcos and physically thrust him into the luxurious, leather-upholstered womb of the bulletproof car. But no bodyguard dared lay a hand on Imelda. So, Marcos himself climbed out of the car, grabbed the first lady, and dragged her into the limo. He sprained his wrist in her rescue.

Of course, Ver's loyalty was well rewarded. And in the course of the Marcos regime, this "chauffeur" drove himself to the height of power and influence.

Later, General Ver became a suspect in the August 1982 plane-side assassination of Benigno Aquino, upon his return to the Philippines from an exile in the U.S. Aquino had been tabbed by political observers to win the Philippine presidency. Of course, his widow, Corazon, succeeded Marcos in an internationally observed election after the dictator fled the country for sanctuary in Hawaii. Ver was tried and acquitted of Aquino's murder in 1985.

Had I been in the Filipino guard's shoes, I probably would have shared his fears, but I don't give a damn about anybody like General Ver if he gets in my way during a protection situation where I am in charge. I don't believe any American Secret Service agent would succumb to such intimidation.

I pointed my Uzi at the shaking Filipino and repeated, "Give me that key!" He continued to clutch it. And though I realized that he, too, had orders to follow, I couldn't give a shit. I uncocked the Uzi and handed it to the policeman. Then I jumped the bodyguard with my full weight, grabbed him in a headlock, snatched his hand, and twisted it beyond nature's design. I almost strangled the poor guy, and I broke his arm in the process, but yes, he dropped the key.

When I saw the key fall, I shoved the guard to the ground, picked up the key, and raced through the commodious apartment to the president's bedroom. I twisted the door handle, but it had been locked from the inside.

"Mr. Marcos! Mr. Marcos! Are you okay?" I yelled.

A muffled response. "Yes, I am all right." Or at least I *think* that is what he said.

I heard a shuffling noise behind me. I spun around, crouching with my .357 magnum pointing in the direction of the noise, and was about to yell a challenge when, in the diffused light, I saw the limping figure of the Philippine security man from whom I had taken the key. In the flashlight beam, I caught a very frightened man—scared not only of me, but also of what General Ver might do to him if he failed in his job.

He protested, "That's the president…"

I ignored him.

"Mr. President, this is the Secret Service. Open the door!"

I had thought that perhaps somebody was holding him hostage, so I demanded confirmation of his safety.

I received that assurance at the point of a Colt .45 shoved directly into my face. When the door opened cautiously, there stood President Marcos, in fine silk pajamas, finger on the trigger. At that instant, I realized that he probably slept with two mistresses: one by his side, the other under his pillow.

"Mr. President, the electricity in the hotel has gone out, and we don't know the cause. We don't know if it's an accident or if someone is trying to get to you."

Then I pointed behind me to his quaking security man and gently admonished, "Mr. President, please tell this security man to leave the key in the door and to cooperate with us, because when you are in the United States, you are under *our* protection."

In their native tongue, Marcos spat some fast-paced verbiage to the Filipino agent. Even in the darkness, I could see the blood drain from the face of this beleaguered, injured man. The poor guy looked at me as though I had been responsible for pulling the handle on the guillotine.

With the lights restored, I began a quick round of inspections of the hotel. When I returned to the Marcos' suite, the key had been replaced in the lock. The Filipino bodyguard was nowhere to be seen. The hotel could not explain the blackout, and because it's my job to do so, I could only speculate that the anti-Marcos factions might be testing our security arrangements and our reactions to a perceived threat.

The next night our protection detail was shifted to an Imelda-owned home above the cliffs of Waikiki Beach, where one of the first lady's famed parties was in high-decibel swing. When we arrived and took up our post at the bottom of a steep driveway, I was directing a police car to block the driveway when someone yelled that two people were stealthily making their way up the private road to the beach house.

Still nervous about the real possibility of an assassination, I grabbed a flashlight and my Uzi and dashed up the driveway. Two silhouettes could be seen in the moonlight, so I illuminated them in the strong, eight-cell beam to see if they were wearing the ID pins that the Secret Service issued to members of the Marcos staff. No pins were visible.

At that point, I cocked the Uzi and commanded these shadowy characters to lie facedown, spread-eagled on the asphalt. Then I slowly approached them with the muzzle pointed at their heads. Only a few seconds ticked by before I was joined by a Philippine security man who responded to the alert. Lifting the suspects' heads up by their hair, the security man let out an audible gasp, as though General Ver had kicked him in the solar plexus. And no wonder. I had captured General Ver and one of his lieutenants, neither of whom was wearing his Secret Service ID pin.

"You can get up now, General," I permitted, and both men stood. "You know, you could've been dead, General. Next time wear your pin or someone's going to blow your ass away." Ver squirmed, knowing he couldn't behead me as he might any of his own underlings who dared to lecture him.

As I began my shift at the hotel the next evening, I noticed the absence of members of the official Philippine party in the halls. As a matter of fact, uncharacteristically, not one person from the Marcos entourage was visible. The reason? It was later explained by one of General Ver's henchmen: "You Americans have a crazy man on the midnight shift."

It was one of the finest compliments I have ever received.

When I got back to LA, the people in the field office told me that they had heard that several presidential security men had been beheaded back home, and that I personally probably sealed their fate. One agent who had spent many years in the Philippines reported that his contacts there phoned him the news that the children of one of Marcos's security guards were now orphaned. I really began to feel guilty, until I saw the conspiratorial smiles and realized that my Secret Service brethren were enjoying my discomfort with their gag.

Still, it wouldn't have surprised me altogether if General Ver *had* ordered the demise of his guards. His men treated him as if he were a god. A god to be feared.

Though Marcos did regard himself a god, and Ver considered himself at least next to god, to me these two were just another assignment. And I was the crazy American on the midnight shift.

Chapter 25

THE HAPLESS HACKER

THE UPS MAN grunted repeatedly as he stepped down from his patented brown delivery truck, the unwieldy-sized boxes he carried adding to his difficulty. Several of them were imprinted with IBM and COMPAQ. After stacking the boxes expertly on his hand truck, he trudged to the front porch of the house to which his load was addressed.

"What are you doing?" an elderly neighbor called out from next door. "Where are you going with those boxes? That house has been empty for nearly a year."

"Doesn't Dr. Hamilton live here?" the UPS driver asked.

"No, he doesn't. Never has. I'm telling you, that place is empty!"

He and other UPS drivers had made numerous deliveries to this address. But with the old lady watching and yelling again that no one lived there, he realized that maybe the house did look unoccupied. Putting the boxes back in his truck, he left an "attempt to deliver" notice in the crack of the door with instructions to call the local UPS number for pick-up information.

Jack Kemp, head of security for UPS, began a cursory investigation of the packages returned to the distribution center. He contacted the mail order company whose labels were plastered over the boxes, which contained more than $10,000 worth of computer and electronic equipment. The company reported that everything had been ordered by phone and charged to a credit card. He contacted the owner of the credit card to confirm the high-tech purchases. The physician who owned the card stated that he had not purchased any computer equipment. The obvious conclusion: credit card fraud. Kemp immediately called the Secret Service.

The next morning, I went to meet Kemp. We hypered on coffee while waiting for the telephone call we hoped would inquire about the packages for "Dr. Hamilton." The call came through.

"Excuse me," a youngish male voice said politely, "do you have packages there for Dr. Hamilton?"

"Lemme check," Kemp said, with a mixture of warehouse gruff and customer service courtesy. He put the phone on hold for a couple of minutes, as if he were back in the "will-call" section of the warehouse.

"Yeah, I got some stuff for Dr. Hamilton."

"Well, Dr. Hamilton asked me to pick it up. I can be there in an hour," the boy said.

"It's okay by me, kid," Kemp said.

Kemp and I were in UPS uniforms and waited behind the will-call desk. Kemp directed the other employees to clear out. Two teenagers—we estimated them to be about seventeen—drove up in a red Toyota pickup and parked in front of the office. They walked in confidently.

"We're here for packages for Dr. Hamilton."

"Yup." We nodded. "Just sign here..." Kemp presented a receipt form, "...and give me some ID."

Looking at the driver's license, Kemp said, "Hey, your name ain't the same as on this address label, kid."

"Er, um, he's, um, my stepfather," the boy stammered.

The kid signed his name, and Kemp and I dutifully went back to retrieve the computer equipment. After we hefted it into the back of the Toyota, the kid thanked us profusely, climbed behind the wheel, and slammed the door. At that point, I motioned to him to roll down his window. When he complied, I reached into the car, grabbed him by the throat, and literally pulled him through the window.

"Guess what, kid…?" I said as he stared at me fearfully through bugged eyes. "You're under arrest!"

My backup agent, who seemed to appear from nowhere, put a bruising grip around the bicep of the second boy and said, "Ditto, amigo," as he pulled him out of the passenger's seat.

At that point two patrol cars from the local Police Department screeched up in a flanking maneuver. You could say it was overkill. But, then, we never know. And to say the boys were thrown into instant shock would be an understatement. These were not hardened criminals. Looking at their white skin, scrawny arms, and zitty faces, I doubted if they were even old enough to have had a hard-on, except maybe over Nintendo. Even though the kids were too scared to run, the police cuffed them before putting them in the back seat of their patrol car.

In the interrogation room at the jail, we grilled the boys, told them what we knew, and that they were going to spend a lot of days in jail dreaming about their favorite computer games. Pools of tears welled large in one boy's eyes. We knew he was going to "roll over."

"The only thing that's going to help you, son, is for you to help us," I counseled him.

The boy sat there crying and scared, thinking about his predicament. Finally, he sobbed, "His name is David… He's a senior at Loma Linda. He's a computer hacker. David hired us to pick up all the stuff at the old house. He paid us fifty bucks each for the trip."

"Who knows about this activity?" I asked.

"Everybody knows," the kid blurted.

I just looked at the others in the room, shook my head, and shrugged my shoulders in disbelief. Larceny starts so young these days. At that point, I suggested to the police that we pay a visit to the high school and that we use our two minor "pigeons" for bait.

With their truck loaded with the stolen equipment, the two boys drove to the high school. They pulled up in front and waited. As if there were some telepathic communications, kids started pouring out of everywhere to survey the booty, to high-five the boys either in greetings or congratulations. They milled around for a while, until a similar pickup painted black drove up.

Here was David, the ringleader. But David wasn't getting out of his car. He remained imperiously behind the wheel of his truck, as if his minions knew exactly what to do. When his boys began transferring the hot computers to David's truck, we rolled. The police pulled right up to David's bumper so he would have no possibility of escaping. I jumped out of the car, ran to his truck, grabbed him by the back of the neck, and pulled him halfway out of the window.

"Secret Service, you're under arrest!" I informed him.

The local police arrested the two co-conspirators similarly in dramatic fashion. The crowd of admirers swiftly changed into gawking, scared kids. Their conquering heroes had abruptly become conquered bums.

Unlike his two "go-fers," David complained that we were mistreating him. His macho facade demanded an immediate face-lift, what I like to call an "attitude adjustment."

"David, how old are you?"

"Eighteen," he said.

"That means prison, David! Not the California Youth Authority," I emphasized. "Do you know what happens to young inmates in prison, David?"

He knew, or at least he had heard stories. The threat of bunking in a small prison cell with a "hardened" criminal encouraged David to tell all.

"Okay, I've been hacking for a long time. Several years. People in the network know me as Scorpion."

People outside the esoteric world of bits and bytes knew that David was an A-student at the high school and that he had received an appointment to West Point. His father was a respected psychiatrist at Loma Linda Hospital.

"How did you gain entry to credit card files?" I inquired.

David told us how he would go "trashing," at one or two in the morning, jumping into the huge refuse bins outside major banks and S & Ls to look for corporate passwords into credit agencies like TRW. His next step involved sharing the passwords with members of his secret hackers' association—whose masking monikers ranged from Rumpelstiltskin to Dicky Boy. These bulletin board buddies also would trade stolen SPRINT and MCI telephone access codes, which, when used properly, precluded the tracing of their calls. Once inside the TRW system, David would wander around the electronic files with impunity.

When it came time to purchase needed equipment and other toys, like bicycles and tennis rackets, David would let his fingers walk through the telephone directory to search for the names of doctors and lawyers. Once David selected a name, he would again "enter" TRW to review that person's financial status. The ideal prey in this electronic hunt were Gold Card holders.

We waited for more amazing revelations from this late twentieth-century *wunderkind*. He sat in a straight-back chair, just shaking his head from left to right as he talked. All of us were rapt by the audacity, tenacity, brilliance, and success of David's activities. And, quite honestly, we wanted to hear more.

"Boy," he said, "when my dad hears about this, he's going to be pissed."

"Why is that?" I asked.

"Because I stole a bunch of numbers from the hospital, and they are all my dad's friends."

THE HAPLESS HACKER

After this confession, we drove to his home to meet his father.

"No, not *my* son," David's father insisted.

Slight of build, sporting a manicured goatee, David's father appeared to be the stereotypical image of an academic. He adamantly refused to admit that his straight-A angel could engage in such malfeasance.

I reasoned that the only way to support our charge was to have David demonstrate his computer prowess.

"Show your father what you did," I ordered.

And, with practiced ease, he complied. His computer spit out a printed road map of his course through wires and circuits, a document which we seized as evidence. Meanwhile, David's father, whose job it was to help people communicate their problems, stood speechless.

Disbelieving, the father said nothing, until David revealed that he had used all his dad's friends' credit cards to make his many purchases. At that news, the psychiatrist came unglued. Mostly in words of one syllable, he called his son every name in the book.

Because David's computer was used in a federal crime, we confiscated it as well as all his peripherals. Then we had our resident computer engineer download the stored data from its hard drive.

The information that spewed forth would have made a seasoned spy blanch. An entire CIA manual printed out—on everything from how to assassinate people by mixing and pouring certain innocuous chemicals together into a car's gas tank so that when the temperature in the tank rises, so does the entire city block, to how to conduct financial robbery.

There's no doubt that David was brilliant. He was so smart that he believed he was invulnerable.

However, with all his genius, he simply forgot to factor in one UPS man and one old nosy neighbor woman.

Chapter 26

Rudy Montoya

THE **FBI** WAS investigating him and his group for kidnapping, narcotics import and distribution, and for transporting stolen cars across state lines. The DEA (Drug Enforcement Agency) was scrutinizing activities of group members, looking for narcotics violations. ATF (Alcohol, Tobacco and Firearms) was sleuthing for firearms violations and smuggling. The Los Angeles Police Department was examining various group members for homicide, kidnapping, auto theft, burglary, assault, and fraud-related crimes.

The California State Banking Commission was looking into money laundering in Canada and the Philippines. The Orange County California district attorney was checking out charges of real estate land fraud and bank fraud. And the Secret Service was conducting investigations of credit card theft, forgery, fraud, and counterfeiting money.

Representatives of all these agencies, plus detectives from several Southern California police departments and investigators for various banks met at the federal building in Los Angeles with an organized crime strike force attorney to discuss our mutual criminal cases and to determine a strategy to attack the Montoya crime family. Each agency one by one revealed their evidence on the Montoya gang. When it came our turn, I let our case agent, Ken, outline our case. The FBI went last. When their agent advised they had nothing, every jaw in the room dropped, realizing they had gathered all the intelligence on every department's case and typically revealed nothing about their case.

When the meeting broke up, an FBI agent approached me and Huffer and asked if he and his partner could have a private meeting with us. I invited them up to my office. Once behind closed doors, they began questioning me and Ken about our case. Thinking they were there to cooperate, I gave them a full accounting of our case and our strategy. After I finished, I asked the two agents what the FBI case consisted of. The senior agent then said, "I'm sorry, but we have instructions from our supervisor that we cannot discuss our case." I stood up and told them to get the hell out of my office or I would throw them out.

I then called their supervisor at the FBI and told him what a scumbag I thought he was to refuse to share intelligence information on the Montoya gang. But in law enforcement, the FBI is known for siphoning information from other law enforcement agencies and not sharing their information.

Montoya first came to the attention of law enforcement when he was arrested for violation of federal narcotics laws. He was tried and sentenced to five years in prison, which he served at the Terminal Island Federal Prison in San Pedro, California.

Upon his release, the unrepentant ex-con immersed himself in more criminal activities—drugs, grand theft auto, and insurance fraud. A gregarious fellow, Montoya hammered out long-lasting relationships during his incarceration, and these contacts would serve him well in his future criminal enterprises. He had surrounded himself with a potpourri of characters—other ex-cons, strong-arm enforcers, street junkies, hookers, drug smugglers, counterfeiters, car thieves, French nationals illegally in the U.S., and larcenous businessmen used as fronts. Almost all of the Montoya associates possessed impressive criminal rap sheets.

Montoya skulked under the nameplates of various enterprises. One was the Montes Auto Body Shop, where his auto-body "magicians" transformed the identities of stolen Mercedes-Benzes and other fine cars. He also operated two shell companies called Worldwide Products and GenStar, Inc., which he controlled from the fourth and nineteenth floors of a very chic Wilshire District LA high-rise. Montoya's always-gleaming burgundy Rolls-Royce Silver Shadow lent credibility to the upscale image of both his operation and the marble-and-glass "Miracle Mile" building in front of which it was religiously and pompously exhibited. From these offices, he head-honchoed the crimes that would involve the Secret Service—counterfeiting, lines-of-credit documents, and my bailiwick at that time, credit card fraud.

We learned of this Montoya specialty through an informant. A contemporary of Montoya's at Terminal Island, who was slowly fading away from cancer and wanted to die with a "degree of self-dignity," identified a number of Montoya players for us including a man who manufactured counterfeit credit cards, using names lifted off stolen microfiche from the Wells Fargo Bank and also made counterfeit California drivers' licenses as added identification to support the ersatz credit cards.

The microfiche from the bank had been fenced to Montoya by another cohort, a drug user/pusher who had a regular heroin-injecting customer positioned in the bank. This semi-cooperative informant gave us some more intel because she was "mad as hell at Montoya, because he owes me money and I'll do anything to get back at him."

Via our first informant we learned about Richard Galloway and Allen Grant, two clothiers in the LA garment district who helped

Montoya by issuing false credit card receipts filled out with the filched Wells Fargo names. These men earned a percentage of their "sales."

Next was Marcel Ragon, a French national and con artist who was practicing his art in the United States. Montoya instructed Ragon (who willingly cooperated) to become a 51 percent "paper" owner of Galloway's and Grant's businesses. Ragon, who theoretically could easily take flight to France if necessary, would become the "fall guy" in absentia when and if authorities ever traced the fraud to Galloway and Grant. Should that happen, both would claim that as minority partners they couldn't know, and didn't realize, that their associate was ripping off the system.

Galloway and Grant opened merchant accounts at two banks and began depositing credit charge slips worth $30,000 to $50,000 a day, using the stolen Wells Fargo list, then withdrawing at least $20,000 shortly thereafter. It took nearly a month for the banks' investigators to discover that the institutions were not being repaid by the cardholders—that, in fact, none of the cardholders had ever shopped at Galloway's or Grant's stores. The banks then called the Secret Service.

I assigned two of my best agents to investigate, Ken and Tom. They unraveled the scam immediately, listing Galloway and Grant as suspected co-conspirators. Ken was assigned to work closely with the Los Angeles Police Department Organized Crime Squad, and Tom Vacarello would conduct the link analysis and document the leads.

Both "innocents," Galloway and Grant, of course named Ragon as the probable culprit but stated they hadn't seen him since the banks had put holds on their business accounts.

Ken and Tom visited the last known address for Ragon. The landlord said that Ragon and his wife had disappeared owing a month's rent. A check with U.S. Customs showed Ragon had flown to Paris two days earlier. I wired our Paris bureau, and with the cooperation of the French national police, who ferreted out the Ragons for us, the Secret Service paid a surprise visit to their address. Threatened with extradition and a long prison term, Ragon agreed to cooperate with us fully.

Back in LA, we obtained a full statement of admission from Ragon, and as a condition of "freedom," we persuaded Ragon to volunteer to work for us. It was a dangerous undertaking for him, for Montoya had booted Ragon out of the country with the explicit warning "not to return for a long time if you know what's good for you!"

Ragon told us he believed that Montoya had murdered people in the past and believed he could suffer the same fate. To say that our French turncoat was scared is the understatement of the decade. Nevertheless, we dropped him off at the Wilshire District high-rise for a surprise visit to Montoya's headquarters. Ragon entered the sprawling GenStar offices unannounced and stood there stonily, just waiting to be noticed. He didn't have to wait long.

"Wha' the fuck!" Montoya said incredulously. "What the fuck are you doing here?"

Ragon stuttered in his French-accented English that he and his wife couldn't find work in Paris. "We had to come back. We had to find a way to make more money."

Montoya wasn't buying the story. He walked brusquely over to Ragon, grabbed him by the shirt, and forced him into the wall. With his face almost touching Ragon's, Montoya fixed a murderous gaze on the Frenchman's face and then forced him to a back office, where he threw him into a chair. Ragon felt Montoya's hard slaps to his cheeks—palm-side and backhanded.

Then Montoya directed two beefy goons who were standing nearby to strong-arm Ragon out of the chair and pull his shirt above his head.

"I don't trust you, asshole. You got a bug wrapped around your stomach?" Montoya demanded.

Ragon's fleshy stomach shook as they spun him around in their search for an electronic bug. Finding none, they shoved him roughly back into the chair.

"You're stupid, Ragon. But stay in touch with Nataf and Arel. We'll let you know what we're going to do with you. Now get out of here!" Montoya's henchmen tossed Ragon toward the door.

Nataf was Jean Paul Nataf, another French transplant. He operated a print shop and was being investigated separately for printing duplicates of insurance checks that Montoya had received through his body shop. Nataf, in fact, had introduced Ragon to Montoya, and had brought another Frenchman into association, Paul Arel.

Using monies earned from drug smuggling and sales, Arel had bought into Montoya's auto body operation. In addition to reworking stolen cars, Arel worked a credit card manufacturing scam. He ultimately moved the operation from the auto-body shop to the GenStar offices.

Several blocks away from GenStar, we picked up a visibly shaken Ragon. "You're going to have to go back there in a couple of days," I informed him. Ragon dejectedly nodded his head. "Let's work you back in through Nataf or Arel," I suggested. Ragon looked relieved. He didn't want to confront Montoya again.

Ragon persuaded Arel that he could be of help to the Montoya operation, that he had proved his loyalty before. Montoya soon agreed to meet with Ragon again to determine if he could bring him back into the fold. Again, for Ragon's own protection, we sent him up unwired. And again, Montoya's men ordered Ragon to hoist his shirt. Somewhat reassured that Ragon was not a snitch, Montoya began discussions on money-laundering strategies.

Our evidence was mounting impressively. We were close to obtaining arrest warrants for Montoya and his gang when the assistant U.S. attorney announced that he had been promoted to a post in Washington and a new strike force attorney would take over. Things ground to a halt. The new attorney was a fledgling who became inundated with the flood of paperwork and was hampered by her unfamiliarity with the case. It did take time to come up to speed, and we understood, but it was a bit of a blow. Investigations continued, and we were depending mostly on information from the inside. Ragon was working back into Montoya's trust…we thought.

One afternoon Ken came to my office with Tom to advise me that they had been working with two LAPD detectives at OCID, but the detectives had suddenly stopped sharing information with them and sealed them off from any meetings.

I called the captain of the Organized Crime & Intelligence Squad and asked him to meet me for lunch in Chinatown. Over lunch the captain revealed that he had received a call from the FBI agent who supervised their white-collar fraud unit and was told, "Don't work with the Secret Service; they can't be trusted."

I then explained what had occurred in the meeting with the FBI in my office, and the captain agreed to work again with us and share all information.

One evening, I received a call from "someone."

"Your informant is in danger. They've got a fifty-thousand-dollar contract on his head, and they're gonna whack him."

The phone went dead.

I called the LAPD and requested that a squad car speed to Ragon's address. Ken and I red-lined our government-issue Plymouth to his apartment, rushed in, and jam-packed his suitcase so that we could get him to the airport ASAP. We had our office arrange for airline tickets back to France. We would protect Ragon until the plane lifted off.

The Secret Service takes *contracts* very seriously. We take our opponents seriously too. For all the formal training *we* receive, they, too, learn well. They get their training in the streets, and it continues in prison. And I don't mean the kind of training or learning opportunities offered by the state.

A diligent professional criminal can leave the brig with the equivalent of doctoral and post-doctoral degrees in murder and mayhem as well as a broad and creative variety of cerebrally oriented illicit activities. However, the downfall of most criminals is that—although they are cautious—down deep they believe they're not going to get caught. The Secret Service hopes they keep thinking that way.

As we shoved Ragon into the car, we began an evasive drive down darkened streets. Always alert to possible tails, I noticed a car about ten lengths behind us, shadowing our every turn. A quick glance at Ken was the only signal he needed to look around and evaluate the situation.

"Step on it," he advised coolly.

I tried to shove the gas pedal through the floorboards, but the tail stayed close behind us. While we leaned somewhat perilously around the corners, the tail seemed rock steady as it whipped through the turns. I felt a little like an African wildebeest futilely attempting to outsprint a cheetah. Despite that, fear mixed with a sense of duty meant that I would do everything in my power to outmaneuver whoever was closing on us.

We wove between slower cars and dared oncoming traffic to move over as we raced through the early evening traffic. Ragon moaned with fear. I don't know which was more frightening—Ragon's moans or seeing the car behind us creeping closer.

"Ken," I hollered, "get on the radio for help!"

Ken radioed the duty agent at headquarters that we were being followed by an "unknown."

The radio crackled back, "Williams! It's Tom! Where the hell are you flying off to?"

"Oh, shit," I said. "Is that you behind me, Tom?"

"Just trying to keep you alive, man. But you won't let me."

"Thanks for pinching my sphincter. You damned near scared our witness to death. Whose side you on, anyway?"

From that point on, we continued our trip to the airport within the posted speed limits. Huffer and I escorted Ragon to the Air

France terminal, where we disappeared into the airline's swank VIP lounge. As soon as the door closed behind us, we whisked Ragon out a back entrance to the tarmac outside the terminal. There, an airport security car sped us to a waiting Swiss Air 747. We ushered Ragon up the boarding ladder, bade him farewell, and sent him to protective custody in Switzerland. We wanted him untraceable. We wanted him safe. And we wanted him back alive to testify.

We accomplished all three goals.

Meanwhile, more evidence against Montoya came from across international borders. The Royal Canadian Mounted Police (RCMP) called to advise that they had a "confidential informant" whom they apprehended with engraved counterfeit $100 Federal Reserve Note plates.

The informant, who I will call Joe, said that he had been approached by an underworld associate from Montreal named Tune who asked if he wanted to buy the plates. Joe identified Tune's stateside contact as a man named Arel, and a quick check verified his phone number belonged to GenStar on Wilshire Boulevard in Los Angeles. We arranged an LA rendezvous between Joe and Arel.

We met Joe and a RCMP officer upon their arrival in Los Angeles. As arranged, Joe then called Arel, who suggested that he himself taxi the Canadian to a meeting at GenStar. We followed.

Joe agreed to find out who was involved in this particular counterfeiting connivance as well as where and when the work would take place. The meeting was chaired not by Arel, but by Rudy Montoya himself.

To establish his credentials, Joe claimed that he was involved in a $12 million computer transaction involving counterfeit blank U.S. Treasury notes and that his contacts included organized crime groups from Los Angeles to San Francisco and Vancouver, B.C.

Arel laid out the plan, named the printer they would use, and assigned someone from the team to fly with Joe back to Canada to check out the plates. Arel said Joe would stay overnight at Arel's home that night, and on their way there they stopped at Montoya's auto-body shop to introduce Joe to another excellent printer, Jean Paul Nataf. Nataf's advice was that to print engraved plates would be "much too costly and take too much time." He said they would be better off using the offset method here.

Montoya and Arel accepted Nataf's advice and opted for the faster, cheaper photo offset process, using their existing plates rather than using the painstakingly engraved plates. This despite the fact that six months earlier, $3 million worth of patently false Montoya 100s printed via offset looked so fake that they had to be dumped in a dumpster behind the print shop.

Joe did his job as informant. While touring the auto shop, Joe claimed to have observed forty cases of Uzi machine guns, stacks of gold plastic credit card blanks, and an embossing machine. Later at Arel's home, Joe was shown negatives of $10, $20, $50, and $100 Federal Reserve Notes, enough weapons to threaten the nearby Pacific fleet, another embossing machine, and boxes of blank social security cards. He also stated that Nataf said he would not do the printing for Montoya and Arel, but that he would allow use of his print shop. No worries. We got Nataf later on collusion.

The next day Arel told Joe that if their next production of counterfeit was of poor quality, they would contact Joe after he returned to Canada, to coordinate with a man they had there who would manufacture fine quality negatives. Arel told Joe either he himself or Montoya would call. Satisfied that a new ally had joined the Montoya organization, Arel deposited Joe and his suitcase at the curb outside Air Canada.

"Hello, sir," the airport redcap said to Joe. "You can come this way. I'll expedite your baggage."

No one noticed that the redcap looked remarkably like one of my agents. Joe was handled safely, and three months after we began our investigation, the Secret Service, the LAPD, and other heavily armed agencies swarmed the offices of GenStar and Worldwide Products.

Totally surprised and caught off-guard, Montoya and his henchmen surrendered quietly. We simultaneously raided the residences and all businesses of Montoya, Arel, and Nataf, and confiscated equipment and supplies.

The LAPD together with the Secret Service and the U.S. Attorney's office held a press conference in the Secret Service conference room announcing the arrest of the Montoya crime family.

The search warrants and the arrests were done without the assistance of the FBI. The blowback was instantaneous. My boss, the special agent in charge of the Los Angeles office, called me into his office to advise that the FBI had made a formal complaint to the Secret Service director complaining that we had interfered with their case. It was obvious the FBI had a wiretap on the Montoya crime family and felt we had jumped the gun on getting the gang prosecuted.

I understand that after I wrote an after-action report with the backing of the captain from LAPD, the director of the Secret Service told the director of the FBI they had failed to cooperate and to go pound sand.

A few months later Montoya and his gang were convicted and sentenced. Any "family reunions" would now have to be held in prison.

Chapter 27

ATM Assault

It's a classic tactic in any battle: Strike when and where the defenses are weakest, using the greatest numbers of personnel and weapons available, and do it in the shortest period of time. Cleverness should always be considered a weapon.

Mark Koenig was clever. Koenig, a computer programmer subcontractor who had unlimited access to countless credit card names and numbers, engineered a techno-scheme he believed would garner him and his greedy group nearly a million dollars. He could do it over a three-day holiday weekend using thousands of counterfeit ATM cards at widely dispersed teller machines.

Despite the brilliant simplicity of his design, Koenig failed to factor in one small thing: a confidential informant coming into the scenario.

The CI, who I will call Max, confessed that Koenig's wife, Jackie, had first telephoned him and asked if he would be interested in making $250,000. In her seductive presentation, Jackie assured Max that this plan was "foolproof." She explained her husband had engineered a scheme wherein he could manufacture counterfeit ATM cards and that he had tested them, and it worked. She told him Mark had already gotten $5,000.

Max alerted the Secret Service to the upcoming scam and listed the names of the suspected co-conspirators. We immediately began round-the-clock surveillance of Koenig's apartment.

"What's the deal?" Max asked.

"You take out whatever you can and return fifty percent of your proceeds to us. We are putting a lot of work into this. Your part is the easy part."

"When do we start?"

"President's Day weekend. All the banks are closed. They won't know anything has happened until Tuesday evening."

Jackie told Max that he would receive at least 100 ATM cards with the PINs encoded on them.

"You can use them anywhere in the United States at various ATM machines," Jackie informed him. "We have others doing this too because they know it's such a safe scheme," she assured him.

Unfortunately for the Koenigs, the phone conversation between Jackie and Max was recorded by the Secret Service. The scheme wasn't so safe, after all.

Max met with Mark and Jackie at their Los Angeles apartment. Also attending—via a bug wrapped around Max's torso—were five agents who were all clustered around a sensitive receiver positioned inside a nondescript surveillance van parked outside the Koenig residence.

During the meeting, Jackie described how she was making the ATM cards by cutting up standard poster board to the proper measurements. The secret to the cards' success was the magnetic tape strips carefully encrypted with numbers stolen by Mark. He explained that as a computer consultant at the phone company's data processing center, he could access processing transmissions of encrypted ATM transaction data from various ATM machines to their respective ATM account holders' banks.

Further, Mark said that the data processing center retains a disc tape file of all ATM transaction data passing through their phone lines. With surprising ease, Mark intercepted the file and simply copied its data onto a disc file tape from his office. He then transferred the data to a floppy disc, which he hid at home.

Once at his own personal computer, Koenig wrote his own program in COBOL computer language to decode the encrypted data. He then wrote a program in a PASCAL language to encode the new fake cards. It was laborious and technical but doable for him with his brilliance.

When all of the pertinent data was obtained, all that was necessary was to encode the data onto simple magnetic tape through the home-built interface device connected to Koenig's PC. The programmed magnetic tape—similar to that found on a reel of tape recorder ribbon—then could be cut, properly placed, and glued onto the poster board ATM blanks.

This is how they did it back then.

"We've already got six thousand cards stacked and ready over there," Mark bragged to Max—and to the listening agents.

The next morning, another of their crew, a man named Robert Hussey, parked his bright red Porsche near the Koenig apartment. He walked purposely to their place, clutching a brown leather briefcase.

Again, the wire did what it was supposed to. The agents merely smiled as Hussey told the Koenigs and Max that he wanted 3,000 cards for himself, and that he intended to use the cards in San Diego, Los Angeles, San Francisco, and Sacramento. He estimated that in three days of marching up the state, he could bring home $300,000.

Hussey said that he had devised his own part of the plan: He would buy a car from an individual not a dealer—never identifying himself to the seller—then use the car unregistered just in case the license plate was picked up on ATM surveillance cameras. Hussey stated he was going to hit the ATMs between the hours of 5:30 p.m.

and midnight. Any time after that, he felt, police might think he looked suspicious. He also explained that he was going to disguise himself by stuffing his mouth with toilet paper, wearing a bandage across his face, and dying his hair with washable hair color. Once finished working his ATM *blitzkrieg*, he would burn everything he had worn.

That night, agents followed as Koenig and Hussey visited an ATM. Using a card of their own origination, they withdrew $200 from somebody's account.

The next day, during a recorded phone conversation between Mark and Max, Mark suggested that Max travel with Koenig's brother, who lived in Nebraska. They could use their home-brewed ATM cards at Midwestern banks. Mark would fly out to join them the day after his co-conspirators began their assaults on the ATMs of California. By sweeping through the Midwest like a Kansas tornado, Koenig estimated that they could rake in a two-day take of at least $300,000.

After a week of eavesdropping and confidential reports from Max, at a moment when the suspects were all gathered in the Koenigs' apartment around their makeshift credit card assembly line, the Secret Service commenced its raid on the premises.

As the agents quietly gathered down the hall from the apartment, Jackie Koenig opened the front door unexpectedly. She spotted the assembled agents, then just stood there, staring in shock for a moment before she quickly ducked back into her apartment. Strangely, she left the door open. Concerned that the suspects might destroy evidence, the agents formed a flying wedge and stormed the apartment. The front line of an NFL team couldn't have been more imposing.

"Police! We have a search warrant!"

The stunned suspects didn't move.

Hussey and others were seated at the dining room table, wearing surgical gloves to eliminate any possibility of fingerprints. Jackie, also wearing rubber gloves, froze where she stood in the living room. Mark was missing. We began an immediate search—and found him sitting serenely on the toilet, concentrating on things other than credit cards. Perhaps there couldn't have been a better place to make an arrest.

During our initial search, we located nearly 1,500 counterfeit ATM cards already encoded and stacked on a bookshelf adjacent to the dining room. We counted over 4,000 unencoded cards with magnetic tape already attached, waiting for encryption. There were too many magnetic tape strips to count, but these lay in a jumble in a bowl on the dining room table, next to the encoding device, which was attached via umbilical to the computer.

If that weren't enough evidence, we found six sheets of 8 1/2" by 11" lined yellow paper outlining a *modus operandi*: "Buy car for cash in San Diego…Clean it for prints before selling in Sacramento…hit San Diego, Los Angeles, San Francisco, Sacramento… Disguises…"

Though Koenig's crime was very sophisticated technologically, his escape strategy was simple: Use PIN numbers exclusively from one large bank. Should the crime be discovered before the action terminated, investigators logically would begin their search in the bank system, believing it to be an inside job. How many hundreds of employees had access to the computer codes? Clever!

When it came to computer programming, Koenig was a certifiable genius. Unfortunately, he wasn't as precise when it came to reading people.

Over the years, I have marveled at the ingenuity of some of the criminals I've been…what is the phrase…"associated with." Too bad these kinds of guys do not use their genius for good. We could have cured cancer by now.

Chapter 28

"Don't Open the Trunk!"

Another faceless phone call. Another criminal looking to soften his time.

"Mr. Williams, my name is Jim Hopper. I'm calling to give you some information, but if I give it to you, you've got to help me out of my sentence."

"Where you calling from?"

"Terminal Island…"

Terminal Island is aptly named because it rests beside the giant docks for both passenger and cargo ships in San Pedro Harbor, adjacent to a Coast Guard base, and because it is the terminus for thousands of convicted federal criminals.

"What you in for?"

"Counterfeiting."

"Talk," I said tersely.

"I know someone who's getting ready to print counterfeit money again."

"Go on."

"I'm not saying no more. We gotta bargain first," Hopper insisted.

I promised to visit the bargainer at the seaside "federal resort" the next morning. But before I could say goodbye, he interrupted. "Just one more thing, Mr. Williams. I gotta be discreet, cuz if anyone here finds out I've been talking to you, I'll be labeled a snitch. And I wanna get out of here on my own two wheels."

"Agreed!" I promised.

After hanging up, I ran a computer check on him and reviewed his extended dossier: arrested six times for counterfeiting. Convicted three times. Currently into the third year of a ten-year term at Terminal Island.

My next call was to the prison. I apprised them of the sensitive nature of my pending interview with Hopper and that Hopper feared for his safety if our *tête-à-tête* ever became public. We agreed that I would log into the prison for the purpose of "routine federal prisoner review," and that Hopper would be ushered to some office other than the warden's. They'd think of some explanation if anyone questioned Hopper's movement outside normal prisoner areas. Then when both of us were in place, Hopper would be moved surreptitiously from his location to mine. Only one other officer would know of this rendezvous.

Entering a prison has to be one of the most depressing experiences any person can have. It's a gray world full of angry sociopaths all jammed together in a survival environment. It's further dispiriting because every inmate knows that on the other side of thick, rock walls topped with razor wire, a vibrant world exists, while their years crawl by. It never fails at the end of every visit I make to a prison or jail; I can't wait to fill my lungs with free air from outside no matter how smoggy it is.

I met Hopper and told him if his information proved correct, I would tell the appropriate people about how he helped us in a case, but that I couldn't guarantee any time off his sentence. He appeared to accept this thread of hope.

"Here's what's going down, Mr. Williams. A guy named Migdol is going to get out of this joint in a week, and he's getting ready to print counterfeit money. Migdol told me about his new scam and asked me if I would help him make contact on the outside. He said that if I did that, he'd take care of me and my family."

I assumed Hopper assumed that Migdol meant he'd take care of him financially.

"I told him to call my sister and she'd set him up with a contact."

Of course, I—and many other agents assigned to the counterfeit squad—had been aware of the Migdol name. Migdol was being released after serving his *sixth* term for counterfeiting.

One week after I met with Hopper, Migdol was out on the streets. He immediately called the sister, who then called me as part of our arranged plan.

"I told him I knew a guy who was interested in doing business, and to give me a couple of days to find him," she said.

The Secret Service tailed Migdol, who had found lodging with several other ex-cons in a house in Westminster, California, one of the many nondescript cities that comprise Orange County. We learned later that while waiting for Hopper's contact, he spent his hours developing a Monopoly-inspired game he called "Convict." Each square on the game board was imprinted with a different crime or sentence. He even managed to appear on a local TV talk show in an attempt to introduce his game to the marketplace. As far as I know, this may have been one of Migdol's rare attempts at honest marketing.

I teamed with Secret Service Agent Jerry Petievich, who later wrote the successful movie *To Live and Die in L.A.*, and together we scribed our own cops-and-robbers play to bring down Migdol. We set up the first scene at the sister's house in Garden Grove, where we coached her on her lines to set up a meeting for Migdol with Petievich.

"Gimme a week," Migdol promised. "I'll have some great samples for you."

"Why don't we meet first? How do I know you're not the heat trying to set me up?" Jerry challenged.

"Hey, man, I just got out of the joint. I ain't no cop."

"So, when are we going to meet, man?" Jerry asked again.

"Tomorrow night at eight," Migdol decided.

We got there early. I sat in the bar, while Jerry waited near the hostess station. Migdol walked in, accompanied by another man, who also looked to be in his sixties. I didn't expect to see older men, but when I reflected that Migdol had served six terms in the federal pen for counterfeiting, the gray hair and lined face—aggravated by years of chain-smoking Camels—it made sense.

Jerry approached. "You Migdol?"

Migdol nodded "yes," then tilted his head toward his gruff-appearing associate, whose gnarled hands rested in his coat pockets. "Meet Bruno. Just in case you're trying to con me, I've brought my own bodyguard."

Ever so discreetly, the heavily tattooed Bruno lifted his Hawaiian shirt, revealing the wooden butt of a .38 tucked into his waistband.

"That won't be necessary, Migdol," Jerry said.

"You never know."

They sipped coffee between strained conversation, each trying to feel the other out to see if they were being set up. Finally, Jerry said, "Listen, man, fuck this game-playing. Call me when you've got a sample. You've got my number." Unknown to Migdol, of course, that number was an undercover line assigned to this particular case.

The trio soon left the restaurant, each giving the other conspiratorial nods.

The next morning, we reviewed Migdol's arrest record. Interesting. In five out of his six apprehensions, he had been snatched in undercover, hand-to-hand transfer of counterfeit for currency that had been withdrawn from the trunks of cars in restaurant parking lots. In four out of the five arrests, the signal for Secret Service support agents to close in was the lifting of the car trunk lid.

I couldn't help but recall an old lesson from freshman psychology class: Even rats in a maze learn to change their pathways when an unpleasant stimulus is repeatedly introduced. But we decided that when we took Migdol down, we were going to test the old felon's memory. Jerry's signal to me and the backup agents to move in would be the old "lift-the-trunk-lid" maneuver.

A few days after the restaurant rendezvous, Migdol called Jerry. "Got the stuff," Migdol bragged.

"Okay, bring three or four thousand so I can get a feel," Jerry demanded.

Migdol offered, "I'll bring ten thousand dollars counterfeit for two thousand real."

"Okay. I wanna see it first, though. If it looks good, it's a go."

That night at 10 p.m. they met in the hotel parking lot of the Holiday Inn in Long Beach right off the 405 freeway, and again, we were set up at the hotel early, searching the area to make sure Migdol didn't get there before we did. After all, he was a sophisticated criminal despite the fact that he had been arrested in such a stakeout six times before. We knew that he knew the routine of surveillance and tails.

Jerry drove up in a black Lincoln a few moments before the appointed hour. Migdol arrived two minutes later, again with the pistol-toting Bruno riding shotgun. Another agent and I were stationed in the van about forty yards away.

"Let's see the package," Jerry ordered.

Migdol responded quickly, reaching into the breast pocket of his coat. Our hearts stopped for an instant, but he slowly withdrew his hand, holding a thick envelope. Jerry took the envelope and riffled through the counterfeit money.

"Now gimme the two grand," Migdol shouted. We could hear him through the siding of the van.

Jerry stood there for a second before saying, "Wait a second, I'll get it out of my car…"

A troubled look crossed Migdol's face. Like he'd been there before. He had to have been remembering all the times he had been busted "out of the trunk of a car."

Abruptly he burst out, "Forget the deal! Don't open the trunk. Forget it, man. Don't open that trunk!"

Jerry smiled at this unexpected outburst, surprised that Migdol kept pleading with him pathetically not to open the trunk. As Petievich lifted the trunk hatch, he looked directly at the melting Migdol and dramatically parodied a classic crime movie line: "Yes, Migdol, the trunk is up…"

When the lid sprung open, that was our signal. We burst out of the van, guns drawn, and shouted for everyone to put up his hands. But Bruno almost made a fatal mistake. He reached into his waistband but thought better of it when he saw a couple of Uzis pointed his way. He raised his prison-tattooed arms resignedly instead—as if he had been down this path before.

Both Bruno and Migdol were sent back to federal penitentiary. Migdol, who possessed the dubious honor of being arrested by the Secret Service more times than any other criminal, developed cancer while doing term number seven. The Bureau of Prisons let him out early on humanitarian grounds, and he died shortly afterward.

Our informant Hopper was released from prison six months later. And no one, to my knowledge, has ever developed a board game about being a convict. If they do, they should call it Crime Doesn't Pay.

Chapter 29

This One Takes the Prize

Kerry Ketchum, one of the more colorful subjects in Secret Service files, was called "a virtual tornado of deception across the entire country" by one attorney, and even his own defense lawyer said, "Let's face it, Kerry's a rascal."

Ketchum was a wanted man for many reasons, in many states. He came to my attention in January of 1988, when I received a call from the operations manager at a bank in Anchorage, Alaska. A keen employee there had discovered a problem worthy of our interest. Two men had both listed their address as the same post office box in North Pole, Alaska, and were delinquent in paying their VISA cards issued via that bank. The unpaid amount totaled more than $10,000. The bank manager doing further research discovered that the two had also been granted VISA cards one month earlier through another Alaska bank, and these cards, too, had unpaid debts amounting to more than $15,000. As on her bank's applications, the cardholders had listed the same North Pole post office box.

Suspecting fraud, the bank contacted postal inspectors, who examined the PO box, finding numerous past-due credit invoices from many credit cards, as well as a Social Security check belonging to a Kerry D. Ketchum.

Routinely, the postal inspectors ordered examinations on the Ketchum name and Social Security number, plus a run on several sets of fingerprints lifted off the PO box door. Both the number and several of the fingerprints did, in fact, belong to Ketchum.

Ketchum's name then was forwarded to the National Crime Information Center in Washington, DC. It took only minutes for a response: Ketchum was a fugitive from the state of Indiana, wanted on a no-bail warrant issued by the state police for defrauding a financial institution and for forgery.

With that information provided to us by the postal inspectors, we picked up on the investigation. I contacted the Indiana State Police, who confirmed their search for Ketchum. Ketchum apparently had visited a local BMW dealership, where he conned the salesman into letting him test drive a "Beemer" without the salesman riding along. For identity, Ketchum provided an Alaska driver's license bearing the name Patrick Quinn, one of the names on the credit cards and PO box. Quinn/Ketchum never brought the Beemer back.

But that wasn't all. Ketchum/Quinn visited a local bank and arranged a loan for the down payment, which he received promptly. Then through private sources, he arranged to cash the check at a discount.

Three things then disappeared from Indiana without a trace: the BMW, the down payment, and Ketchum.

In addition to the Indiana caper, the evidence for credit card fraud in Alaska was overwhelming. We had a face and a proper name, as well as some well-used AKAs. But the trouble was Ketchum was now underground. He'd be more difficult to locate than the proverbial snowflake in an Alaskan snowdrift. It would become a waiting game, until he decided to emerge from hibernation.

In the meantime, we issued a "wanted" photo to the media in our forty-ninth state, detailing Ketchum's fraudulent activities and seeking information leading to his arrest. His picture, borrowed from the files of the Alaskan Department of Motor Vehicles, ran in the *Anchorage Times*.

Two days after Ketchum's picture was in the paper, the bank manager called again. One of her tellers reported that she had seen Ketchum.

"Where? Did he come into the bank?" I asked.

"No, she saw him on TV."

"…on the news?"

"On *Super Password*. He won a lot of money!"

Until Ketchum's game show debut, everyone involved in the investigation believed that he was holed up in some wilderness cabin. It now appeared that Ketchum had holed up in Hollywood. The Secret Service was going to have to go show-biz too.

The office manager at the game show confirmed that a man purporting to be Patrick Quinn did in fact win $58,600 on *Super Password,* and he became the "highest single-day winner in the history of the game show."

She confirmed that Ketchum/Quinn had taped a series of shows in December and that those contests were aired in January, but that Ketchum's winner's check "had not yet been cut."

Our agents showed Ketchum's picture to the producers and to the game show's host, Burt Convy. They reconfirmed that Ketchum was Quinn. Convy also told the agents he found it strange that Ketchum/Quinn appeared on his show. Convy explained that Ketchum/Quinn had confided in a conspiratorial whisper that he was a CIA agent on leave and was due to return to the Middle East very shortly. Therefore, he needed his winnings as soon as possible. Burt Convy thought this was very odd and didn't make sense.

Now Ketchum, the most successful player in the game's five-year history, had been calling every day for his check. "We advised him just today that his check would be ready by eleven o'clock tomorrow morning," we were told. This was, indeed, great news. The Secret

Service would be right there to greet him on the "payday."

At 10:30 a.m. the next day, a comely receptionist ushered two of our agents into a glass-walled conference room just off the lobby of the executive offices of Goodson Productions, where they were met by Julie Stevens, the office manager, and the company's productions manager. They were ready for Ketchum's 11 a.m. arrival.

About twenty minutes before the hour, Ms. Stevens got up from the conference table and ambled over to the doorway, where she could see down the hallways of the office complex. Unexpectedly, her eyes locked onto a visitor who was pacing tensely, head down, in front of the receptionist's desk.

With a second sense doubtlessly honed from years of "hide-and-seek," Ketchum felt Ms. Stevens' gaze. He lifted his head and gazed back. But Ms. Stevens' next move must have triggered the fugitive's survival alarm bell. She looked back over her shoulder, where the Secret Service agents waited. This body language was the only communication Ketchum needed. He pulled a "180" and bolted from the office toward the building's emergency stairs.

"There he goes! He's running away!" Stevens screamed. The agents took off after Ketchum. Just like a classic foot chase in the movies, they raced on slightly out-of-condition legs down ten flights of stairs. They burst through the lobby doors, guns held muzzle up, startling a gaggle of people waiting for elevators, then dashed outside to take up a more horizontal pursuit up and down the block.

But Ketchum was quicker than they had imagined. He quite simply disappeared as quickly as if someone had flicked the channel changer of the TV set.

Disappointed and breathing heavily, Agent Ken Edwards returned to the building and decided to go to the restroom in the restaurant adjacent to the building lobby. While standing at the urinal, he noticed that all the doors to the toilets were open except for one. Common enough, except that there were no feet resting on the floor in the closed stall. There were no sounds of any kind emanating from the stall either—no newspapers rustling, no coughs, dripping or flushing sounds. Very unnatural, Ken thought.

After he finished and zipped, Ken pulled his gun, walked over to an adjacent toilet, and muttered, "Damn diarrhea…" When he closed the door, instead of sitting down, Edwards climbed up on the toilet seat, peered over the top, and spotted Ketchum crouching on the toilet seat.

Pointing his gun downward, Edwards announced calmly, "Mr. Ketchum, you're under arrest."

When Edwards frisked his prisoner, he found identification for everyone but Ketchum. However, under interrogation, Ketchum admitted who he was.

With so many different agencies interested in getting their legal claws into Ketchum, it finally was decided that Ketchum be remanded to the custody of the FBI and held without bail. Ketchum was sentenced to five years in prison for mail fraud—staging an elaborate hoax in which he faked his wife's death to collect on a $100,000 insurance policy.

He was separated from his wife when he filed the claim, and she was unaware of the scam, but the man certainly had an interesting past. Ketchum had been a deputy sheriff, but he had resigned from the County Sheriff's Department in Dayton, Ohio, only after he had been convicted in federal court of stealing and then fencing more than $200,000 worth of military equipment while he was a sergeant in the U.S. Air Force. For that caper, he exchanged one blue uniform for another and eighteen months in Leavenworth federal prison.

He was smart though. And maybe even contrite. According to a *Los Angeles Times* story that ran after his conviction, he stated, "One of the reasons I went on the game show was to use my own intellect for something other than bad."

His case spawned a silly joke around our office.

"Ketchum?"

"Caught 'im."

Chapter 30

BCCI Bank-London

IN THE EARLY 1980s, a counterfeit $100 bill appeared that was flawless.

The U.S. government prints federal reserve notes from paper manufactured at the Crane Paper Mill in Dalton, Massachusetts. The "paper" is 25 percent cotton and made to last at least eighteen months in circulation. Printing of the notes is conducted at the Bureau of Printing and Engraving in Washington, DC, with specialized ink and printing methods.

The new counterfeit hundreds were printed on similar top-quality paper, with the same expensive intaglio or raised ink and typographical or indented printing. Most counterfeits at that time were printed lithographic offset wherein the ink lies on the surface of the paper. These new bills were so good, they were being cleared by the Federal Reserve Banks, and the case became a top-secret investigation.

A confidential informant was developed, and the intelligence information indicated that Iran had backed Hezbollah in Lebanon to print three billion dollars in counterfeit 100-dollar bills in the Bekaa Valley. The motive was to distribute the money to various terrorist groups and into the worldwide distribution system to destroy the American economy.

Agents who were assigned to investigate this "supernote" were sworn to secrecy. Some were sent to Cyprus to monitor the case and work with informants to track the distribution of the counterfeits.

One of the terrorist groups that reportedly received over $20 million of the fakes was the Irish Republic Army, aka IRA, in Northern Ireland. The notes were distributed through the Pakistani-owned BCCI Bank (Bank of Credit and Commerce International) located in London. I was assigned to the American Embassy to work with Special Agent Dennis Crandall of the Secret Service, who was stationed in London, and with Scotland Yard to determine if the BCCI Bank had indeed acted as a distribution point for these supernotes.

My contacts at Scotland Yard were Reggie Leonard and Brian James. Both of these men had a great sense of humor and were delightful to work with.

One of our first meetings was an appointment to go to the Bank of England and examine their vaults to determine if any of the counterfeit bills had been received and stored at the bank. We spent all day examining money but found no supernotes. I was told that I was the only foreign citizen to ever be allowed into the vaults at the Bank of England.

One afternoon we adjourned to the bar in the basement of Scotland Yard to have a pint. The table seated ten and when we joined the group, we filled out the circular table. Sitting to my left was a rather skinny detective with a distinctive long nose and narrow face. Brian James sat immediately to my right. After about ten minutes of social conversation, the fellow on my left said in a loud voice and disparaging tone, "President Eisenhower's mother was a maid."

I looked at him thoughtfully and calmly said, "I think it's wonderful that Eisenhower could be so successful coming from a humble background."

Although the comment was completely out of place, I decided to forget it until about ten minutes later, when he sneeringly said again, "Did you know Eisenhower's mother was a maid?"

This time I gave him a mad dog look and said, "I think that's wonderful, but what's that got to do with anything?"

Skinny Long Nose did not reply. Brian, realizing I was becoming agitated, leaned over and whispered to me to just ignore the fool. I told Brian, "If he says it again, I'm gonna deck the bastard."

Ten minutes later, this nitwit yet again said in his condescending attitude, "President Eisenhower's mother was a maid."

I stood up and slammed my fist on his pointed nose and knocked him off his chair. He remained lying on the floor, still conscious but now quiet, while blood gushed from his nose. I looked down at him and said, "That's for Eisenhower's mother."

Brian and Reggie ushered me out of the bar, while some of the other detectives attended to their comrade. Later, the detectives who were present apologized to me and said the bloke had it coming. They urged him not to file a complaint as they would support me for punching him out. Thus, my name from Brian James became the "Prince of Darkness." I dubbed him the "Prince of Wales." We have remained friends to this day.

Brian, Reggie, and I went to the BCCI Bank on Leadenhall in London to examine the premises. The bank and all assets had been seized for operating a criminal enterprise. The CPA firm of Deloitte & Touché was there conducting an inventory. I noticed a steel door hidden from view at the side of the bank. I tried to open it but it was locked. We asked the Deloitte manager what was behind the door, but he had no idea. He said the door had never been opened even though they had been at the bank for weeks. So we summoned a locksmith.

It took the locksmith two hours to get through the lock. When the door was opened, we saw stairs, about thirty steps, going down underneath the street. Brian, Reggie, and I clambered down the stairs to discover cages filled with counterfeit money, counterfeit bank certificates, as well as drugs and other items of illicit activity.

We confiscated the illegal items even though the manager of Deloitte & Touché objected because he cited the fact that he was responsible for the audit and all inventory. While Brian argued with him, Reggie and I were busy cleaning out the cages and putting the items in a truck from Scotland Yard.

Ultimately, the standoff was solved when we allowed the manager to document for his records the items we seized. Although we could never prove the counterfeit money was targeted for distribution to the IRA, we at least kept what we found out of their hands. And anyone else's.

The investigation went on for years as top secret, until someone in our government revealed the counterfeit investigation to the *60 Minutes* TV program, and it appeared on a Sunday night segment.

That was a frustrating setback since we were getting close to the operation and had successfully foiled attempts to distribute the supernote. The counterfeit operation was moved to North Korea, well out of reach of the Secret Service. Or so they thought.

For many years, the North Koreans tried to spread the counterfeit dollars throughout Asia, but the Secret Service kept the lid on the investigation and continued to seize vast quantities of the supernote.

Chapter 31

Fidel Castro

I WAS PART of the detail providing security for Fidel Castro during his visit to New York to address the United Nations in October 1979.

Prior to his arrival, nobody could—or would—clue us in as to the exact date of Castro's visit, so we occupied our time at orientation meetings provided by our own people, the FBI, CIA, and state department.

Perhaps the most enlightening of the briefings was a film about Alpha 66—a group of Miami-based expatriate Cubans bent on the violent overthrow of the cigar-chomping, fatigue-attired dictator. Alpha 66 members were the hardest core of the hard-core Cubans whom the Central Intelligence Agency had trained for the ill-fated Bay of Pigs invasion in 1961, as ordered by President John F. Kennedy. Though some Alpha 66ers had been killed or captured by Cuban defenders, enough were withdrawn from the beachhead to continue their single-minded mission from the security of the U.S.

Throughout our briefings, we were told that intelligence sources had reported that Alpha 66 would use Castro's visit to take him out—and that if they had to "sacrifice any U.S. agents in the process, they would unhesitatingly do so."

Our moods became dour, our dispositions sour. All we could do was wait impatiently at our hotel for word of the date of Castro's appearance. Finally, after a week of boredom, we were collected and shipped out on a small Air Force executive jet to New York.

Again—after many "agains"—we were warned *not* to reveal why we were in town. This was to be a totally secret assignment. Additionally, we were told that we had to stay together as a group, and if we were to go out at night, we had to inform the command center duty agents where we'd be.

Where we'd be was called "Septembers," a favorite haunt of the Secret Service where drinks were anything but counterfeit. After a couple of days of evenings at Septembers, with no word about Castro's arrival, we began to relax and enjoy ourselves.

We were extraordinarily laid back when one of the guys from HQ rushed into the bar at 12:30 a.m. and ordered us to get back to the hotel. "Get suits on! A bus will pick you up at 2 a.m. Castro's comin' in!"

Not even the State Department had known when Castro was to arrive. Like us, they had to wait until the Western Hemisphere's Marxist *supremo* decided when he was going to leave Cuba.

At two o'clock sharp, a commercial bus picked us up and drove us to a remote section at LaGuardia Airport. Literally, a small army of agents and policemen awaited Castro's Russian-built transport there.

Castro didn't know how lucky he was to be guarded by so many law enforcement professionals, for most of the men with whom I spoke privately couldn't have cared if an Alpha 66 bullet ricocheted around the interior of Castro's skull. Such was the disdain America had for him.

However, none of us was going to let that happen if we could help it.

I was assigned to the motorcade in the police tail car. At three in the morning, all the streets along our route into the city were declared "clean." Still, we were nervous, for we knew that the Cuban exiles—with keen intelligence of their own—were well aware of Castro's comings and goings. Our skittishness was compounded by the announcement that the NYPD had just discovered the theft of several police cars, along with dozens of police uniforms.

"Oh, oh, it's started," an agent mumbled to me just before I climbed into the back seat of the patrol car. For all I knew, the rather swarthy driver of my car was an Alpha 66 assassin. I kept my service revolver loose in its holster.

Without fanfare, Castro stepped out of his jet and, with a few henchmen a respectable distance behind him, walked among his own bodyguards to his own limousine for the unpublicized and circuitous ride to the Cuban consulate in Manhattan. Forty-five minutes later, his car disappeared into the basement of the building, leaving behind a concentrated security force the size of which not even our own president enjoyed.

An entire four-block area surrounding the consulate had been cordoned off. No one wanting or needing to enter the security zone was above suspicion. To that end, all security personnel were issued armbands—a different color for each day Castro was to be there—so that we could easily identify the "good guys." Every resident, business owner, and employee within the zone was given a perimeter pass. Whoever requested or received a pass was checked out by the Secret Service.

Secret Service anti-terrorist snipers patrolled building tops throughout the zone. Occasionally, we could see the glint of sun off their binoculars or the high-powered scopes resting atop their high-powered rifles.

On the third day in New York, word came down that Castro was finally going to the United Nations. I was assigned to cover the front gate of the General Assembly building at U.N. headquarters.

Despite the fact that I wore a bulletproof raincoat and carried a twelve-gauge magnum-loaded shotgun, in addition to my standard weaponry, I felt uncomfortable that Cuban security people were stationed behind me. I kept thinking, *If this thing breaks loose, what do I worry about most: Alpha 66 or Cuban security?*

The area around the UN was sanitized too, the facility itself transformed into an armed fortress. When Castro arrived in his high-security convoy, protected by an extended awning, a phalanx of agents and other security types closed around him. As quickly as this cluster of men grouped around Castro's limo door, they reversed course and ushered the dictator into the General Assembly building.

Though a tall man, Castro must have been stooping to walk, or the Service assigned agents of Sequoia proportions to surround him, for nobody outside the protective circle could get even a glimpse of black curly hair. After Castro's two-hour-long diatribe to the General Assembly, he left almost the same way he had entered. It was like watching a movie sequence in reverse. Then we convoyed him to his airplane. His departure was as surreptitious as his arrival.

Security around Castro was stitched so tightly that, in review, it was estimated that from the time of his arrival, including his descent from his aircraft into the limousine, his ingress and egress from the U.N., return to the limo, and back to LaGuardia, then to the gangway for his departure, he had been exposed to the outside world for less than fifteen seconds. A bee—let alone his enemies—would have been hard put to penetrate our defenses to sting him.

Of all my protection assignments over the years, Castro was the only head of state on whom I never laid eyes. But whether he knows it or not, we saved his life.

Chapter 32

SMOKEY THE BEAR

IN AUGUST 1980, my boss called me into his office. "The Fresno Resident Agency is open for an agent in charge. I'm recommending you for the position if you want it."

The Fresno office had just three agents and two secretaries, but if I wanted to go, it would be a great opportunity to run my own show and learn how to administer and manage an office. After two years I could be eligible for a promotion to come back to Los Angeles as a GS-14, assistant to the special agent in charge.

I said yes.

The Fresno Resident Agency was staffed with three agents plus me, and for the next two years, we outperformed our home field office of Sacramento with twelve agents there by making twice the number of arrests and doubling their criminal cases closed.

On my third day in the Fresno office, I had a visitor named Mike Eagles, who wanted to welcome me to Fresno. Mr. Eagles, whose real name was Malcom George, literally bounded into my office wearing white tennis shorts, white tennis shoes, and a white tennis shirt, carrying a tennis racquet.

"I'm here to introduce myself because you will be protecting me when I announce I am running for President of the United States."

Eagles took a seat across from my desk and proceeded to tell me how I should address him and how he wanted to be protected after he announced his candidacy. After ten minutes of listening, I told him, "Thank you for your time today, but I have other business that I have to attend to. Please leave."

The man became incensed and told me, "You work for me, the taxpayer, and if I want to sit in this government office all day, I will."

With that, I came around my desk, grabbed Eagles by the hair and the seat of his pants, and pushed him toward the door. I yelled at Elsie our secretary to open the door as I picked up speed carrying Eagles toward his final destination, the hallway. When I reached the doorway, I gave him a final liftoff and threw him across the floor. Little did I know they had just waxed the floor, and to my surprise, he slid all the way across the floor, hitting the elevator.

I looked up from my successful shot put of the man and realized three men in business suits had witnessed my toss. The first FBI agent said, "I saw nothing." The second FBI agent said, "I heard nothing." The third FBI agent said, "I don't know anything." The three agents then did a pivot and walked back down the hall, retracing their steps to their offices.

For the next week, Mike Eagles called my office at least fifteen times a day, harassing my staff and trying to get me on the phone. I thought he would eventually give up, but he became obsessed. So, one morning I got up at five and called his home telephone number, deciding to turn the tables.

The phone rang one time when he answered, "This is Mike Eagles, President of the United States. Now what the fuck do you want?"

I said, "Isn't your name Malcom George?"

He became irate and said, "I'm Mike Eagles! Now who is this, the FBI?"

Sensing my opening, I replied, "Yes, this is the FBI, and we have you under surveillance."

Malcom George/Mike Eagles screamed that he was the President of the United States and surveillance by the FBI was illegal. At that point I knew mission accomplished, and I hung up the phone.

The next day I got a visit from Charlie Sullivan, the resident agent in charge of the Fresno FBI office, informing me that Mike Eagles had started calling their office repeatedly, accusing the FBI of unlawful surveillance and harassment.

"You wouldn't have instigated this now, would you, Williams?"

"I know nothing," I replied.

The Malcom George episode started a war of practical jokes between me and the Fresno FBI. Both our offices were on the fifth floor of the Fresno Federal Building. The culmination of the jokes came one day when I arrived early and the elevator happened to open on the fourth floor, where the Forest Rangers had an office. Standing in front of their office was a seven-foot-tall plastic Smokey the Bear with his arm extended and finger pointed. I got off the elevator and walked over to Smokey and gave him a nudge. To my delight, he was not that heavy and not tethered down. I got back on the elevator and went to my office to secure a dolly. I returned to the fourth floor to retrieve Smokey; I placed him in front of the FBI office and hung a sign on his finger that read: NEW FBI AGENT.

Later that morning I walked into the employee cafeteria to get coffee. Several FBI agents accused me of stealing Smokey and putting him in front of their office. Of course, I was offended and vehemently denied their insulting accusations.

That afternoon, which was a Friday, at two o'clock, Elsie rang my office and said the U.S. marshal was there to see me. Accompanying the head U.S. marshal were three FBI agents. They surrounded my desk, and the marshal advised me I was under arrest for the theft of Smokey the Bear, because he was official government property. I stood up to tell them to exit my office when they grabbed me and placed me in handcuffs. They then marched me to the elevator and down to the marshal's lockup, putting me in a cell with a young Mexican man. He asked me what I had been arrested for, and I looked at him without missing a beat and said, "For killing a Mexican." He screamed to the guard to get him out of the cell.

After an hour, I was escorted down a corridor behind the courtrooms. When the marshal opened the door to the courtroom, all of the federal employees in the building had been invited to attend my trial and were sitting on the benches. As I walked in, they all stood and shouted, "Hang him, hang him."

The prosecuting attorney was a young Black man named Adrian Farver from the U.S. Attorney's Office. My attorney was Vaughn Hall, one of the agents who worked for me. The judge stepped through the door into the courtroom, and the bailiff said, "Order in the court. We are here for the case of the *United States vs. Ron Williams* for theft of Smokey the Bear."

I jumped up and said in a loud voice, "Your Honor, before these proceedings begin, I want to file a complaint that my civil rights have been violated."

Adrian Farver stood and said, "Your Honor, Williams is not Black and he's not a Mexican; he doesn't have any civil rights. Sit down, White boy."

The judge pounded his gavel and said, "He's right; sit down, White boy."

On the stand, they had placed Smokey on the witness chair. The prosecuting attorney asked Smokey if he had been stolen that morning and if so, did he see the culprit in the courtroom.

Someone with a deep voice behind Smokey said, "Yes, I was stolen this morning and forced to stand in front of the FBI office."

"If the thief is in the courtroom, can you point him out?"

The person behind Smokey started turning the big bear with his finger pointing directly at me.

"Let the record show that Smokey is pointing directly at Mr. Williams."

The trial lasted one hour, at which time I was found guilty and a scathing probation report was read. I was accused of being an alcoholic who was sexually attracted to small, furry animals, among other heinous accusations. The judge sentenced me to appear at the cafeteria every day the following week to buy each federal building employee a cup of coffee and a doughnut.

At the end of the week, I had spent over $300 buying doughnuts and coffee. Of course, the FBI agents went through the line several times.

Who says federal agencies can't get along? That is how we did it in Fresno.

Chapter 33

SHORTY

"SECRET SERVICE, RON Williams," I answered the ringing phone.

I heard only laughter on the other end of the line.

"Who is calling, please?" I asked politely.

"Rick Nelson." I knew that this was the Bakersfield Secret Service agent, not the youngest brother of *Ozzie and Harriet* TV fame.

Nelson said, "Bakersfield PD received information from an informant about a counterfeit operation that's gonna start up any day. Informant's name's Shorty Lewis." Nelson erupted in laughter again. Obviously, he knew something I didn't.

Agent Nelson continued, telling me that the bad guy's name was Robert Jensen. Jensen told Shorty that he wanted to buy paper so a local printer he knew could churn out $5 million bogus. "How good is Shorty?" I asked.

"Bakersfield police have used him before. Some of his information was good, some not so good. They wouldn't vouch for his reliability."

I called Sacramento and requested that additional agents be

assigned for an undercover operation. Two days later, Nelson and I, plus four more agents, rendezvoused in Bakersfield, that central California town known for its oil, agriculture, and home-brewed Country/Western singers Merle Haggard and Buck Owens.

Nelson introduced us to our snitch, Shorty. Shorty the Snitch. It had such a great ring to it.

Shorty was appropriately named. He wasn't just short. He was a certifiable midget. An obnoxious, abrasive midget who swore—literally and figuratively—that he was telling the "fucking" truth. He would introduce our contact agent, Vaughn Hall, to the suspect in their favorite bar.

We set up the meeting for eight the next evening. Two agents were undercover in the bar at a table with a clear view of the entire room. Nelson, Hamilton, and I waited outside in the parking lot.

At 8:05 p.m., Jensen waddled into the bar—all 6'5" and 270 pounds of him. Jensen's wide leather belt strained to surround his distended stomach, which I'm sure blotted out any visual contact with his cowboy boots. The buttons of his Western shirt must have been triple-stitched in order to contain the chest girth.

Jensen had a police record of mainly DUIs, not much more, so we weren't expecting much trouble from the fat guy. He clomped right up to the bar next to Hall and Shorty. Almost the exact second his global-sized butt hit the barstool, his hand went up in what had to be a well-practiced move. The bartender responded like a well-conditioned dog in Pavlov's kennel, handing out double scotches all around.

Shorty made the intros, and before Hall could say "Glad to meet you," the double had evaporated. Jensen's hand went up again, the barkeep kept pouring and serving, and Jensen and Shorty kept slugging them down.

An undercover agent is coached to get in and get out—no excessive chatter. The longer an agent remains, the greater the chances he can be tripped up on small talk. But there was no small talk, just toasts and tosses. The drinking went on for at least three hours. Meanwhile, our agents at the table were loading up on Cokes, to the vexation of the waitresses.

Suddenly, Shorty screamed from his barstool, "I want to hear some music!" With that, he twisted his body so that his stomach rested on the stool seat, legs dangling above the ground. He rested suspended like that for a few seconds before he felt confident enough to let loose; then he slid down the legs.

After three hours of downing doubles nearly nonstop, Shorty wasn't any too stable. He weaved across the dance floor, not so much to escape the boots of the stompin' cowboys, but to compensate for severely impaired equilibrium. About stage center, he stopped, looked around, squealed, then fell on his face. The dancing stopped. People pulled away to give the little guy space and air. He just lay there for half a minute before he summoned sufficient energy to raise his head and wave his arms, much as a beached turtle struggles to inch forward.

Then he screamed, "Elevator! Elevator!" But the only person to respond was Hall, who rushed over to his little snitch and picked him up like a mother hefting a fallen child. Shorty twisted around so that he clung face-to-face with Hall, grasping him like a child would hug its mom for security.

"Take me to the jukebox. To the jukebox!" Shorty commanded. Hall had to stuff several quarters into the slots while Shorty hung down and pushed buttons randomly.

"To the bar. To the bar!" Shorty insisted next. Like an obedient servant, Hall ported the midget back to his stool.

This "meeting" lasted until midnight, at which time Hall finally gave the ream of paper to Jensen. Unlike Shorty, Jensen stored his consumed alcohol with greater efficiency than a cask. He left the bar with the same "grace" as when he entered, waddled back to his beat-up Chevy, stuffed himself behind the wheel, and began what amounted to a nonstop tour of Bakersfield.

We followed.

Jensen drove almost as if he expected a police tail. He skirted through alleys, turned in to cul-de-sacs, then waited facing outward, sped up, and tried to ditch any followers in shopping center parking lots. At one point, he pulled a rubber-burning 180 and sped toward us, veering away at the last moment. Either he was very good, or very drunk.

This cat-and-mouse game lasted two days and nights. Jensen literally led us to every honky-tonk bar in Bakersfield. Finally, Agent Hall signaled us and said, "I've got to end this before I become a total alcoholic. Besides, he's not telling me where or when he is going to get the money printed."

Because this case was taking too much time and money, I decided to arrest Jensen, which we did outside another bar on the third day.

I approached him as he sat in his car. With gun drawn, I commanded him to get out. Instead, Jensen death-gripped his steering wheel, refusing to move. Finally, a Bakersfield police officer came to the open window, leaned in, and repeatedly karate chopped Jensen's wrists until he agreed to ooze out of the car.

Fear causes strange reactions in people. And Jensen filled his boots with fear. It took a full spray can of Lysol disinfectant in the detective's interview room before any of us would enter. And when we did, all Jensen would say was, "I know Shorty's working with you, and I ain't gonna tell you anything."

In the end, the U.S. attorney declined to prosecute, and the case died a natural death. Shorty Lewis submitted a bill for his services to the U.S. Government for his fine work. Frankly, I don't know if it was ever paid. But maybe his liver eventually died a natural death too.

Chapter 34

Mariposa—A "Royal" Tragedy

Fresno is a Spanish word meaning ash tree. It's also the name of a city in Central California which was first settled by Mexican ranchers in the early 1860s. Historians surmise that these early settlers saw *fresnos* growing in the region and chose to christen the area after the tree. It probably was safer than risking a fight over whose wife or girlfriend the area should be named for. Located in the fertile San Joaquin Valley, Fresno is America's leading agricultural county, whose productive farmers raise more than 200 different crops.

In 1980, when I was assigned to head the Secret Service office there for three years, I remember joking that I probably was going to spend my career investigating counterfeit peas and carrots. I came to learn that this farming region of more than half-a-million people was more than a mecca for vegetables—it was a productive center for forgery and fraud.

My introduction to the region started with an examination of a large topographical map taped to the office wall. I learned quickly that our area of responsibility spanned the huge Central Valley plus several of the counties whose territories climbed through the fabled California gold country and high up into the majestic Sierra Nevada mountains. This region is world-famous for the incredibly august, glacially carved Yosemite Valley, and its redwood forests, whose towering evergreens are the largest living things on earth and date back to before the time of Christ.

It is undoubtedly in large part due to these natural wonders that in December of 1982, I received a teletype message announcing that Queen Elizabeth intended to visit the Yosemite National Park sometime in early March of 1983. A pre-advance team from Buckingham Palace and the White House would be visiting the area on January 2, to—as the Brits explained—"reconnoiter." I was to join the advance party at a dinner hosted by the valley management group, known as the Camp Curry Company, at the rustic, yet posh Ahwahnee Hotel in the park.

This arrangement would provide a perfect opportunity to get to know the players, for ultimately, I would be responsible for coordination and route security for the royal entourage. My office mate, Senior Agent Vaughn Hall, accompanied me to the dinner.

About fifty representatives of Her Royal Highness attended the banquet, perhaps an indication why British taxes were so high. They were accompanied by another Secret Service agent, Bob Alberi, whom I had known for a number of years. Bob and I enjoyed a camaraderie reinforced by similar senses of humor. During the banquet, we stood back to watch officialdom at work, the wonderfully cultured act of sincere superficiality. The power-playing was as heavy as Sierra slush, that unforgiving, weighty form of snow that blankets the Sierras every winter. It was high-altitude theater-of-the-absurd, as local politicians and British and American staffers played their roles according to the script each had written for himself. The more wine that Alberi and I sipped—our little fingers appropriately angled away from the stems of our glasses—the more absurd this drama became, because the "actors" were their own best audience. We merely stood in the wings as casual observers at a very off-Broadway play.

About an hour after the cocktails began, the formally attired maître d' rang the bell for all of us to repair to our assigned tables. Happily, Alberi and I were seated at the same table, across from one another. Some long-nosed representative of the queen had the pleasure of sitting next to me (or did I have the pleasure of dining next to him?). I neither remember his name, nor his pedigree, but his demeanor demanded that I show him uncommon respect, for he was very prim, arrogant, and foppish. In short, he was a dickhead.

The captain of the royal yacht, HMS *Britannia*, sat next to Alberi. He seemed to be a regular kind of guy. Conversation at the table was reserved, consisting mainly of "Chap, won't you please pass the Worcestershire," and other survival dialogue. To say the least, it was a well-behaved and boring dinner.

At one point, one of our very starched waiters came to the table and asked, "Who will order the wine?"

"I'd be pleased to," I responded ceremoniously. I selected two California wines, Fetzer chardonnay and a cabernet sauvignon. The waiter returned promptly with both bottles; the Fetzer had been uncorked. He poured a sample in my glass for the customary evaluation.

I turned to the royal Sir Dickhead, nodded, and said, "Please let our guest do the honors."

With great pomp, he swirled the glass and held it up to the light of the chandelier above. He inhaled the vapors. He took a sip and let the wine settle on his tongue, then swallowed. He closed his eyes, tilted his head slightly back, and licked his lips. Then he spat, "Ooooooo! Horrid! Horrid! Away with the bottle. Away!"

The waiter looked at me dumbfounded, but he returned in an instant with another bottle, whose contents surprisingly passed the jerk's taste bud test. "It's somewhat bettah," he clipped.

"Asshole," I mouthed to Alberi, then ordered the waiter to pour for the table. I thought I perceived a slight smile on the face of the captain.

No one said very much during the main course—mostly formal grunts of pass this or that. Veddy borring! Finally, I put down my fork, looked at Alberi, and asked formally, "Excuse me, Mr. Alberi, may I ask you a question?"

"Why, of course, Mr. Williams."

I paused for effect, gently wiping the corners of my mouth with my starched napkin. "Tell me, how do you feel since your sex change operation?"

"Oh, thank you for asking, Mr. Williams," Alberi replied, adding, "I feel absolutely wonderful. So…o…o…o liberated."

The eating stopped. The diners all froze mid-chew, but Alberi and I continued eating solemnly with nary a smile across our faces. We watched with contained amusement as the men on either side of Alberi slid their chairs as far away as possible. No one said a word for the next five minutes.

"May I ask you another question, Mr. Alberi," I chimed.

"Of course, Mr. Williams."

"Is there anything you miss about not being female since your operation?"

Alberi responded, "Yes, there is one thing I miss."

Throughout this questioning, the *Britannia's* skipper kept spooning sweet baby peas into his mouth.

"And what is that?" I pressed Alberi.

At that point, Alberi delicately put down his fork, cupped both hands under where his breasts would have been, and moved them up and down.

"I miss my big ol' tits!" he screamed.

The *Britannia's* skipper spit his peas across the table. They struck the dolt next to me like harmless shrapnel. The rest of the table exploded into laughter. With one sentence, the British glacier had melted, save for the Royal Ice Cube next to me.

The skipper stood up, raised his wineglass, and toasted, "That's it, chaps. Let's adjourn to the bar."

Later that evening, I asked the captain if he thought I should apologize to the queen's representative.

"Don't waste your time, ol' chap. He's an arrogant, pompous ass. It's probably the first time in his life he's ever been splattered."

Toward the end of the evening and after still another rather raucous toast, the representative from Scotland Yard approached me and said, "I know the queen and her party will relish Yosemite Park to the utmost, and we will feel confident in your hands."

The Brits and other U.S. officials departed the next morning to catch their flight from nearby Castle Air Force Base to begin their trips to wherever; then Vaughn Hall and I left for Fresno to begin the protection plans for the queen.

In February I conducted a law enforcement briefing at the headquarters of the Mariposa County Sheriff's Department. Mariposa, nestled quaintly in the Sierra foothills, is one of many picturesque towns that sprouted during the California gold rush of the 1860s. Those attending my route-planning session included representatives from the Atwater Police Department, Merced Sheriff's Department, Mariposa County Sheriff, the Yosemite Park Rangers, and the California Highway Patrol. Specifically representing Mariposa County were Sheriff Ken Matthys and Sergeants Rod Sinclair and Rod McKean.

I laid out the strategy thus: Lt. Bob Haworth of the California Highway Patrol (CHP) was to be in charge of the royal motorcade. He agreed to provide a lead car, two scout cars, a tail car, and a helicopter.

The Atwater PD would secure the route from the main gate of the Air Force base along a one-mile strip of Buhach Road. Merced PD would secure intersections within the city of Merced, and Merced County Sheriff's Department would block all appropriate intersections through which the queen was to pass.

Mariposa's Sinclair and McKean said they'd secure intersections along Route 140 through Mariposa, a distance of 50.4 miles, with an estimated motorcade driving time of one hour fifteen minutes. Yosemite Park rangers said they'd barricade all intersections within Yosemite Park.

Discounting any unexpected happenings, I had calculated the queen's 93.4-mile driving trip to take two hours and sixteen minutes.

There are many considerations in planning a motorcade. One of those is communications, a problem exacerbated by the many police agencies involved. Not all police services enjoyed CLEMAR, a statewide, interagency communication system used then. This was something I had to solve during my dry runs with the CHP along the route. Mariposa County sheriffs were not tied into this network, which meant a reassessment of their responsibilities. They now would be assigned to rooftop and high-ground security; the CHP would provide route and crowd control.

Also, CHP Lt. Haworth and I agreed that we would insert a "route and intersection" patrol car to precede the motorcade by twenty minutes. Via loudspeaker from the CHP patrol car, the officer would activate intersection control, during which time the assigned police agencies would stop both oncoming and perpendicular traffic, but allow travelers heading in the same direction as the procession to continue. We notified each agency as to this change. Everyone accepted the changes professionally, except for Mariposa's Sgt. Sinclair, who voiced anger at Mariposa's diminished role in the procession.

Sinclair then asked me if I had planned to place a SWAT team in the motorcade. I explained that the Secret Service saw no need to include Special Weapons and Tactics since we had no "adverse intelligence." I quipped that we didn't believe that the Irish Republican Army was currently operating in the Sierras. I began to get a feeling that Sgt. Sinclair was going to get on my nerves—big time.

On March 2, Sgt. Larry Cappa of the CHP and I drove the entire route to a meeting I had called in Yosemite to review the queen's proposed visitation sites. This latest meeting included the CHP, Special Agent Vaughn Hall, my advance man, and Park Ranger Norm Hinson. When we arrived at the Yosemite law enforcement office, however, we were greeted by two uninvited guests: Mariposa Sgts. Sinclair and McKean. Someone must have innocently mentioned our meeting during a phone conversation down the mountain.

During lunch at the swank Ahwahnee, I had the distinct displeasure of sitting next to Sinclair. Fat and sweaty, Sinclair literally leaned in my face during my lunch, simultaneously spewing both breadcrumbs and proposals about his "special protection plans." I lost my appetite.

Sinclair explained that he wanted to insinuate a Mariposa County Sheriff's car—driven by his most capable driver, himself—between the CHP number two scout car (positioned five minutes ahead of the motorcade) and the lead car. He called it his "sweep car."

"Why?" I asked tersely.

"Well, if there are any bad guys along the route, I'd be able to recognize 'em," he stated. Additionally, he wanted to place a Mariposa SWAT car in the motorcade to counter any terrorist attack.

This would have turned an already long motorcade into an unwieldy serpent.

"No!" I said. "It is my position that a sweep and a SWAT are not needed."

Sinclair became visibly agitated but proceeded to tell me about his anti-terrorist training. I just sat there, thinking what a giant blowhard this man was. Little was accomplished at this luncheon meeting, so I adjourned the group and drove back to Fresno with my CHP cohort.

On March 3, the CHP called and left word that a massive mud-and-rock slide had blocked the primary route, the result of unusually severe rains that winter. The route was now closed to all but emergency equipment. A state geologist confirmed that another giant slide could occur at any time. I contacted Agent Hall in Yosemite Park and directed him to find an alternate route (which he did in very short order) and to notify the critical police agencies. The motorcade would now drive Route 140 to Highway 49 south, intersect Highway 41, then turn north into Yosemite. Yes, the queen would miss seeing the burg of Mariposa.

Literally within minutes of my receiving the new map description from Hall, I received a phone call from a rude and ruffled Sgt. Sinclair.

"What are you changin' the route for, Mr. Williams? You're gonna disappoint a lot of people, you know," he said accusingly.

He heard nothing but silence from my end of the phone.

"We can get the slide cleaned up before the queen's visit," he persevered.

I said nothing.

"The Mariposa Chamber of Commerce has decided to place a man on horseback to gallop through the town announcing her approach, as Paul Revere signaled the approach of the Redcoats," he explained.

It was quite clear to me that Sinclair wanted to be the town hero. Plain and simple.

"I don't care if your people in Mariposa will be disappointed," I said. "I'm strictly concerned with *the queen's safety*. As a matter of fact, *you* should be more concerned with the queen's safety!"

Still later that day, Park Ranger Henson phoned to say that there had been three washouts along Highway 41, and that road, too, was deemed unsafe.

I immediately contacted the captain of the CHP in Merced and requested that his people recommend an alternate route, which they did after an officer ran the course: Highway 59 North to Highway J 59 to Highway 132 to Highway J 20 to Highway 120 directly into Yosemite. Though not as scenically spectacular, the latest itinerary offered broad shoulders and gently sloped hills. The chances for washouts or landslides were minimal. But the best news for me was that I got to call Sgt. Sinclair to inform him that we no longer needed the service of the Mariposa County Sheriff, for the new route covered only seven miles within his county.

I could "see" his carotid arteries pulsating angrily alongside his fat neck. "Anyway," I said, "your cars don't have the radio frequency we need, so there's no need for you to attend tomorrow's planning session. Goodbye, Sinclair." I hung up the telephone feeling just great.

My elation was short-lived, though, for during the briefing at the Merced CHP office the next morning, Sinclair erupted from the back of the room to announce, "We can now participate because we've installed both CHP and Park Ranger frequencies in my car, and I've got twenty-eight deputies ready to go."

I was just about to tell him delicately to "kiss off" when a CHP officer chimed in, "We are strapped for bodies; maybe we could use the support."

A sincere but inopportune comment by the officer pinned me. I had to relent. "Okay, Sinclair," I ordered grudgingly, "you and your men will be responsible for the intersection control from the county line to the town of Coulterville."

I thought to myself, *What damage could he do with only a seven-mile long ribbon of responsibility?*

On the evening of March 4, I briefed the Secret Service agents who were flown in to assist in security operations and gave them their assignments. At the end of the session, my immediate supervisor asked if there had been any problems. Little did I know how prophetic my answer would be: "There has been one BIG problem. Sgt. Rod Sinclair of the Mariposa County Sheriffs. Look out for him. He's an accident waiting to happen!"

After the session, we went to our motel rooms near Castle AFB to await the arrival of the queen.

I awoke early the next morning to the sound of heavy raindrops pummeling the roof of our motel. Mini-Niagara Falls cascaded over clogged rain gutters to fill inconveniently situated "lakes" in the parking lot—most of them forming unerringly at the doors to our cars, and much deeper than the height of our wing-tip shoes. From the dry security of my motel room, I began a series of calls to fix our schedule for the day.

Queen Elizabeth was slated to touch down at 10 a.m., approximately twenty minutes after the press plane. The media would be accompanied by two Secret Service shifts, the twelve midnight-to-8-a.m. crew and the 4-p.m.-to-midnight team. Obviously, the on-duty team would be accompanying the queen on her flight, along with her own security people from Scotland Yard.

I had ordered six rental cars—the Dodge "K" mid-size series—for the two off-duty groups, for I felt it would be wise for each team to have at least one spare car.

When the press plane arrived at 9:45 a.m., a Sacramento agent assigned each team to their cars, then hopped into the lead car to guide the 8 a.m. shift immediately to Yosemite.

A Fresno agent was to lead the second group to the park, but instead was instructed to take up protective perimeter posts at the Air Force base for the pending arrival of the queen's jet. It touched down twenty minutes ahead of schedule. This caused minor confusion because general staff and other VIPs from the Air Force base had to muster quickly at the ramp to greet the queen. The ceremony was about as perfunctory and brief as one could orchestrate. Then, with practiced grace, Queen Elizabeth entered her bulletproof limo for the journey to Yosemite.

As the lead advance agent on this protection assignment, I chose to ride in the California Highway Patrol lead car along with White House advance man and the agent in charge of the Sacramento office. The three of us were jammed shoulder-to-shoulder in the back seat, while the CHP's Lt. Haworth, the man in charge of the motorcade escort, and his driver sat uncrimped in front.

The next car in the motorcade was termed the "spare car," but it was occupied by then White House Chief of Staff Michael Deaver. The queen's limousine followed immediately behind, tailed closely by two Secret Service follow-up cars.

Next came three staff limousines, then three press vans. A U.S. Park Ranger communications vehicle and a Secret Service intelligence car trailed along, and a CHP tail car played caboose. About one mile back, we positioned an ambulance for the unexpected, for the unthinkable, which is what Secret Service agents are paid to think about always.

Above us and slightly ahead, a CHP helicopter provided route and high-ground coverage. We were all upbeat as we left Castle AFB. Hundreds of people along the motorcade route strained to glimpse the queen behind the tinted limousine windows as the motorcade zipped by at the prescribed speed. The five of us in the CHP lead car were engaged in idle talk when, twenty minutes into the ride, we were interrupted by a call from another CHP unit that there had been an auto accident up ahead.

"Probably some farmer got too close to the highway," I said calmly, but I was annoyed at the thought that some tractor driver had strayed onto the highway, lost control, and dumped hay bales across the road. I didn't want anything to impede our progress.

We traveled another five minutes when the radio crackled once again: "Are you aware of those involved in the accident?" the caller asked tonelessly.

"No," Haworth responded.

"We've got three dead Secret Service agents," the CHP unit informed us in the same monotone.

It was like a death shroud had enveloped our car. We sat in shocked silence as our CHP driver maintained his prescribed course. People kept on waving at us along the roadway, totally oblivious of all the tragedy that now clouded this parade. I almost became physically sick at the incongruity of it all. All of a sudden, the queen's visit became almost inconsequential compared to the grief and shock that we all felt.

We drove for nearly twenty-five interminable minutes to cover twenty never-ending miles before we came onto the accident scene on Highway 132, between the towns of Coulterville and La Grange. We slowed, but never had to stop, for the accident had occurred adjacent to a short spur road that paralleled the highway.

The agents' crumpled "K" car lay inert on its roof ten feet down an embankment, almost equidistant between the highway and our detour road. The bodies of Agents George "Pat" LeBarge, 41, Donald Bejcek, 29, and Donald Robinson, 38, also lay equally inert in an ordered row, each alone beneath his own white sheet within fifty yards of our motorcade.

The death scene played out just inside the Mariposa County line. If the queen didn't turn her head to look away, she had a front row seat to a real-world tragedy.

Of the three deceased agents, I knew only LeBarge. We had met in 1974, in Kansas, when he had been sent as the lead advance agent for President Nixon's visit to Kansas State University. Pat had particularly enjoyed this assignment, for his parents lived in Junction City, Kansas, and he had served on that city's police department for two years. He took me to dinner with his folks the evening before the president arrived.

Now I flashed on how proud Pat's parents were of him. Pat was a very sharp guy, and I've no doubt that the other agents were equally sharp, respected, and loved.

As we drove slowly by, I noticed that the other car involved was an all-white Pontiac. Not just *a* Pontiac, but a high-speed version belonging to the stable of the Mariposa County Sheriff's Department. Though its front end was accordioned, the car remained upright on the highway. An ambulance crew was tending to the driver, whom we later learned was forty-three-year-old Deputy Rod Sinclair. His passenger was Deputy Rod McKean.

Sinclair had raced back from the other end of the county just so he could place himself prominently in front of the motorcade as it passed through his territory.

Our motorcade was directed around the accident, and, for a moment, we alone occupied the detour. But suddenly, a four-wheel drive Ford Bronco appeared in front of us, its rooftop red-and-blue lights flashing officially. Behind us I spied the SWAT car of the Mariposa Sheriff. This escort was in complete contravention to the arrangements I had made with the Mariposa Sheriff, whose people were limited to participation in intersection control.

I radioed to this uninvited "lead" car: "Move over and let the motorcade through! Move that vehicle off the road! We don't need you. We don't want you. Get out of the way!"

The deputy did as ordered, but as I learned later, he had been led to believe that all had been coordinated by the Secret Service and Sinclair.

The motorcade proceeded to Yosemite Valley—*the valley of the shadow of death…*

About five miles from the Ahwahnee, Michael Deaver requested that the motorcade be stopped so that he could advise the queen of the events. We sat about ten minutes before word passed forward to continue.

At the hotel, one of the supervising agents came to us and said that "the queen issued sad condolences."

As we approached the hotel parking lot, we saw to our left the olive-drab Navy Med-Evac helicopter, another forethought should the queen become ill.

Tragedy hung around us like the pall of forest fire smoke as we were ushered into the Ahwahnee Hotel elevator for the second-floor festivities. The queen and her husband, Prince Philip, had already gone up. Standing quietly with me were several other agents, various government staff, and an officious Marine major who served as a military aide. When the elevator door glided shut, the major bellowed, "Who was the son of a bitch who got that military helicopter to Yosemite?"

I just looked at him. "I did."

"You had no authorization—helicopter's out of here!" He didn't seem to care that three of my comrades had been killed.

"That helicopter stays," I said. "If we need it for Med-Evac, that's the quickest way out of here. If you don't like it, that's tough shit!"

I just couldn't imagine anyone with such a lack of foresight or compassion. We stood nose to nose, each trying to stare down the other. Frankly, I wanted to tear the head off that starched and pressed asshole right there, and I might have, except that Agent Bob Alberi separated us just in time.

Trying to cool down, I walked to the Secret Service command post and entered just as the other team members arrived. They had seen the accident and were devastated and despondent. The Service made arrangements to send them home and to replace them on the midnight shift. That night, more than at any other time in my career, I wish I could have packed it in.

On the drizzly morning of March 5, we had scheduled the queen to visit Lookout Point, a promontory above the valley that affords a panorama not even famed photographer Ansel Adams could capture—though he, more than anyone else, was able to embrace its essence on his photo plates. Just as we had ushered the queen into her limousine and our mini-motorcade was about to roll, I received a radio call from Agent Hall, my advance agent up the mountain, advising me that it was raining hard, the roads were icing, and the weather was deteriorating.

"Dangerous?" I asked.

"I believe so," he stated.

I sat there for a moment, evaluating the situation. Just as I stepped out of my car, the Scotland Yard agent approached. "What's the hang-up, ol' boy?" he asked.

"We're not going up. Too dangerous!" I told him. Scotland Yard looked at me as if I were a pusillanimous schoolgirl.

"You don't understand, ol' man. *The queen* wishes to go up. That's what *the queen* wants to do."

I blurted back, "*You* don't understand, ol' man. *The queen* isn't going up there. And while she's in the valley, I'm in charge of her safety."

We argued—no, *he* argued—for a futile moment, until I said, "Okay, okay, the queen can go up. I hope she enjoys her walk, 'cause these cars ain't movin'." I just loved battering the English language when I talked to Brits, especially officious Brits, especially officious Brits in a huff.

I caught a glimpse of our military aide off to the side. If looks were hand grenades, he had pulled the pins on all of them.

"Look," I said, "I've been advised by a man who knows the area, a man whom I'd trust with my life, and he says no! So I'm not going to lose anyone else on this trip!"

Even if the agents hadn't been killed, I would have made the same decision, for I grew up to respect weather conditions like these. Protection was my duty, and that meant protection from dangers other than assassins' bullets or knives.

The Scotland Yard agent trudged off to inform his superior, who had to tell his superior, who then had the job of informing his superior, who had the job of informing the queen. For the next forty-five minutes, we just sat there with our engines idling, while waiting for the next plan to filter down through their clumsy chain of command. Finally, the Scotland Yard man came back to me and reported, "The queen will go for a stroll through the woods."

Walking with a queen in the woods is more than "a stroll." It's a military maneuver. Like point men on a reconnaissance patrol, forest rangers—keeping well out of sight—bushwhacked 100 yards on both flanks of the well-manicured trail. I assigned agents to advance us on the path while two other agents and I surrounded the queen. Five more members of the queen's official party joined us.

One hundred yards back, hanging in like an irritating hemorrhoid, followed the Marine major, whom I could hear apologizing to some uppity Buckingham Palace official for the Gestapo tactics of the Secret Service. His voice carried through the mist. I heard him say, "…I think it should be entirely up to the queen…"

This whole event seemed surreal to me. Here we were, all dressed in fine clothes, strolling through a dripping forest and stomping through mud. It brought to mind Rudyard Kipling's oft-quoted phrase, "…only mad dogs and Englishmen out in the noonday sun." The "sun" dripped on us for ninety minutes before Her Majesty's representative came up to me and announced that "we shall drive through this beautiful valley."

This was my first experience with British royalty and its entourage. My impression was that these people all lived in an unreal world. The queen was treated like a goddess. To me, this class structure seemed stifling. Each individual had his proper class and place.

In the early morning hours of March 7 (in my book, 3 a.m. *is* early), park rangers called to report that a severe snowstorm had hit at 1:00 a.m. and that all of the roads out of Yosemite were closed. Again, Mother Nature posed the danger.

All available snowplows had been marshaled and were already scraping the roads, the rangers reported. They'd know by 5:30 a.m. if the queen could continue her royal exit.

As if by regal decree, the blizzard ceased its soft bombardment, and our motorcade drove cautiously out of the valley. The clouds parted dramatically, and the sun lanced the valley with warm spears of light. It truly was an Ansel Adams kind of morning, and the queen marveled at the broad view which I (and God) had denied her the day before.

Just before we left Yosemite, I phoned the Mariposa Sheriff and spoke to Deputy Dave Beavers, who took Sheriff Sinclair's place on the spur road following the deadly accident.

"Mr. Williams, Sinclair feels sorry and apologetic for what happened," Beavers said.

"He should. He killed three agents, and one of them was a good friend of mine," I said bluntly.

After a pause, Beavers said, "We'll be prepared in Mariposa, and we'll put into effect the security plan that Sinclair gave me."

"What is that plan?" I asked.

"Lead car and SWAT car to follow," the deputy replied.

This was the first time anyone confirmed that Sinclair obviously intended to follow his own personal agenda, despite Secret Service orders. From the very beginning, I had been quite direct and clear in declining Sinclair's involvement and in reassigning the sheriffs to *intersection control only*.

"We don't need or want a lead car!" I yelled at Beavers through the phone. "The Secret Service doesn't want the sheriffs there… PERIOD!"

I slammed down the receiver, punching the wall out of frustration.

The return drive to Castle AFB was beautiful, although uneventful. As we drove through the guard gates of the airfield and approached the queen's waiting plane, I was greeted by an old friend, Agent Dave Carpenter, who had been in the third Secret Service car and had witnessed the tragedy. Dave and I stood on the tarmac beneath the giant jets, looking at each other with tears in our eyes. Neither of us needed to say anything. We just hugged.

Later I learned that the bodies of three dead agents had been loaded aboard military planes for their final flights to their respective homes. Agents Jerry Henson and Dean Terry had guarded their dead brethren throughout the night at Castle AFB. Henson later said that it was one of the eeriest experiences he had ever had, and he had reflected all that night on his future and how fleeting life really is.

On March 28, 1983, a report by the California Highway Patrol's Multidisciplinary Accident Investigation Team (MAIT) concluded that Sheriff Sinclair had been solely responsible for the fatal accident, "…the result of a wrongful operation of a motor vehicle by driver Sinclair…"

When CHP officers handed this report to Mariposa District Attorney J. B. Eckerson, he asked, "Before I read this, tell me who is at fault."

The officers obediently summarized the lengthy and scientifically arrived-at report.

"Bullshit! A bunch of lies!" Eckerson shouted, throwing the report at the officers as he kicked them out of his office. Eckerson literally "became unglued," as was later described to me.

Subsequently, because of the continuing media interest, the CHP called a press conference to announce the findings of its own investigation. And following this event, D.A. Eckerson called a press conference of his own to state that Sheriff Sinclair had not been at fault and that he was hiring an accident reconstruction expert to examine the crash. Thus began a media war between the CHP and Eckerson, who accused the CHP and the Secret Service of collusion.

The next media volley also came from Eckerson. In a five-and-one-half-page press release issued on September 28, 1993, he announced that "major discrepancies between two (accident) reports submitted by CHP Central Division MAIT…" had led to his decision "against prosecution (of Sinclair) in the matter of the fatal accident on Highway 132 on March 5, 1983. It is my opinion that the facts presented…are not only contradictory, but in comparing the final reports with the (CHP's) rough notes, misleading."

Eckerson tagged his press release by stating, "The disparity between purported evidence and formulas used in the two reports and the wide divergence of witness statements are not sufficient to make a clear showing of either the cause of the accident or the party or parties responsible, therefore. This necessitates my decision to decline prosecution."

The CHP, outraged at Eckerson's manipulation of the facts in his press release, refuted Eckerson point-by-point in a ten-page, single-spaced press announcement that Agatha Christie would have praised for evidentiary accuracy and Sherlock Holmes for logic.

Much of the CHP report covered technical information, such as skid marks; presumed impact speed; approach, impact, and departure angles; linear and rotational movement of the vehicles, and post-impact sliding distances.

Eckerson charged that the Secret Service car was at fault for having crossed the center line of the highway. His fierce battle against the facts puzzled, frustrated, and maddened me. But as the years went by, I finally found the answers to the puzzle.

The truth is that the Mariposa story goes far beyond the accident that killed my compatriots. No crime fiction writer could manufacture such a convoluted web of intrigue and conspiracy as that unearthed in Mariposa County: rampant corruption that ranged from murder to drug distribution in Yosemite Valley by Mariposa deputies; to bank embezzlement by the daughter of the Mariposa sheriff; to money laundering for "respected" area businessmen suspected of international drug smuggling in their private aircraft; to collusion between Sinclair, an official with the Camp Curry Management Company in Yosemite National Park, and a U.S. congressman who resigned under suspicion.

People who got too close to exposing the goings-on met their untimely demise. Perhaps the best-known person of those who died under suspicious circumstances was Mariposa Deputy Ron Van Meter. Van Meter traveled on his off-duty day to Sacramento to secretly meet with the Department of Justice to outline criminal acts being perpetrated by the Mariposa County Sheriff's Office and their deputies. He revealed that sheriff's deputies, led by Sergeant Sinclair, were protecting a major drug dealer, Mickey Corcoran. Corcoran would bring in drugs to the tiny airport in Mariposa late at night and store the drugs in a storage facility near the city. He would then arrange for the sale of the drugs by his enforcers inside Yosemite Park to tourists as they camped out in the park. The deputies were also engaged in seizing cars inside the park as well as weapons and reselling them.

Unfortunately, John Van de Kamp, the attorney general, had gone to Hastings Law School with Bruce Eckerson, the Mariposa district attorney. A call to Eckerson alerted him that Van Meter had provided information that the Mariposa Sheriff's Office was corrupt.

Several days after Van Meter returned to work, he was called into Sheriff Paul Paige's office. Van Meter was informed there was not criminal corruption in Mariposa and to forget his visit to DOJ.

Seven days later, on June 24, 1980, a deputy picked up Van Meter at his home to go out to Lake McClure in Mickey Corcoran's speed boat for a day on the lake. He never returned. According to a Mariposa Sheriff's report filed by Sergeant Sinclair, the deputy driving the boat hit a wave, and Van Meter was thrown from the boat and drowned.

Van Meter's wife revealed that when two deputies came to the house to tell her of the accident, they did a search of the home and took out a briefcase belonging to her husband that contained evidence of criminal corruption.

Years later I examined the sheriff's report signed by Sinclair. It was one page and simply stated that Van Meter drowned, and his body was not recovered. Van Meter's body was recovered in September 1990 when the lake went down, and Van Meter was found with a fish net wrapped around his body and a fire extinguisher inside the net.

Another was Carolle Clark, a county supervisor who died in an auto accident. Clark had told Sheriff Ken Matthyes that he (Clark) possessed information that had to be shared. But Clark never made it to reveal his information. The brake lines of his car had been bled, so he was unable to slow down to negotiate a sharp mountain curve. Authorities found him badly injured in the crumpled wreck of his car at the bottom of an embankment. He died within hours. An autopsy found that Clark's injuries had not been fatal, but that he had been "allowed" to bleed to death by officers on the scene.

Even ABC-TV's weekly *20-20* investigative program profiled the Mariposa story in November 1991. But their necessarily truncated work only turned over rocks, when in fact there were boulders to upend.

Unfortunately, official jurisdiction precluded my immersion in the shadowy events in Mariposa, so I can only relate events germane to the Secret Service.

I began by asking what caused Sheriff Sinclair to cross the center line on that fateful March day and smash the lives out of our agents?

A few weeks after the accident, I received a phone call from a confidential informant, a detective within the Merced Sheriff's Department, that Sinclair had been a dope addict and had been treated "for psychological problems and addiction on two occasions at a local hospital prior to the accident."

In August of 1983, I received a phone call from Agent Craig Winstead of the California Bureau of Narcotics Enforcement. He said that he had information that was "pertinent to the accident that killed your agents."

The information he shared with me that stifling Monday morning was explosive. While doing a routine survey of Schedule II prescriptions at Rayley's Pharmacy on Route 50 in Oakhurst, about thirty-five miles outside of Mariposa, Winstead came across what he felt was evidence of a suspicious amount of Class II narcotics being prescribed for Sinclair by a Dr. Dahlem. The drugs included Seconal, Demerol, and Percodan, in "high dosage amounts."

Not coincidentally, Dr. Dahlem also happened to be a director of the Yosemite National Bank in Mariposa. His daughter-in-law, Perca Dahlem, was the bank's internal "auditor" during a period of rampant embezzlement by former Sheriff Paul Paige's daughter, Elena, who worked nights there. Her activities had been discovered and reported by the night janitor—the former newspaperman for the *Mariposa Gazette*.

Elena subsequently was convicted and sentenced to state prison for three years. Upon her release, she was hired as the assistant county clerk of Mariposa, and Dr. Dahlem made sure that the bank's janitor was fired.

Agent Winstead had asked the pharmacist about the large amounts of narcotics going to Sinclair. "This looks like an exceeding amount for a single individual," he commented. The druggist responded, "These were prescribed for the sheriff who killed those Secret Service agents."

Upon completing his report, Winstead forwarded it to his own agency in Sacramento, underscoring that "this is suspicious."

Hearing nothing about his report, he followed up several weeks later to ascertain what action his superiors wanted him to take. The agency told him to "forget and bury it…don't get involved!"

His conscience wouldn't let him turn his back on this pertinent evidence when three men had been killed. I told Winstead that I had to use the information. He said he knew but that once I did, he would "be fired." He nonetheless gave me the reports, and he was subsequently fired. To this day I honor Craig Winstead for doing the right thing even though he knew it would end his career with the Department of Justice.

At that point, I became livid because I was convinced that Sinclair was a known dope addict who had been allowed by the Mariposa power structure to "take charge" of security for the queen, and under the influence of drugs had killed three Secret Service agents. I called Joe Carlin, the assistant director of investigations in Washington, DC, and advised him of this new information. He asked me if the Secret Service should get actively involved in the investigation, and I said no because there was already enough bad blood between the Secret Service and the officials in Mariposa. I suggested that I had a meeting with the U.S. attorney and the heads of the FBI and DEA in Fresno to initiate an investigation. Carlin gave his approval to proceed.

On March 29, 1984, a division investigator for the DEA

conducted a survey of Schedule II prescriptions issued by Dr. Dahlem and found that of eighteen of this type of prescriptions retrieved from two Oakhurst pharmacies, thirteen had been issued to one patient: Roderick Sinclair. All for Seconal. When questioned if 1,250 dosage units was unusual, the pharmacist replied that he had "never seen a similar situation."

The chief pharmacist at Rayley's said that he had noted the prescriptions for Sinclair, and the number had raised doubts in his mind about their legitimacy, for the doctor and patient both resided and worked thirty-five miles away.

The investigation revealed that Sinclair had cashed in numerous prescriptions for Class III drugs as well.

On April 2, 1984, Dr. Frederick Meyers of the Department of Pharmacology at the University of California, Berkeley, was consulted concerning the amount of the Class II narcotics prescribed by Dr. Dahlem. Dr. Meyers said that it was difficult to imagine that the condition of Sinclair would justify the prescribing patterns, and that the prescribing of Seconal to a police officer "is suspect" since it could significantly interfere with his official function.

The investigation concluded that "Dr. Dahlem had been distributing narcotic drugs to persons who have no legitimate need for the drugs in violation of Title 21, U.S. Code Section 841-A."

In reviewing the CHP report, the on-scene officers indicated that no drugs or alcohol had been found in any of the victims. This was important. Unfortunately, the CHP never thought to check Sinclair for drugs since, they said, he was a lawman. For the same reason, the hospital staff conceded they never checked Sinclair's blood for drugs or alcohol. Interviews of Sinclair's fellow deputies after the accident indicated that they did not see Sinclair take any prohibited substances.

However, in 1989, when I interviewed former Deputy Sheriff Dave Beavers, he offered the opinion that "Sinclair had to have been on something because of the way he was sweating and acting all hyped-up."

Approximately one week after I had shared all of my intelligence with the U.S. attorney and the FBI, one of the attorneys representing the wife of deceased Agent Pat LeBarge came to my office to announce that the wives were about ready to settle for $250,000 apiece. "They just want to get this thing over with," he said.

I advised the lawyer to postpone the settlement, for something was about to happen that would greatly affect the settlement. And that something was this: The search warrant for Dr. Dahlem had been served and was about to be returned to the clerk of the court in Fresno, thereby becoming a public record subject to review by anybody.

When the DEA agent called me to advise the evidence had been obtained in the search warrant, I placed an anonymous call to a newspaper reporter, Gene Rose of the *Fresno Bee*, who—along with co-writer Joe Rosato—jumped on the story. The next day's front-page headline read:

INVESTIGATION TIES DRUG ORDERS TO SERGEANT
-- U.S. looks at driver in Mariposa crash—

"Heavy doses of Seconal may have been illegally prescribed to the Mariposa County sheriff's sergeant who drove the patrol car involved in the collision last spring in which three Secret Service agents were killed during Queen Elizabeth's visit to Yosemite National Park.

"Documents on file in U.S. District Court in Fresno contend that Sgt. Roderick Sinclair received more 1,250 doses of Seconal, a fast-acting, short-lived sedative, during a two-year period. In addition, other drugs were prescribed."

The story reviewed the chronological events of the crash, then picked up more on the prescription scandal:

"Based on information obtained…the government has 'probable cause to believe Dr. Dahlem…illegally prescribed' the drugs to Sinclair and two other people, all of whom 'have no legitimate medical need for the drugs.'

"Though Dahlem has not been charged with any crimes to date, the investigation is continuing.

"According to the PDR, the drug may be habit-forming, and prolonged use may result in psychic and physical dependence. Its use, warns the reference, may impair the performance of potentially hazardous tasks, such as driving a car or operating machinery…"

In large part due to the story by Rose and Rosato, the three Secret Service widows split $4 million rather than receiving only $250,000 each, as offered by Mariposa County.

No amount of settlement can assuage the hurt and loss of loved ones. No amount of anger or even justice can bring back their lives.

But in a small way, I believe that our investigation and my tip helped the wife and children of Pat LeBarge, and the families of the other two heroes, whom I'm sorry I didn't have the opportunity to know.

In 1985, I was transferred back to the Los Angeles District to run the Riverside Resident Agency office. However, I could not live with the information I had about the accident and the corruption I discovered in Mariposa.

After some research, I discovered information on the internet that piqued my interest. An extensive article, "The Last Circle, Mariposa," written by Cheri Seymore, a reporter for the *Mariposa Gazette,* piqued my interest. The article was an exposé of the criminal conduct and corruption not only by the sheriff's department, but there were serious allegations about some other high-level county representatives.

I called Cheri Seymore, and she offered to meet with me as well as contact former Sheriff Ken Matthyes, who had retired and moved to Wyoming.

I took several days off and drove to Mariposa. It was an eerie feeling to return to the site where three of my colleagues had died.

I met with Cheri Seymore and Ken Matthyes in her living room. At first, Matthyes was reluctant to talk with us about crime and corruption in Mariposa, stating that if he told everything he knew, "they will kill me." Eventually he opened up Pandora's box and revealed the following story.

Matthyes said that a cache of non-issue automatic weapons plus a suspected "C-4 bomb" had been discovered in the trunk of Sinclair's accordioned patrol car at the crash scene. This corresponded to a statement made to the FBI by Mariposa Deputy Rod Cusic that he had witnessed a booby-trapped incendiary device explode at Sinclair's home after being accidentally tripped by Sinclair's son. Additionally, Cusic testified that he was told by Rod Sinclair to lie to the grand jury about any connection Sinclair's former drug addiction might have with the fatal accident that occurred on tour of Yosemite National Park.

During our interview, Matthyes confirmed that Sinclair had been "doing narcotics," and that a local doctor, Dr. Arthur Dahlem, had been prescribing drugs in prodigious quantities. Another recollection: Three days after the accident, Matthyes, concerned about one of his men, visited Sinclair and told him to "just take it easy. The county will take care of you."

Sinclair looked up from his hospital bed and responded, "I'm not worried about anything. Bruce Eckerson is going to take care of me, because if he doesn't, I've got enough on him to send him to jail for a long time."

Matthyes said that he had been a detective on the Los Angeles Police Department before retiring and moving to Mariposa to get away from the big city and crime. Shortly after he took up residency, Carolle Clark approached him and asked him to run for sheriff of

Mariposa County. Clark said the current sheriff was crooked and the sheriff's department needed to be cleaned up.

Sometime after Matthyes announced to run, Clark had the fatal accident.

Matthyes said that while he worked for LAPD he had been reprimanded and suspended for a minor violation. After he was elected sheriff of Mariposa, one day he walked into his office and found a copy of his reprimand on his desk. He said he knew the deputies were out to get him because they knew he was elected to clean up the department.

Matthyes said that he called the Merced Sheriff's Department and asked them if they had an informant they could send up to Mariposa to meet with him to work undercover to determine if his department was involved in drug distribution.

Merced sent him an informant who had successfully worked for their department. The informant met with Matthyes in a wooded area near Mariposa, and Matthyes briefed him on his concerns. Matthyes gave the confidential informant (CI) his private home telephone number and asked him to call him every night to report in.

Matthys said that five days went by, and he got a call around 11 p.m. from the CI reporting that he just made a buy from Mickey Corcoran in the woods and that two Mariposa deputies in uniform driving a Mariposa County squad car covered the buy. The CI told Matthyes, "I'm out here; it's too damn dangerous."

Matthyes said that the reason no drugs were found in Sinclair's blood after the accident is because deputies stole the blood samples that were taken at the Fremont Hospital in Mariposa and altered the report.

Matthyes then dropped the bomb. He said he decided to retire and move away from Mariposa to Wyoming because he discovered that Tony Cohelo, a Democratic congressman from Merced, Bruce Eckerson, the County DA, and Ed Hardy, the head of Curry

Company in Yosemite, were involved in a cabal to obtain junk bond loans in $100,000 increments from Valley Federal Savings and Loan, in Van Nuys, California. The junk bonds were to finance a scam to build a theme park outside of Yosemite Park that never materialized. Matthyes also said that Eckerson was involved in keeping money when estate sales occurred after the death of a Mariposa citizen.

The allegations by Matthyes were never substantiated. However, Tony Cohelo was investigated by the FBI for fraudulent junk bond loans, and although he was a rising star in the Democratic Party, he abruptly resigned during the investigation in 1989.

Rod Sinclair died from cancer in October 2001.

I portioned the California State Legislature to put a monument commemorating the death of the agents on Route 132. They passed the legislation, but California Transportation was going to charge the Association of Former Agents of the Secret Service $100,000 to build an inlet off the highway.

I called Joanne Drake, the administrator at the Ronald Reagan Library, and requested permission for a plaque to be hung at the library in honor of the three fallen agents. The board of directors approved, and on March 29, 2015, a ceremony was held, and the plaque was hung at the Reagan Library in the Secret Service exhibit.

Chapter 35

THE COUNTERFEIT COUNTERFEITER

THE ONE "VISITOR" the wife of a Secret Service agent can always expect at dinnertime is the telephone call. It usually comes either right in the middle of the main course that took all day to prepare and must be served piping hot or just before the birthday cake. Thus, came the inevitable ring one cold Friday evening, this time from a desk sergeant at the Fresno Police Department.

"Mr. Williams, I've got a little guy in front of me who alleges (police like to use that word) that a man approached him to print counterfeit money. Interested?"

"The food will be in the fridge. Set the microwave to two minutes when you get home," my wife instructed as I left her and the girls at the kitchen table. We all knew the routine. I kissed my family, mumbled something eloquent, like "see ya," and drove unexcitedly to the police department.

Waiting there was one of the most anemic-looking men I had ever seen. Pale and tiny and thin and almost cartoonish. His thick glasses distorted his eyes so that they resembled those of a bubble-orbed goldfish in one of those cheap, round tanks—the kind you win in the Ping Pong ball toss at the school carnival.

I introduced myself and extended my hand, a veritable catcher's glove in size compared to the little one's dainty paw. We shook hands, I not daring to squeeze too hard.

He said his name was Thomas—not Tom, Thomas! he insisted—and he claimed to be a printer of fine works and books from Oregon, who had to move to the Central Valley for health reasons. *Sure*, I thought to myself, *he moved here because too many lumberjacks threatened to chop his little tree.*

"Tell me why I'm here," I said to Thomas.

"When I was a printer, the people I worked for introduced me to a man named Wayne Powell. I told Wayne that I was planning to move to Fresno to work at a print shop. He recently called me here and had me meet him for dinner. Then he said he had a proposition for me."

"I'll bet he did." I chuckled to myself.

"Mr. Powell said he couldn't tell me about it in the restaurant, but that I should go to his motel room with him. Mr. Williams, I was really scared, because I thought he might be…well…you know…but I said okay anyway. We drank a couple of beers in his room, and then he told me that he likes me and knows I am a good printer. He said he was planning to open a print shop and asked if I would be willing to print counterfeit money for him. He promised that I could make lots of money."

Thomas looked at me blankly and continued. "I told him that I couldn't possibly do that kind of work, but I had a friend just out of prison who might be interested in taking the job. And then I notified the police."

He couldn't remember Powell's room number at the motel but recalled that there was a late model blue Ford Thunderbird parked in front. So, with Thomas as passenger, we cruised the motel's parking lot, and outside Room 115 sat a blue T-bird sporting Oregon license plates.

I placed a call at the motel to Mr. Wayne Powell, but the operator said no one by that name was registered. Luckily Thomas then remembered that when he first met Powell in Oregon, he had introduced himself as "Wayne Carson." I dialed the operator again, and she confirmed that a Wayne Carson was registered in Room 115.

"No message, I'll call back," I said.

We drove to a nondescript truck stop on Highway 99, outside of Fresno, and I had Thomas call Powell to tell him that "I ran this by my buddy, and he said he wants to meet you. He's real interested. Meet us in the coffee shop at Buck's Truck Stop on Highway 99 at one a.m."

I was not surprised when Powell showed up, but I was surprised by his appearance. Powell stood six-two and probably registered 165 pounds on a generous scale on a humid day. His clean-shaven face looked like a pasty moonscape, pale and cratered. He also stank from cheap cologne.

From the beginning, I tried to intimidate Powell with a tough demeanor and the strength of my grip. I stared at him, letting him know through body language that I wasn't to be messed with, yet through countervailing signals indicating my "pliant, cooperative nature" since he was "the man in charge" with the checkbook.

Having attended a university in Oklahoma, I had no problem playing the part of a reticent Okie—"yups" and "durns" and all that. We ordered some Buds, and he gulped them down faster than an AA failure falls off the wagon. I could see that he didn't handle even light amounts of alcohol very well.

"What's your background?" Powell mildly slurred.

"Out of Oklahoma State Pen about a year. Lookin' fer full-time work—maybe as a printer or truck driver. Right now I got a part-time job at a piece-o'-shit print shop, but they pay crap. I need ta git full-time work, man," I said.

"How can I get in touch?" Powell asked.

I gave him my undercover phone number that played into

our small Fresno Secret Service bureau. Powell shook my hand. I squeezed his hard and saw him shake the pain out of it as he left.

The check we ran on him confirmed my suspicions: lengthy criminal record for fraud, credit card theft, embezzlement. His latest antics involved the torching of a small business for the insurance money. Here was a typical dickhead who forged a career out of trying to beat the system.

About a week later, Powell called me on the undercover line. Since I supposedly was employed in a printing shop, I turned on the teletype machine that was positioned next to the phone. Its clacking sound seemed close to the noise of a cheap printing press. Could a Hollywood sound-effects man have done any better?

"Still interested?" Powell asked.

"Shore am," I responded.

"I'm still up here in Oregon, clearing up some business, but I'll be driving down your way in about a week," he said.

He was lying, for further tracking of Powell through the Oregon Parole Department, plus a credit card report, placed him not in Oregon, but in residence with his mother in Glendale, California.

"Just call me when you git here," I said. "Be seein' ya." I hung up abruptly and called a local printer with whom I had become acquainted during a series of seminars I conducted on counterfeiting.

"Sam, Ron Williams, Secret Service. I need a favor."

Sam Jones ran a successful printing business. His father before him had been a printer, and his father before him. Sam agreed to give me a crash course in printing over the next week. I think he enjoyed his secret role of advisor to the Secret Service.

When Powell showed up the following week, I made sure that residual ink showed beneath my fingernails. In his hotel room at the Holiday Inn, Powell painted a beautiful scenario for me. I'd be printing $10 million cash for him and his financial backers, which they would then smuggle to South America and exchange for various goods and services.

"I'm personally gonna make five hundred grand on this one," Powell boasted.

Of course, I tried to act big-eyed. I whistled a big "wow!"

From that meeting on, Powell called me just about every day, and he continued to feed me information guaranteed to make a starving printer salivate. "You're gonna make more money than you ever thought possible, Ron." "I'm buying our very own print shop." "The best equipment you can buy." "And you're gonna be a partner, Ron."

Powell called with such frequency, I figured that I had better switch the undercover line to my house, just so my "cover" couldn't be botched accidentally by the other agents in the office. This proved to be an inadvertent stroke of genius, for my wife normally spoke with a definite Texas drawl—the perfect complement to my Okie accent. When she answered the phone, the arrogant Powell just assumed that my "ol' lady" was another dumb Southern bimbo. Wrong! She had been the recipient of countless "business" calls over the years and was an expert at playing telephone charades.

But then, almost as suddenly as he appeared, Powell evaporated. I communicated this turn of events to the Los Angeles office, who counseled, "Just lay low. The grease-ball will resurface."

Powell floated back two months later.

"Hey, Ron, bet you wondered what happened to me. I've been shopping around for a print shop, and I think I've found one in Anaheim. I'll be in touch."

Then the LA Secret Service office received a call from a printer from Anaheim who reported a couple of suspicious buyers for his shop—equipment and all. Powell and his partner told the printer that they were agents for the CIA, and they needed an obscure print shop for some real "hush-hush" work.

Powell called me again. "Want ya to come on down to LA to look at the operation and see if it'll work for us," he ordered.

"You buy the ticket, man," I said. Powell wired the money to me, and I caught a flight to Los Angeles the next day.

Powell was there to meet me. So were several Secret Service agents, blended into the crowds. So they couldn't lose sight of me in the crowded concourse, I wore an obnoxiously large black ten-gallon cowboy hat. My cowboy boots elevated me another two inches. We ambled outside the terminal to Powell's waiting car, a brand-new Pontiac Trans Am.

"Just got it for my wife," Powell bragged proudly, seeing me look at the car. He didn't know we knew that his wife had divorced him right after the Oregon conviction, and he hadn't rehitched.

Roaring out of the airport, I set the pattern of my "lifestyle." "Hey, man, stop at the next liquor store so's I can git some beer and chaw. Cain't live without it."

I also wanted to make sure that the following agents were on our tail. They blinked their headlamps when they saw me leave the store and walk back to the Trans Am, hefting three six-packs.

Once back in the car, I popped a can of Bud ("Hey, man, keep that down on the seat or the chippies'll pull us over") and simultaneously tore off a chunk of chewing tobacco. God, that stuff is awful, but, hey, this was show biz. I kept chew between the gum and lip long enough for effect. Then, with the practiced move of a lifelong chewer, I spun my head and spat the viscous mess out onto the freeway. Only…

…Only the chew, it never got that far. Powell had closed the passenger window while I was in the store, and I hadn't realized it. The brownish bolus splatted on the window and began its slide into the inner workings of the car door. I was mildly surprised, to say the least. But Powell went fuckin' nuts.

"You crazy Okie. What the fuck is wrong with you?!"

I just stared at him hard, and my crazy gaze quieted him somewhat. He mumbled more invectives as he jerked the car off the freeway to the shoulder.

"Clean it off, asshole!" he commanded. So I did, all the while hoping that our tail hadn't zipped by us. I had to know. So under the guise of doing a super job, I got out of the car and looked around. My guys were nowhere behind us. My stupidity meant that I was now alone. Climbing back in the Trans Am, I managed a weak apology, which seemed to mollify Powell somewhat. We accelerated off the shoulder, back into the traffic flow, nearly clipping a gray Plymouth that raced us from an on-ramp in a futile attempt to cut in front of us.

"Look at those fuckers!" Powell snarled. "They ain't gettin' in front of me!"

He punched the gas pedal. The Trans Am roared into a stomach-wrenching fourth dimension as we maneuvered right next to the gray Plymouth in an attempt to force them back into their own lane.

"EEEEEE-ahhhhhh," I shouted in the best Rebel tradition. In reality, that was the sound of my sphincter slamming shut.

I grinned wildly at the three "businessmen" in the conservative car as we edged them nearer to the shoulder, and then flipped them off like a wild man. It's not often you get to give the bird to fellow agents who are shadowing you.

"You know, man, if I do this deal with ya, I'm gonna have to bring down another guy to help me print. I know him from Oklahoma, and he really knows how to engrave. Anyways, I need someone to help me run the place," I told Powell.

"Can I trust the guy?" Powell wanted to know.

"Man, he's solid gold…knows his stuff. Watched out for each other in the joint," I assured him.

We reached the print shop, located in a run-down industrial section. As we walked through the modest printing plant, I feigned appreciation of the small presses that Powell thought would soon make him a gazillionaire.

"Love those presses, man," I exclaimed to the present owner. "Any one of these'll do fine," I approved, winking at Powell. The owner, well prepped by LA Secret Service as to who I was, could barely contain his conspiratorial smile.

"You smile a lot," I chided him. "You got somethin' you ain't tellin' us, man?" I punctuated my question with such a fierce gaze that I could feel the chill working its way down each of the poor guy's vertebrae. He didn't grin again during our survey.

I took Powell aside and told him that this arrangement was exactly what I needed to do the deal, but I still needed my buddy to help me run the operation. I cautioned him not to put down any money until I contacted my guy. But Powell had already presented a down payment check for $5,000.

"Get your guy," Powell commanded, so I excused myself and went to the small office, and instead of calling my printing pal, I called the LA office.

"Call Sternad. It's a go!"

I pretended to stay on the line far longer than my three-word message took. Five minutes later, I reported to Powell, "I called him. It's a go."

Powell drove me back to the airport. At curbside outside the terminal, I shook Powell's hand—crushing it again—and said, "See ya in a week, pardner." I looked over my shoulder to see him shaking off the pain.

Fellow agent and printing genius Gary Sternad flew in from his home base in Milwaukee. Though only 5'10," he outweighed me by at least fifteen pounds. His distended stomach spoke eloquently to one of his favorite Milwaukee pastimes: pub hopping. A full face-smothering beard made him look like one of the Smith Brothers on the box of those cough drops. He had been a printer in his pre-Secret Service life, the perfect preparation for his career specialty for the past two decades, which was conducting nationwide sting operations in print shops.

Sternad was a virtual encyclopedia of printing. There wasn't a piece of equipment he couldn't operate, a piece of technology he didn't understand, a counterfeit bill he couldn't print convincingly.

After a leisurely drive down California's Central Valley, we checked in to a cheap motel a short distance from the printing plant. Even though the desk clerk obviously had catered to a motley group of customers, he looked fearfully at us, as if we were two Vikings about to rape and pillage. Later we drove to the print shop to meet Powell and to take delivery of ten reams of 100 percent cotton fiber paper, plus $1,000 in crisp twenties, fifties, and hundred-dollar Federal Reserve notes.

These bills were to be our "pattern" notes, from which we would make our photographic printing plates. The plan was to use the offset printing method, whereby ink is spread across a "positive" image of the money, then chemically transferred to a rubber roller that picks up the appropriate ink image from the plate. This image is backward on the roller, but when paper is pressed against the inked roller, the resultant image is transferred to the paper. Offset printing is a photographic process and is the most common type of printing done today.

Sternad and I took the money, promising Powell that we would stay up all night to manufacture "the best durn plates you'll ever see, man."

After Powell left us to do our artistry, Sternad got on the phone to the counterfeit division at Secret Service headquarters in Washington. The results of that call arrived early the next morning at LAX by commercial jet and were then relayed to our motel via special government agent. What we had to show Powell were perfect plates of $20s, $50s, and $100s. As far as he would know, overnight we had produced the highest quality plates he ever hoped to see.

When we showed Powell the plates, he was so excited that he started to give me a spontaneous hug. I just stood and stared so fiercely at him that he backed off. He started to offer his hand to me but thought better of it when he remembered that I made a hobby out of crushing his bones. He just said, "Great, man. Great!"

"If they're so great, man, why don't you go out and buy us a coupla six-packs. Keep us happy, man," I suggested.

"While you're at it, buy us a fan. It's friggin' hot in here," Sternad added.

As Powell left, we started running the $20s. Though Sternad wasn't being too careful, the bills looked pretty decent. We must have run two reams and stacked them on a table to dry when we heard a knock on the front door. A phone company service man had come to take out a phone. I told him to wait a minute while Sternad and I covered the stack of bogus bucks.

It took him just a couple of minutes to disconnect and remove the phone. As he was walking through the print area, his tool belt snagged the cloth covering the stack of $20s. He looked down, did a fast double-take, and hurried out to his truck.

"We got trouble," I told Sternad. "The cops are going to bust this place."

I was right. Twenty minutes later a cop came to the back door, gun drawn, and ordered us to raise our hands. We complied quickly. We saw that this rookie was so nervous even the slightest involuntary jerk would have been cause for him to pull the trigger.

I tried to calm him down. "I know why you're here, Officer. But I've got to make this fast. We're Secret Service agents working on an undercover investigation."

I started to lower my hands, but the language end of his .38 revolver told me to raise them again. "Listen, let me go out to my truck to get my ID. You keep Sternad here covered," I bargained.

Confused and only partially convinced, the officer okayed my request. I rushed to the truck and grabbed the handheld radio to call the LA office.

"Call the cops and tell them to pull out. They're going to blow the action," I said. Then I rushed in with my ID. Five minutes after the rookie left, still not sure whether he had been scammed or not, Powell returned. He grabbed some samples and disappeared. We continued to print.

About five that afternoon, Powell stormed in to announce, "My partner thinks this is crap."

Sternad fired back in a great display of extemporaneous creativity: "You expect us to print good shit with the quality camera I had to use to make the plates? Man, that camera is older than your grandmama!"

Powell pondered that for a moment, then told us to stop printing;

he'd call us at the motel later that night.

And he did, at 10 p.m., to announce that he had just purchased a new Kodak plate-making camera. "Meet us at the shop," he ordered.

We washed our mouths out with some beer (not wanting to be out of character) and drove to meet Powell and his partner, Donald Vanbrunt, whom we had never met.

Vanbrunt obviously didn't want to be seen. He sported a trench coat with the collar turned up and a large-brimmed hat, which he pulled down over his face. He stayed in the shadows and never faced us directly. His communication consisted of a few unintelligible grunts of agreement with Powell.

Put off by Vanbrunt's bullshit secret-agent behavior, Sternad hefted a bottle of beer, walked straight over to him, stooped, and stuck his face right below the brim of Vanbrunt's hat, then flashed his teeth through his sagebrush beard and roared, "Howdy there, pardner! How ya doin' under there?"

Repulsed by the furry face thrust up so close to his, Vanbrunt signaled Powell that it was time to leave. Sternad and I told them we'd stay late and print up some "new beauties" for them.

In actuality, Sternad had brought out some fine samples of previous work and was going to present the bills to Powell and Vanbrunt at the appropriate time. That time was about to occur. Sternad and I left in our pickup, driving evasively in case a tag had been placed on us. We discussed strategy during our maneuvers and decided that we should issue a search warrant for the print shop, then arrest Powell and Vanbrunt the next day.

We went to the shop early in the morning to set up the sting. When Powell and the still behatted Vanbrunt came into the shop, we proudly displayed the "freshly printed" samples. They were literally awestruck at the beauty of the bills. And rightfully so, for they had been printed by a master "counterfeiter," Sternad himself, for another sting operation.

Powell lovingly laid each denomination out on the ground, and the two hugged the floor with magnifying glasses, marveling at the quality, congratulating themselves on investing in the new plate-making camera.

As they focused their attention on the money, Sternad hand-scrawled a note which he placed on the printing press. It read: AGENTS, 7; BAD GUYS, 0.

What Powell and Vanbrunt didn't know was that I wore a wire which was transmitting our conversations to a Secret Service arrest team waiting out front to storm the print shop. The code for the agents to smash in was "When this is finished, I'm going back to Fresno for some bass fishing." Between Powell's and Vanbrunt's oohs and ahhhs, I blurted the code.

"What you say, pardner?" Sternad asked, as if he hadn't heard.

"When this is finished, I'm going back to Fresno for some bass fishing!" I bellowed so loud it must have blown out the eardrums of the agent on the receiver outside. Thirty seconds later, a team of agents blasted through the front and back doors, guns drawn. They smashed Powell and Vanbrunt down to the floor and cuffed them quickly.

A couple of agents "roughed up" Sternad and me, and one of them uncoiled a punch in my stomach for the sake of "reality." While I was doubled over in pain, he whispered, "That's for giving us the finger on the freeway."

"You assholes set us up!" I accused Powell. "You assholes!"

Sternad and I were cuffed and escorted out the back while Powell and Vanbrunt were marched through the front door.

The next day I went back to Fresno. Sternad returned to Milwaukee to wait for his next printing job. Vanbrunt cooperated and received a mere one-year sentence. Powell refused to cooperate and was sentenced to all of two years.

Perhaps it was my wife who learned the biggest lesson from this case. From then on she unplugged the phone during dinner.

Chapter 36

Robert Mugabe

Every year the United Nations holds a meeting in New York for all the heads of state of every country in the world. In 1986, I received orders to report to New York, assigned as the detail leader for Prime Minister Robert Mugabe of Zimbabwe.

As the detail leader, you must report two days early to make preparations for the protectee you are assigned to. To that end I met with the consul general of Zimbabwe to discuss the visit. I was informed the Mugabe party would consist of the prime minister and ten military officers, and they would be staying at the Waldorf Astoria Hotel. I advised the consul general that the motorcade would consist of three vehicles: the limousine for Mugabe, a Secret Service follow-up car for the shift agents, and a station wagon for the party's baggage. I told the consul general that he would need to rent a separate vehicle for the ten military officers. He shook his head as if he understood.

On the day of Mugabe's arrival, I positioned our three vehicles curbside at Kennedy International. I asked the consul general where his vehicle was, and he replied, "We will ride in your follow-up and baggage cars."

I said, "Your folks will not ride in the Secret Service follow-up vehicle, and the baggage car will be full of suitcases. You need to arrange some transportation." He just shrugged his shoulders as if to say, "It's your problem."

When Mugabe arrived, ten military officers in full uniform were with him. As we removed Mugabe's suitcase from the plane, I asked the consul general where the bags for the military officers were. He stated, "They have their clothes with them."

It was then I noticed the officers were each carrying a medium-sized gym bag. My immediate thought was, how can they stay in New York at the Waldorf Astoria for ten days with just a gym bag?

I opened the back-passenger side limo door for Mugabe while the consul general went around and got in the back seat on the driver's side. Meanwhile, the military officers were like ants trying to get into the Secret Service follow-up vehicle. The agents in the follow-up locked the doors and denied them entrance. The officers then scurried to the baggage car and started piling in without any order. I silently watched as chaos ensued and the station wagon back end got lower and lower until the back bumper was almost on the ground.

I finally decided enough was enough and got in the right front seat of the limo and told the driver to go. There were two Zimbabwe military officers still trying to get in the baggage car. As the three-car motorcade pulled away from the curb, these two men ran and dove through the rear window that had been lowered.

The problem was that only half their bodies made it through the window. As we traveled into New York, their lower bodies were literally hanging out the back window. Every time the baggage car hit a pothole, their legs would fly over the top of the car as the back bumper hit the pavement. As I watched in the mirror, I couldn't stop laughing. Mugabe, wondering what was so funny, turned in his seat and looked through the rear window to see his two military officers dangling from the back window of the station wagon. He, too, started laughing, one of the few times I ever saw him show any expression during the entire visit. When we finally pulled up to the Waldorf Astoria, I was relieved that we had not lost any of his aides lying on the street somewhere in New York.

The next seven days with Mugabe's crew were excruciating. The military officers obviously did not know what the showers in their rooms were for. Each day the stench from their unwashed bodies got worse. When Mugabe moved, they insisted on being right there with him. Instead of walking behind the prime minister, the Secret Service agents assigned to the detail started walking in front of the party so they could breathe fresh air. I, as the detail leader, unfortunately, had to walk directly behind Mugabe. The body odor was so bad, I thought I would lose the hairs in my nose, or that the wallpaper in the hallway of the Waldorf would peel right off the wall.

On the fourth day of the visit, the consul general came to me to advise that the prime minister would be attending a Third World cocktail party at the United Nations that evening.

The foreign dignitary command center put out a directive that only the head of state and their detail leaders would be allowed to enter the United Nations building and go up to the ballroom where the cocktail party would be held. I informed the consul general that Mugabe's military aides, including him, were not allowed at this party, and it would be advisable if they stayed back at the hotel. He acknowledged my request.

That evening we ushered Mugabe down the Waldorf elevator and escorted him to the limo. I then realized the consul general had not passed my directive to the military officers, because they sat in a van (that the consul general had finally rented) behind our follow-up car. I again told the consul general they were not to get out of the van when we arrived at the United Nations. He shook his head as if to acknowledge my instruction.

When we arrived at the entrance to the United Nations, the van doors were flung open, and the officers jumped out and ran like a pack of mice to get inside the building. The agents in the follow-up were concentrated on protecting Mugabe, so they were not able to corral the Zimbabwe officers.

When Mugabe and I arrived at the elevator, the ten officers had already piled inside. The elevator operator turned and looked at me through glazed eyes and said, "Lordy, Lordy!" I could tell the stink was overpowering his nostrils.

When the elevator doors closed, we were pressed together like sardines. The elevator traversed about three feet upward and came to an abrupt stop with a signal it was overloaded. The operator looked at me with a frightened stare. I told him, "Get this damn thing down."

After several minutes, the elevator slowly lowered. When the doors opened, I grabbed the officers one by one and threw them off the elevator. Some I kicked in the butt. As the elevator emptied, the operator started laughing and said, "Amen, brother." When all the officers were off the elevator, I turned and looked at Mugabe, who had a smile on his face. He obviously enjoyed the scene.

At the party, the foreign heads of state stood around speaking English and trashing the United States. The Secret Service detail leaders were pressed into one area, but we were still witness to some of the conversations. It was like we were ghosts in the room.

During seven long days with Mugabe and his party, never once did he speak to me. If he had to address me, he would speak to his consul general in his native tongue, and the consul general would tell me what the prime minister wanted.

The next year when assignments for the United Nations came out, I was once again assigned to Robert Mugabe. When I inquired as to why I was selected, I was informed that the consul general from Zimbabwe had specifically requested my services. I could only think it was because Mugabe had liked the way I kicked his military officers in the butt to get them off the elevator.

Chapter 37

THE HIGHLIGHT OF MY CAREER: PROTECTING THE POPE

A DOZEN MEN crouched behind whatever barriers they could find, waiting for that split-second window of opportunity to storm the building without getting blown out of existence in the process.

Our gun barrels were so hot, they seemed ready to melt. Blue-gray smoke hung perniciously in the air, residual evidence of an intense, protracted firefight. Our ears rang intensely from staccato blasts of both magnums and shotguns as we poured hundreds of rounds into the building.

Thanks to keen international intelligence, we had trapped several—and maybe more—suspected "presidential" assassins, who were identified as having been dispatched on a suicidal mission by a fanatical Middle Eastern dictator. How they penetrated our customs barriers we would never know. Probably they entered North America through Canada, then took back roads across the world's longest, unpatrolled border into the United States proper. Of course, that was irrelevant now. Our only mission was to eradicate these zealots.

Finally, during a lull in our well-choreographed assault, someone screamed, "Lunch break!" We stood down from our realistic exercise to review and renew.

Though those "games" are fun, they're necessary and deadly serious. Always in the back of our minds, we knew that these live-fire rehearsals were extraordinarily important to both peace and peace-of-mind. It's part of our business, the business for which the Secret Service is best known: that of providing security for the President of the U.S. and other heads of state.

I barely had time to clean my guns that October day in 1979, when I was ordered to Washington, then to Beltsville, MD, for a special protection review seminar. I had been selected as a member of the protection team for Pope John Paul II, who was to visit the U.S. just one year after his solemn Vatican installation.

The powers-that-be felt that we "uncultured" agents needed instruction in papal protocol. Being a not-too-committed Protestant from the Deep South, I thought the Pope was going to be just another VIP who needed protection, albeit one who happened to wear his robe out in public.

I was to become enlightened. As our protection teams jetted off to greet the Pope upon his landing in an Al Italia 747 at Boston's Logan International Airport, not even our most experienced planners had the vaguest idea how big this event would become.

Senator Ted Kennedy and his wife, Joan, arguably Boston's most renowned Catholic citizens, stood respectfully in the rain at the bottom of the gangway as the Pope descended the long stairway to kiss the ground, a gesture for which he has become famous. After some plane-side greetings, Sen. Kennedy ushered the Pope to his limousine. Other Vatican and State Department dignitaries scattered to their cars. The caravan proceeded as planned out the secured gates of the airport, en route to the nearby rectory, where His Eminence could refresh himself from his long pilgrimage of grace.

But there was to be no rest soon for either the Pope or for the Secret Service team. As soon as the limo hit the parade route, we jaded agents woke up in amazement at the throngs which lined the streets.

People stood fifteen deep on either side of the roads in a drenching downpour for more than an hour, almost the entire way from the airport to the city, just for a glimpse of the Pope. It was then that I, and most probably all my fellow agents, realized that we were guarding more than just another international dignitary.

Two things impressed me immediately and poignantly. One was that tens of thousands of people would suffer this deluge to glimpse the "Vicar of Christ." But most of all I can never forget this humble man who fended off repeated but well-meaning attempts by his protectors to keep him safe and dry in the limo, choosing instead to stand as tall as he could out of the hatch atop the limousine to wave at and bless his followers. It was obvious to me, watching him, that he answered to only *one* protector.

The Pope next visited New York City, where we witnessed another miracle of numbers. In all my years before or after, I have never experienced such large or enthusiastic crowds. In this city where respect seems to be the exception rather than the rule, the mean streets pulsated with pure love and reverence. I do recall reading afterward, however, that pickpockets, equally faithful to their Deity of Dexterous Digits, had a field day working the pious as they lined Broadway.

As we traveled with the Pope, I tried to detect any personal signs of egocentricity, megalomania, or conceit in His Holiness. After all, having guarded many of the world's most famous leaders, I had become somewhat of an expert in identifying such idiosyncrasies. However, with this man, there was none of that—not even a hint. Throughout his visit, I remained amazed at his humility, his rare gift of reaching out with unconditional love and compassion.

Perhaps this gift was reflected best in his love of babies. The Pope absolutely loved babies. He'd bless and kiss every baby who was thrust within reach. More than once, I thought I'd have to lunge forward to catch a falling infant who may have been knocked loose from its mother's grip by people who felt an overpowering need to touch the Pope.

Too many times I've seen politicians hold, hug, and kiss babies, then wipe their lips and shake imaginary goobers off their hands when they were out of sight from the voters and the cameras. But not the Pope. His love was genuine. His sincere love was his PR. And he couldn't have cared one whit if news cameras captured his expressions of affection.

John Paul's visit to Philadelphia was a reprise of earlier cities. Almost. Here he chose to address students at a small Catholic seminary, where about 300 young aspirants studying for the priesthood waited studiously for what might have been the supreme religious experience of their lives. For two and a half hours, the Pope reached into the depths of his beliefs and lectured and expressed all that which embodied priesthood: service to all men in the name of the Lord, compassion, love, humility, and dedication. The young men were moved to tears. Even I had to sneak in a wipe or two.

"If you have any other agenda in life," he concluded compassionately in his gentle Polish accent, "then the priesthood is not for you."

I can't tell you how privileged I felt to have witnessed the Pope's "pep talk" to a chosen few.

A heavenly hush descended over the chapel as the Pope made ready to leave. He led a seemingly contradictory little procession back toward the ornate wooden chapel doors, with twelve faithful Secret Service agents in tow.

Then the solemnity of the moment imploded. All 300 students collapsed upon the Pope. They were beside themselves with emotion, crying out to be blessed. In their zeal, they were crushing us. I fought like hell (pardon me, Holy Father) to free the Pope. I even threw a couple of novices back over the pews.

Behind me, I heard Bishop Marchinkas cry out, "Be rough with these guys. Do what you have to do. Don't let the Pope get hurt." So much for "compassion."

We finally wrestled our way out. It was a religious experience I'll never forget.

The next day, the Pope held an outdoor mass near the Liberty Bell. We estimated conservatively that more than one million citizens bunched in the streets to hear his words. He spoke of basic human values. There was a depth of spirit the likes of which I'd never witnessed before. And when he finished, I felt uplifted and positive about life.

I thought I had seen it all. One million people packed together in one place. But then Chicago outdid Philly. An estimated two million people sardined themselves into Grant Park to embrace the words and drink in the love of their spiritual leader.

In the motorcade to the park, we literally had to bodily throw people off the limousine. As we crawled along the boulevard, a woman carrying some kind of long projectile exploded from the crowd and rushed toward the car. I was standing on the back of the limo when I noticed her. My impulse was to jump off the back, parry her charge, and send her back to the sidelines. I thought, mistakenly, that I could simply step off the back of the limo. However, somehow my foot got caught in the bumper, and what should have been a nimble, athletic maneuver turned into an embarrassing tumble. I fell to my knees, scraping holes in my best pair of pants. The agents in the follow-up car laughed and held up finger scores for my performance.

The next morning, we accompanied the Pope on a morning stroll. Even early in the morning, hundreds of people outside his rectory waited to see and to touch the pontiff. Suddenly, the police sergeant in charge of a contingent of officers grabbed the Pope's hand, fell to one knee, and started to cry. The Pope blessed him, but we couldn't pry the burly sergeant loose. He had entered a trance, so mesmerized was he by the Pope's presence.

Unfortunately, I literally had to judo chop the officer's hand free. Throughout all of this, the Pope never lost his aura of peace and calm. The sergeant was led away in tears. In his state, I'm sure that he didn't even feel my blows.

From Chicago, we flew to Des Moines, Iowa, where Pope John Paul held a mass for more than 200,000 people in a huge pasture. Standing atop what stagehands call "risers" so he could be seen by all, the Pope was separated from his parishioners by a wobbly snow fence—something akin to a hair net staked out horizontally. Again, he held his people rapt. But after the final benediction, as if possessed with one brain, the crowd surged forward—a human avalanche that the snow fence was ill-equipped to contain. This avalanche truly had us worried. We weren't sure if we could move fast enough to avoid being trampled.

Fortunately (miraculously?), the Pope's helicopter had been warming up, so if we could get him to it before the onslaught, we'd be able to lift him safely above this great, sincere, out-of-control outpouring of human emotion. But we were also worried that those in the vanguard of this human flood would be chopped up by the tail rotor of the helicopter.

Quite frankly, I was worried about myself as well. In our orientation to the Secret Service, we were warned that we might possibly take a bullet aimed for a president, but there was nothing in our contract about taking helicopter blades for a Pope.

Luckily, the immense downdraft of the helicopter's main rotor, coupled with the intimidating roar of the turbocharged engines, slowed the worshippers to a crawl as we lifted above them. The Pope continued to wave earthward until the crowds shrank away in the distance. Finally, he took a deep breath, closed his eyes, and relaxed in his seat.

The Pope's visit was winding down, but still ahead of us were a White House visit, a press opportunity for President Jimmy Carter, and a religious service at the Washington Monument.

On our way to the White House from Andrews Air Force Base, the Pope stopped for a quick mass at the monument. Again, an estimated 200,000 people flocked to see and hear him. This time, the crowd remained calm.

As we left in the motorcade for the presidential audience, we were flanked by policemen on horseback. Most unusually, one of the horses bolted in front of the Pope's limo. I thought the limo was going to strike the horse as the driver slammed on his brakes, but both the policeman and the chauffeur managed their mounts well. I flew forward when our driver hit his brakes, but I managed to wrap my arms around the Pope to shield him from any kind of rib-crunching collision.

"Are you okay, Your Eminence?" I asked after we lurched to a stop.

"That's not the question, my son," he said kindly. "Are *you* okay?"

How could I not be?

It sounds corny, I know, like a replay from a classic Hollywood biblical epic in which Charlton Heston or Victor Mature come into contact with Christ, then segue to the next scene, transformed for life as disciples of the son of God. No, that wasn't my script, but during my ten days with the Pope I had been transmuted from a world of cynicism—largely shaped by aggressive, self-serving, megalomaniacal VIPs and criminal low-lives—by a man of innocence who was truly pure of heart and purpose.

Before his departure back to Rome, the Pope held a private audience for the agents who had formed a halo of protection for him during his visit. Catholic agents knelt and kissed his ring. Being Protestant, I simply shook his hand. Then he draped two rosaries across my open palm for my daughters. To this day, I cherish those strings of beads perhaps more than any other possession.

In my time here on earth, I have been anything but an angel. That I was chosen to help protect Pope John Paul may be the closest I will ever get to God.

If that be the case, I'll be satisfied.

Chapter 38

President Richard Nixon

When I was sworn into the Secret Service in 1970, Richard Nixon was President of the United States. As a young fledgling agent, I was sent to several cities to stand post for Presidential visits. My impression of POTUS was that he and his administration operated like a well-oiled machine. Everything was pre planned with specifics and Nixon's visits were well orchestrated.

In January 1973 I along with 150 other field agents were sent to Washington DC to stand post for the second inauguration of President Nixon on January 20. We were moved from location to location ahead of the President's arrival to secure the area and provide for a secure environment. I got a first-hand look at a President's ball and the excitement that was generated by President Nixon's reelection. At each location the President and First Lady were introduced to a raucous vocal crowd cheering and clapping.

In 1990 I was the agent in charge of the protection squad in Los Angeles when we were notified President Nixon would be inaugurating the Nixon Presidential Library on July 19, 1990.

The inauguration would include a VIP guest list of former supporters of President Nixon as well as former President's, President George H. Bush, President Gerald Ford, and acting President William Clinton. President Jimmy Carter refused to attend the event as a protest for Nixon's renown Watergate fiasco.

There have been many speculations about why Nixon and his minions would authorize a break-in at the DNC Headquarters at the Watergate complex. The poll's indicated Nixon was well ahead of the Democratic Senator George McGovern, and indeed Nixon won the election in a landslide.

In Robert Mahue's book, "Next to Hughes", he alleges the Watergate burglary was instigated to recover evidence that Mahue had delivered $1,000,000 in cash to BeBe Rebozo to acquire a substantial contract for Howard Hughes aircraft company. The payoff was to ensure the Nixon administration would honor his payment. Apparently, a high-level Democrat had obtained documentation of the payoff and the Nixon administration wanted to steal the evidence.

The inauguration of the Nixon Library offered some tactical complications. The library sits just off Yorba Linda Boulevard, a major throughfare in Yorba Linda, California. Across the street in 1990 was a hillside with substantial foliage that overlooked the library and the parking lot area where the ceremony was to be held. Additionally, securing the parking lot without any natural barricades was an issue to designing security checkpoints where guest could be checked and validated.

After extensive review, the Orange County Sheriff's Department agreed to place several officers on the hillside after they swept the area to ensure no one was hiding in the foliage.

To build a barrier we brought in eighteen-wheeler trailers to create a box in the parking lot and put metal shields across the openings at the bottom of the trailers.

On the day of the inauguration, July 19, 1990, the temperature got up to 105%. As the secured area began to fill up, the guest was left no shade and sat on chairs baking in the hot sun.

I positioned myself to the left side of the elevated podium next to the Marine Corp Band. Once the ceremony started, the Sargent in charge of the Marine Corp band tapped me on the shoulder. When I turned to face him, I noted that he was sweating profusely in his dress blues. He had fire in his eyes as he addressed me, "Sir, are you in charge of this event". I said "yes I am." The irate Sargent said, "get those news people off my instruments or me and my men are going to kick their asses and leave." I had no doubt this sweating warrior would relish leading his men to war with the news media, and I would have liked to have seen him tune up the animals representing the news, but I told the Sargent I would handle the matter.

Traditionally, the President hires young neophytes whose daddy gives a lot of money to the President's party to be gophers and low-level staffers. One of their duties is to accompany the press pool and to provide them with some direction in where to park to get photo shots. In this case some of the press pool felt their best position was in the area the Marine Corp instruments were lying on the ground.

I approached one of the assigned neophytes who oversaw the press pool and tapped him on the shoulder and asked him to get the press pool off the Marine Corp instruments. He gave me a condescending look as if I was a mere pawn in his kingdom and mumbled something I could not decipher. As I turned to walk away, I overheard him turn to another neophyte and say, "one of these days I'm gonna kick some Secret Service Agent's ass." At that I returned to the neophyte and got within inches of his face and said, "I heard what you said, and when this event is over, meet me here in the parking lot because I'm gonna give you your wish to try and kick my ass." The wimpy neophyte's face became white with fright and his lips began to quiver. I then said, "now get those clowns off the Marine Corp instruments or the Marines are going to kick their asses and leave."

At the back of the crowd several LBGQ people were holding a protest by shouting and waving signs declaring their rights and protesting the government. Standing alongside the LGBQ members was a Boy Scout troop consisting of ten young scouts and their scout master donned in tan shorts, tan shirt with patches, and a wide brim hat that clearly defined him as the master in charge of his troop.

While President Gerald Ford was speaking, a member of the LGBQ waved a sign that struck one of the boy scouts. The scout master took offense at his fledgling being hit and socked the LBGQ member in the face apparently knocking him to the ground. At that point the crowd around the boy scout troop cheered as the Orange County Sheriff's moved in and led the LBGQ protestor out of the event. President Ford thought the crowd was cheering for his speech and he broke into a smile as if to recognize the crowd's approval.

The ceremony in the parking lot ended, thank God, and the four Presidents and their wives were escorted through the Nixon library.

I have returned several times to this historical site and wondered on each occasion what possessed the leader of the free world to authorize a second-rate burglary that altered history. One can only speculate.

Chapter 39

President Ronald Reagan

JIMMY CARTER, A Democrat and the 39th President of the United States, presided as the President for four long years, enduring the fiasco in the desert in Iran when an attempt to rescue American hostages ended in disaster. The Shaw of Iran had been deposed by an uprising of radical Islamic mullahs and the radicals had invaded the American embassy on November 4, 1979, in Teheran and taken 52 American prisoners.

Inflation rates had ballooned to 18% and there were long lines of cars waiting in line to get petrol. The country was in turmoil, and people were reeling from an inflation rate that was killing small businesses.

As an agent, there is no greater thrill than watching Air Force One land and the President come down the steps of the plane with the band playing Hail to the Chief. But when Jimmy Carter was President, you were never sure he was the President when Air Force One landed.

Ronald Wilson Reagan the Republican candidate for President, ran for President in 1980 and campaigned on cutting taxes, cutting government spending, and building a strong military. Reagan won in a landslide, and he was sworn in as President on January 20, 1981.

I was fortunate to be assigned to go to Washington DC for Reagan's inauguration on January 21, 1981. I was stationed along Pennsylvania Avenue in front of the White House for the parade. Reagan's election was like a breath of fresh air breathed into the nation. It was like the country was being reborn from years of economic stagflation and a lack of leadership.

From 1981 until his term ended, when Air Force One landed and stairs were wheeled up to the side of that impressive plane, you knew who President of the United States was when President Reagan bounded down the steps.

A week after Reagan was elected, he and Nancy Reagan came to Los Angeles. I was present in Chasen's Restaurant when they entered through the front door. The guest inside who had been vetted and cleared stood and cheered for five long minutes. Something else occurred that had never been done in the Carter years. The President insisted the Secret Service Agents and police officers working the security detail be fed. This of course endeared agents and police to appreciate the President even more.

Starting in 1981 and every year after that while Reagan was President, he and Nancy would travel to Rancho Mirage, California on December 29th and stay at the Sunnylands Estate, through January 3, owned by Walter and Leonor Annenberg.

To prepare for the President's first visit, Agent Dave Cahill and I paid a visit to Sunnylands to meet the Annenberg's and discuss security arrangements.

Sunnylands estate sits at the corner of Bob Hope Drive and Frank Sinatra Dr. and is 205 acres surrounded by a six-foot concrete wall with Oleander bushes behind the wall hiding the property. When Cahill and I pulled up to the main gate off Fran Sinatra, an elderly unarmed uniformed security guard came out of the guard shack to check us out. After identifying ourselves I asked the guard where the cameras were monitored that I had noticed on the walls surrounding the property. The guard replied, "those cameras are fake, we don't have a way to monitor them." A billionaire's property with fake cameras? Wow.

After we drove up the long driveway, we were met at the door by Mrs. Annenberg. I noted that immediately behind her was a solid gold six-foot statute that appeared to be 4" thick. As she walked us through the home to meet Mr. Annenberg, I noticed expensive paintings on the walls with such artist as Rembrandt, Picasso, Vincent Van Gogh, and marble statues worth millions of dollars. All that and fake cameras and old guards without guns.

When Mrs. Annenberg introduced us to Ambassador Annenberg, he looked me and Cahill up and down and said, "you guys look like football players." I responded that "I only played in high school, but Dave played college ball and seven years in the NFL for the Philadelphia Eagles, Washington Redskins, and he was the fifth man on the Los Angeles Rams." The Ambassador was impressed and began a long litany of how he loved football and asked David Cahill questions about his career in the NFL.

After we had gained the Ambassador's confidence, he took us outside to view the property. As we gazed over the beautifully manicured flowers and trees, he asked us if we liked his golf course. I said, "it's beautiful." The Ambassador then stated, "you know why I built a nine-hole golf course on my property?" I said, "no." He then said, "when I moved here, I attempted to join the golf club at the El Dorado Country Club, but they wouldn't accept my application because I am Jewish. So, I built my own golf course. Now when Reagan comes to visit me, I'm going to take him to a New Year's Eve party. Do you know where I'm taking him?" I said, "let me guess, the El Dorado Country Club." He said, "yes and when I walk in, I'm going to say you wouldn't let me join but I'm bringing the President of the United States to your club."

I then said, "Mr. Ambassador, the fake boxes pretending to be cameras are not sufficient for Presidential protection. We need real cameras with a monitoring station to protect the perimeter." He said, "how much is this going to cost me?" I said, "perhaps we can get Secret Service Technical Security Division to install cameras with a monitoring capability." He said, "I like that." And that is what we did.

For the outer perimeter we got the Riverside County Sheriff's Department to utilize suv four-wheel drive vehicles to transition back and forth outside the four corners of the property 24/7 with lighting along the wall at night.

For the middle perimeter we put lights out about 50 yards from the main residence and stationed agents in golf carts.

For the inner perimeter, we had the working shift posted outside the President's reserved house that was on property.

It became obvious that agents stationed in golf carts were dozing off at night. So, after the first visit I recommended that we supplement the agents on the middle perimeter with dog teams. Dogs may doze, but they are trained to alert if there is an intrusion or unusual activity on property. So, in subsequent visits that's what we did.

One year and I don't recall which year, I went out to the Annenberg estate to conduct the advance for the Reagan's visit. When I pulled up to the back gate, I noticed all of the Mexican workers were carrying signs in protest of Ambassador Annenberg. I asked the foreman "what is going on, why are you protesting?" He said, "the Ambassador just gave $100 million to the United Negro College Fund, but he forgot about us Mexican's who come to work for him every day. We want ours."

When I spoke to the Ambassador about the protest I said, "the protest isn't a security issue, but it could be a political problem." He said, "yeah I know I'm gonna have to settle with them before the President arrives." Three days later I again came to the estate, and I noticed all the workers were back to work. I called over the foreman and asked him what happened. He said, "we got ours", as he rubbed his fingers together.

After Ronald Reagan left office, I had the pleasure of being around him and Nancy Reagan frequently because in my last four years I was the agent in charge of the Protection Squad in Los Angeles. Our office frequently supported the Secret Service Reagan Detail.

Ronald Reagan was always a gentleman, and Nancy was always a lady. He had an amazing sense of humor, and she had this inner core of steel that supported her Ronnie.

The Reagan Presidential years were magical. The nation prospered and Reagan defeated the Soviet Union in the cold war. The Berlin Wall came tumbling down, and the world was at peace knowing that a strong leader had imposed his will to make peace.

The thing that was most impressive about Ronald Reagan that Donald Trump never understood is to let insults, and a hostile press roll off your back while his minions fought the battles in the trenches. Trump ruined his vast accomplishments by exerting his ego and sending out nebulous tweets that offended enough Americans that voted him out of office.

On November 4, 1991, I was the lead advance from the LA field office for the opening of the Reagan Library in Semi Valley, California about 35 miles from LA. The library sits on top of a hill with two roads that lead up the hill. The front road is the main entrance, and the back road is non-descript and little used. However, on the day the Reagan Library was inaugurated, we used the back road to bring the motorcades of President's George H. Bush, President Gerald Ford, President Jimmy Carter, President Richard Nixon, and President Reagan to the library.

It was a momentous day with the first time in history that five Presidents of the United States and their wives met and were together for the occasion. There were no incidents that day, but after all the President's spoke, President Nixon's speech stood out as outstanding. He concentrated on America's foreign policy and how we must remain powerful and vigilant in the face of evil.

In 1989, George H. W. Bush was elected the 41st President of the United States. He was a gentleman and was well liked by the Secret Service Agents who toiled on his detail. His foundation was Barbara Bush. Although she looked like a grandma, she was extremely witty, and intelligent. She enjoyed kibitzing with the agents.

When George Bush was Vice President, he and Barbara spent every Christmas in Kennebunkport, Maine. On Christmas Day, the Vice President and Barbara would give each agent on the detail a gift that they personally purchased. Their thoughtfulness was well known and appreciated by the agents who had to spend time away from their families.

One time after George H. was President, Barbara Bush came to Los Angeles for a visit. She gave a speech to the entertainment community at the Beverly Hilton Hotel ballroom. As we were coming down the elevator Mrs. Bush said, "stay close by me boys, I'm speaking to a bunch of liberal Democrats, and I may have to hike up my skirt and make a run for it." One of the agents turned to her and said, "we got your back Mrs. B."

After Barbara Bush was introduced to the throng of over 500 guests, she began to read her prepared speech. After about two sentences she picked up her speech and threw it into the air and said, "I don't like this speech, let's just talk.". She proceeded to tell humorous stories about being in the White House and poking fun at her husband. The audience howled with laughter, and she had them in the palm of her hand. They gave her a thundering ovation that lasted for at least three minutes. She owned the ballroom, and everyone knew it.

In 1991 Mrs Bush was asked to make the commencement speech at Pepperdine University in Malibu. The university sits on a hill overlooking the Pacific Ocean and is home to the elite and movie stars. I conducted the advance and got to meet the President and the Chancellor of the university, Charles Runnels. When I shook hands with the chancellor, he insisted I call him Charlie. My youngest daughter, Renee, had stood on the hillside overlooking the ocean at Pepperdine when she was 12 years old and declared that she was going to go to college at Pepperdine. I remember gulping, knowing that the tuition was much more than a federal agent could afford.

When Barbara Bush was introduced as the commencement speaker, she started her speech with, "what in the world is your mascot, a wave? The only thing I can imagine is that a bunch of students got together at Pepi's Bar and had a few to many cocktails to come up with that mascot." The students roared with laughter, and she owned them.

Barbara Bush was the finest first lady America never really knew. If she had made all of George Bush's speeches, he would have won the election in 1993 hands down.

I closed out my career with George H. W. Bush losing the election to William Jefferson Clinton.

As an addendum, my daughter Renee, went to Pepperdine University. After graduation she went to UCLA law school, and is now a successful attorney with a fantastic husband and two sons who are good athletes.

My oldest daughter, Robyn, has a heart as big as Texas. She graduated from BIOLA University and works for Hope International which is a 501C charity. She has a young son and is married to James, a good husband and father

I remarried to an outstanding woman, Liz, and mother of two daughters. Her oldest daughter is Meghan who attended NYU and Loyola Law School and is a successful tax attorney. She has a young son and a daughter and is married to Chris, an outstanding person.

Melissa went to Cal State San Marcos for two years and then to Fashion Institute of Design and Merchandizing (FIDM). Today she works for 24 Carots, an event and wedding company. She has a little boy and is pregnant with a girl. Her husband Steve is a great guy.

My family of four daughters, four son in laws, and six grandchildren with one on the way is my greatest joy.

Chapter 40

THE LAST CAMPAIGN

AFTER RUNNING THE counterfeit squad and the financial fraud squad, I was assigned as the agent in charge of the protection squad in Los Angeles in 1988. This entailed me to oversee all protection for presidential, vice presidential, foreign heads of state, former presidents, and presidential candidate visits to the Los Angeles area.

We had visits from a number of foreign heads of state such as Yitzhak Shamir of Israel, Tanaka of Japan, and many others, as well as the President and Vice President of the United States.

Yitzhak Shamir's visit in late 1991 was particularly memorable. I received a telephone call from a security officer with the Israeli Consulate stating that Prime Minister Yitzhak Shamir would be visiting LA in November, and they would like to have a meeting to discuss security arrangements. I invited him to come to the Secret Service office. He declined and asked me to come to the Consulate. I responded that I would bring my team the next day. He said the request was for me only. I was annoyed, but I agreed to meet the following day.

When I arrived at the Consulate on Wilshire Blvd., with their armed security around the building and bulletproof lobby, I was asked to show my credentials and to give up my gun. I was then escorted to the elevator and to an isolated office on the fourth floor. The room had no windows, and there were five men sitting at a table. The lead agent sat at the head of the table and introduced himself as Beni Lava. He did not reveal whether he was Mossad or Shin Bet, our equivalent to the CIA and FBI.

Beni Lava was a short, balding man, with a personality akin to a Neanderthal. He offered no pleasantries, and if he had smiled it would have broken his face. Lava immediately began questioning me about Secret Service methodologies and procedures. Instead of advising me about the visit, I realized this meeting was more of an interrogation, and I got more and more irritated. I finally said, "I came here to find out about the prime minister's visit to Los Angeles, not to be interrogated. If you can't treat me with respect, I'm leaving. If you want to talk further, you can come to my office."

One of the other agents at the table tried to make apologies and said it was time to discuss the visit. Lava just stared at me, or I should say he glared at me. I knew he and I were not ever going to be barroom friends, but I had no idea how adversarial it would become.

We left the consulate, and I followed the group of Israelis to the Four Seasons Hotel on Doheny in Beverly Hills, where the prime minister would stay on his visit to LA. Hotel management had arranged for a very pretty young lady to show us around the premises. When we got to the floor where Shamir would be staying, Lava asked the young lady which suite would be Shamir's. She advised that the suite he would be utilizing was currently occupied, but she could show another suite just like the one Shamir would use.

Lava blurted out in a loud, commanding voice, "I said I want to see the suite my prime minister will stay in. Take me to that suite so I can see it. Now."

I saw a small tear form on the hostess's cheek, so I stepped forward and said, "It is against American law to enter a room someone has rented without a search warrant. Today you are not going to be able to see the suite he will be staying in. Now you either see the identical suite or leave."

Lava and I had a stare-down in the hallway, and I thought he wanted to take me on. I was now really pissed off at him for being such a bully and wanted him to make a move. But he backed down.

Two days before the visit, the Secret Service hotel advance agent called to inform me that the preliminary bomb sweep had uncovered a suspicious device. What appeared to be an unarmed explosive was found under a staircase near the floor where the prime minister was assigned to stay. I requested the device immediately be brought to the Secret Service office for further examination, after the LA Police bomb squad ruled it safe to be transported.

We put the device on the first plane back to Secret Service Headquarters to be examined by the Technical Security Division and Army EOD (Explosive Ordnance Detail). The next day I received a call notifying me that the device was made in Israel and was essentially a dummy explosive.

I called Beni Lava and told him we discovered his "little dummy device," and not to try any more amateur tricks. I was angry, so I said a lot of other things but frankly can't remember all the names I called him. He just responded by saying, "We wanted to see if you were on your game."

The first day of the visit was uneventful with Shamir going to a couple of synagogues and a dinner at a very wealthy home owned by a very wealthy Jewish family.

On the second day, we went to the Century Plaza Hotel, where the prime minister was to make a speech to a Jewish organization. Since we were operating like this was a presidential visit, we had a complete LA Police Department motorcade with two lead cars, twenty-six motorcycles for intersection control, and a helicopter.

On arrival at the Century Plaza, the motorcade went underground, and we escorted Shamir to a private elevator and took him to the presidential suite located several floors up.

Our advance team had set up a sterilized path from the suite to a private elevator. The route from the elevator was lined with Secret Service agents and Metro police officers through a labyrinth of hidden tunnels to where Shamir would appear on stage in the ballroom.

When the door to the suite opened and Shamir stepped into the hallway, Beni Lava immediately put his arm around the prime minister and started ushering him the opposite way from our sterilized path. I hacked Beni's arm from the prime minister and grabbed Shamir around the waist and pushed him toward our security. When Lava recovered, he tried to reach around Shamir to change his course again. I grabbed Lava by the throat and lifted him off the floor and slammed him against the wall. I finally released him when the prime minister was safely on the elevator. Lava hacked and coughed and grabbed his throat, but he had lost his voice, so he could only mouth cuss words at me.

When Shamir got on the plane to leave LA, I was relieved the visit was over, and glad I never had to deal with Beni Lava again.

In late April 1992, riots were ignited in Los Angeles after four white police officers were acquitted for the arrest and beating of Rodney King. King, a suspect in an armed robbery, had led the LAPD on a chase. When he was stopped, he refused to give up even after the officers Tased him. It was a brutal arrest because King was a big man, and it was obvious he was high on methamphetamine. A witness videotaped the scene, and that night the videotape hit the news airways and the officers were cast as villains.

The news media refused to reveal that in 1988, Rodney King had beat an Asian store owner with a tire iron and put him in a wheelchair for life as a paraplegic.

Public opinion, especially in the African American community, ran red hot. Buildings were burned to the ground, and there were numerous shooting deaths in the ghetto.

As the riots continued, Arkansas Governor William Jefferson Clinton, a candidate for president, decided to come to Los Angeles and make a campaign stop. His first intended stop was the First African Methodist Episcopal Church in the heart of South Central LA, where the passions and anger were still boiling.

After getting notified of Clinton's visit, I contacted Captain Pat McKinley of the Los Angeles Police Department Metropolitan Division. McKinley and his staff would be responsible for the motorcade and intersection control, as well as posting on the outer perimeter.

On the day of the visit, Clinton's aircraft was due to land at LAX and taxi to Mercury Air, a remote private facility on the other side of the main terminals. When I arrived, the Secret Service airport advance agent met me and said, "We have a problem."

He proceeded to inform me, "Clinton's chief of staff, Bruce Lindsey, told me to send LAPD home. They say it's not politically correct since they were the police department that beat Rodney King."

Pat McKinley overheard our conversation and asked me how I intended to handle the request. I informed him we were not going anywhere without LAPD. With that, I walked into the terminal to find Bruce Lindsey seated on a couch talking on the phone. I respectfully sat down facing him and waited until he was through with his conversation.

When he completed his call, I said, "I'm Ron Williams, the Secret Service agent in charge of Governor Clinton's visit to Los Angeles. I understand that you want to dismiss LAPD and send them home."

He responded by waving his hand in the air and said in his Southern drawl, "Yeah, just git rid of them; it is not politically correct to have them around when we go to South Central LA."

I asked, "Where are you from?"

THE LAST CAMPAIGN

He replied, "I'm from Little Rock, Arkansas."

"That's the problem," I said. "You're from Little Rock, and this is the big city where rioters have stolen thousands of guns from the gun shops in LA. This city is a very dangerous place. We are not about to travel around LA without an LAPD motorcade. You have a choice. You can sign off protection and we will all go home, or you accept the fact that LAPD is going to provide motorcade security."

With that I turned to walk away. That's when Lindsey stood up and said, "You son of a bitch."

I turned and walked back and grabbed him by the tie and pulled him close to me. I said, "Now you just made this personal, and if I don't get an apology, I'm gonna kick your ass."

He apologized and I walked out to meet the aircraft.

When the plane arrived, Lindsey ran up the stairs and through the open door. The Secret Service detail leader came down the stairs and asked me what the hell was going on. He said, "As the plane was landing, Clinton took a phone call and was screaming like a madman."

I told him what had transpired and asked him, "Are you going to back me up?"

He said, "This is your city. We do what you feel has to be done."

Eventually, Clinton and Lindsey came down the stairs and got in the limo. I got in the LAPD lead car, and the motorcade began the trek to the church. As we drove eastbound on I-10, smoke from burning buildings was billowing on both sides of the freeway. When we were five minutes out, the LAPD radio crackled, announcing that the protestors had tried to firebomb the LAPD building in Van Nuys. I radioed the detail leader in the limo and told him to advise Bruce Lindsey what had happened.

When the motorcade was one minute out, the LAPD helicopter advised that sniper fire was coming through the front door of the church and we needed to go to the alternate arrival site. We pulled up in back of the church, the detail leader threw the bulletproof raincoat over Clinton, and we rushed him into the church.

In the church, Lindsey came up to me, and his face was ashen white. He said, "I apologize. This is a dangerous town."

I said, "This is going to be a long campaign; I won't do your job, and you don't do mine."

After leaving the church, we stopped at the Beverly Wilshire Hotel, where Clinton was met and greeted by over 100 members of the LGBT community. We then went on an excursion around LA with Clinton getting photo shots of him walking among the ashes and shaking hands with African Americans.

Clinton made California one of his priority states, and he selected the Loews Santa Monica Beach Hotel as his preferred hotel mainly because of its close proximity to the ocean. Most often, Bill would come to LA without Hillary. On one such occasion, he was a guest at the National Organization of Women Business Owners, where they were having their convention at the downtown Westin Hotel. He was scheduled for a fifteen-minute appearance for photo ops and to shake a few hands. However, after seeing the audience of over 2,000 women, I knew we would be there a lot longer than fifteen minutes.

I have to give Clinton credit. He knew how to work a crowd, especially a room of attractive, successful women. As Bill and Kenny G strolled in from the back of the ballroom playing their saxophones, the ladies swooned with delight, their perfume melting into their skin, creating a euphoric atmosphere. After some brief remarks from an elevated platform, Clinton walked down the stairs into the sea of adoring women. We had to hold the women back as they clamored to shake hands and talk to him. As they would put out their hand, Bill would clasp their right hand, and take his left hand and rub the lucky lady's hand and wrist with his left hand, all the while saying, "I'm Bill Clinton and I hope you vote for me for president."

On another occasion, Hillary accompanied Bill to LA. He was to address a Hispanic crowd at a park in San Bernardino at 5:30

p.m. on a weekday eighty-five miles from the Loews Beach Hotel. At approximately 5 p.m., he and Hillary exited the service elevator and climbed into the waiting limo. I had secured the California Highway Patrol to lead the motorcade and route security for the long trip. This meant the CHP would supply a scout car about five minutes out, a lead car, a tail car, and at least twenty motorcycles and a helicopter for advance scrutiny of the route.

To provide security for a thirty-vehicle motorcade meant shutting down on-ramps and off-ramps to the freeway at least seven minutes out. This meant the over-clogged LA freeways would be a nightmare, and it was.

When we arrived at the park at 6:30 p.m., Bill and Hillary got out of the limo and held hands as they walked up to the platform. They both smiled and waved to the crowd, portraying a loving couple running for the highest office in the land.

The detail leader riding in the Clinton limo came over to me and said, "Williams, I will give you a hundred bucks to switch places with me."

I raised my eyebrows at him. "The entire ride out here, Hillary yelled and screamed at Bill, using some profanities I have never even heard before." After we returned to the Loews Hotel, he said the ride back was even worse than the trip out. "My ears are bleeding from the tongue-lashing Hillary administered."

When the California primary projected Bill Clinton as the winner, preparations were made to have the celebration at the Biltmore Hotel in downtown LA. We had held several events for foreign heads of state at the Biltmore, and our security surveys provided protocols and procedures that could be followed to insure a safe and secure environment.

However, several days prior to the primary celebration, a meeting was held at the Biltmore between my advance team and the Clinton advance staff. The discussion became tense when I discovered the Clinton team wanted Bill to come off the elevator and walk through the crowd to get to the stage. They wanted him to be surrounded by adoring fans to get a television photo op that would resonate nationwide.

I countered with Clinton skirting the crowd and walking around the ballroom via a sterilized passage and coming on the stage from behind a curtain. I reminded the Clinton staff that in 1968, Robert Kennedy walked through a crowded kitchen at the Ambassador Hotel and was shot and killed by Sirhan Sirhan. I also reiterated that the guests that night would not be magnetometered for weapons, and the event was not ticketed for specific guests. In other words, it would be chaos, and we needed to stick to our security protocols.

Their staff, led by George Stephanopoulos, insisted that Bill Clinton should walk through the crowd. Again, I advised that since we could not verify and vet everyone, it would be difficult to provide a safe and secure exit in the event of an emergency. The meeting ended with some very heated words.

I immediately went back to my office and composed a memo to file with my security recommendations, and the Clinton opposition to my plan. I date- and time-stamped the memo and took it to the special agent in charge of the LA office and explained the issue. He asked if there could be a compromise.

The next day another meeting was scheduled at the Biltmore. This time the Clinton advance team laid out a plan to have Bill come down the middle of the ballroom with staffers following him with a rope to separate the crowd, providing a safe zone. They said that when Bill was halfway to the stage, the rope would be dropped to allow the crowd to fill in around him for the photo op.

I responded by stating, "This still exposes him. We can't have exposure and an unsafe environment with no viable escape plan."

They insisted, I disagreed, and we finally agreed that I would talk to my team to see what I could do.

I knew what I would I do. That evening I called Captain Pat McKinley with LAPD Metro. I asked Pat if he could supply fifty officers, at least six feet tall, dressed in dark suits. When I explained why, he said he would do it.

Next I went to Ron and Paul, two huge Secret Service agents assigned to LA. I explained that the Clinton staff wanted to drop the ropes and allow the crowd to surround Clinton as he walked down the center of the ballroom. I told them they were there to make sure the ropes would not be dropped. We had to have an exit path if something happened.

I assembled the agents who were assigned as post standers and instructed them to use hand wands at the security checkpoints and to examine the contents of handbags and to conduct pat-downs for guests who entered the ballroom. I was intent on not allowing a tragedy. Not on my watch.

On the night of the California primary, Bill Clinton, as expected, won.

The agents at the ballroom checkpoints did their best to screen guests as they arrived. All bags were searched, and hand wands were used to detect any weapons. However, hand wands are not that reliable. We also did pat-down searches, and supervisors roamed the crowd looking for anyone suspicious.

The ballroom was filled to the maximum, and the fire captain came to me and advised no one else could be admitted. Soon the crowd got restless and started chanting, "We want Bill." Just when they reached a fever pitch, Bill came down in the elevator and stepped into the back entrance to the ballroom. But instead of seeing a sea of bodies, he saw fifty very tall police officers in suits forming a ten-foot-wide passage for him to walk to the stage.

As Clinton began walking, his staff moved forward to drop the ropes behind him. Paul and Ron on cue stepped in and blocked the staff from dropping the ropes. Clinton literally had to strain on tiptoes to shake hands with the crowd as the police officers stood shoulder to shoulder all the way to the stage.

Bruce Lindsey was livid. He came to me and hissed, "You reneged on our agreement to allow him to be surrounded by the crowd."

I responded, "Yes, but he will live through this night, and I did the right thing."

The Clinton campaign complained about me changing the security arrangements. Fortunately, the special agent in charge of the LA office backed my decision. My memo prior to the event helped to put the security arrangements in perspective. If we had proceeded with the Clinton advance team plan and Clinton had been assaulted, I would have had a difficult time living with myself.

In November of 1992, William Jefferson Clinton from Little Rock was elected as the forty-second President of the United States.

Several days before Thanksgiving, we were informed that the now President-elect Bill Clinton would visit LA again. One of his stops would be the Glendale Galleria shopping mall in the vibrant suburb city next to Los Angeles. The plan was for Clinton to arrive at the shopping center and walk the length of the mall shaking hands to celebrate his election. I thought it made no sense to treat his election as if he were still campaigning for office.

Nevertheless, I made an appointment with the Glendale Police Department, and our advance team together with police officials visited the mall. Our security review showed multiple entry and exit points and too many checkpoints to control visitors who wanted to see their new president. The Clinton advance team also wanted to place the motorcade below a bridge so a crowd could look down on Clinton as he arrived and departed the mall. This idea defied security logic. We could not control who would form on the bridge, and it afforded a potential assassin a high-ground advantage.

Despite my concerns and protest, Bruce Lindsey reminded me that Bill Clinton was now president-elect. His parting words were, "Find a way to secure the location. We are going to the shopping center."

I went back to the office and again composed a memo. I date- and time-stamped the memo to go on record with my concerns.

Clinton did visit the shopping center, and the mall was packed with fans of all ages, sizes, gender, and ethnicities. The Clinton team loved the hoopla, still seemingly oblivious to the security risk. As we fought the crowd to get him through the mall, I knew I never again would be party to such chaos. We finally got to the other end of the mall where the motorcade was waiting. As Clinton got into the limo, Bruce Lindsey glided up to me and whispered, "Now that he's president, we're gonna git you, boy."

I looked him in the eye and said, "Don't bother, I'm retiring."

On January 20, 1993, Bill Clinton was sworn in as the President of the United States.

One day earlier, January 19, 1993, I officially retired from the Secret Service.

Case Closed

I spent over twenty-two years in the United States Secret Service, retiring as the assistant to the special agent in charge of the Los Angeles office. I was fortunate enough to receive the Director's Award for outstanding performance eight times. Although this career was not particularly rewarding financially, my time as a Secret Service agent honed me to be a successful businessman in private industry after I retired. My myriad experiences gave me the confidence and discipline to develop and run a security and risk management business.

So many stories. These that I have shared here are just the tip of the iceberg of all that I have lived through. It has felt good to recount some of my experiences, and even if no one but family reads them, I will be fine with that.

I can only state that if I had my life to live over again, I would choose to be an agent in the United States Secret Service.

Thinking back to how it all began, I recall the first week at Bethany Nazarene College after that taxi driver dropped me off. It was traumatic for me. No one drank alcohol, smoked cigarettes, or used foul language. They were a group of focused young men and women, truly dedicated to a belief in God through their savior, Jesus Christ.

One month after being at Bethany Nazarene College, I accepted Christ as my savior, and met and married Diana Moore, a pretty blonde from San Antonio, Texas. We later divorced but not before raising two wonderful daughters, who we both adore.

My life has strayed many times from the commitment to Christ I made as a young man, but even as I strayed and did some things I am not proud of, the hound of heaven, the holy spirit, never left me.

I am now an "old" man, age seventy-three, as I write this. I wrote this book of stories about my career as a Secret Service agent to leave to my grandchildren. I had a great career, worked with the finest men and women in the world, and had some wonderful experiences. Some of the stories presented are raw, but realistic. That is life. I've always said life is a full-contact sport. It is not for the faint of heart, or those who are afraid of taking a risk.

I have lived long enough to develop some conclusions about what it takes to live a successful life. It is not about power. It is not about money. It is having a faith in God, having a loving family, and developing trusted friends.

Thank you for reading.

www.ingramcontent.com/pod-product-compliance
Lightning Source LLC
Chambersburg PA
CBHW061251230426
43664CB00024B/2915